BIRTHRIGHT

Jean A. S. Strauss is an adoptee who located her birth family in 1988. The author of numerous magazine articles about adoption issues, her first book, *The Great Adoptee Search Book*, was published in 1990. Married, with two young children, Jean currently lives in Massachusetts where her husband is a college president.

BIRTHRIGHT

The Guide to Search
and Reunion for
Adoptees, Birthparents,
and Adoptive Parents

JEAN A. S. STRAUSS

PENGUIN BOOKS

PENGUIN BOOKS
Published by the Penguin Group
Penguin Books USA Inc., 375 Hudson Street,
New York, New York 10014, U.S.A.
Penguin Books Ltd, 27 Wrights Lane, London W8 5TZ, England
Penguin Books Australia Ltd, Ringwood, Victoria, Australia
Penguin Books Canada Ltd, 10 Alcorn Avenue,
Toronto, Ontario, Canada M4V 3B2
Penguin Books (N.Z.) Ltd, 182–190 Wairau Road, Auckland 10, New Zealand

Penguin Books Ltd, Registered Offices:
Harmondsworth, Middlesex, England

First published in Penguin Books 1994

1   3   5   7   9   10   8   6   4   2

PUBLISHER'S NOTE

This publication is designed to provide accurate and authoritative information in regard to the subject matter covered. It is sold with the understanding that the publisher is not engaged in rendering legal or other professional service. If legal service or other expert assistance is required, the service of a competent professional person should be sought.

The identities of some of the individuals described in this book
have been changed.

LIBRARY OF CONGRESS CATALOGING IN PUBLICATION DATA
Strauss, Jean A. S.
Birthright : the guide to search and reunion for adoptees,
birthparents, and adoptive parents / Jean A. S. Strauss.
p. cm.
Includes bibliographical references.
ISBN 0 14 05.1295 0
1. Strauss, Jean A. S.   2. Adoptees—United States—Biography.
3. Adoptees—United States—Identification.   4. Birthparents—United
States—Identification.   I. Title.
HV874.82.S77A3   1994
362.8'298—dc20   93-36064

Printed in the United States of America
Set in Galliard   Designed by Claudine Bianco

Dedicated with love
to my Mom and to Lee,
without whom
this book would not
have been possible

FOREWORD

The practical, psychological and spiritual needs and challenges of *all* members of the adoption quadrant—the child, birth parents, adoptive parents, and facilitators (secular, religious, legalistic and familial)—are all deserving of much more inquiry and analysis than has previously been given during the fifty-plus years of institutionalized adoption in North America.

Adoption is one of the most compelling and complicated matters in human affairs. It reaches far beyond one family wanting a child to love and care for, and another family loving but unable to provide for their child. It is, in fact, a complicated dance that all partners in the adoption quadrant must take upon themselves in order to bring peace and harmony to all concerned.

Birthright is a useful and clearly written book for adoptees and their loved ones who are coming to terms with the practical and emotional concerns surrounding the search for the parents of one's birth. Ms. Strauss focuses on many important issues of search and reunion in a very sensitive, non-intrusive and helpful manner. Her work is a poignant contribution to the ongoing dialogue about adoption in our time.

> —Clarissa Pinkola Estés, Ph.D., Psychoanalyst, and author of *Women Who Run With the Wolves* and *The Gift of Story*.

AUTHOR'S NOTE

Out of the seventy contributors to *Birthright*, sixty-seven were more than willing to be known by their full names. Unfortunately, in the eleventh hour it was decided that using complete names might present a legal problem. Hence, for the most part throughout the book, only first names are used, and some names and locations have been changed in order to protect the privacy of third parties.

This change was a source of frustration for many contributors. It was their feeling, as well as my own, that to obscure identities only prolongs the secrets and stigmas surrounding adoption. It is our combined hope that the stories in *Birthright* will help others to understand the far-reaching effects that secrecy and judgmental attitudes can have on individual lives and families. Collectively, we look forward to a day when individuals will be valued for who they are, not how they came into the world.

CONTENTS

CONTENTS

INTRODUCTION

THERE ARE OVER SIX MILLION ADOPTEES in the United States. Double that figure and you come close to the number of birthparents as well as the number of adoptive parents in this country. That's 10 percent of the population. This does not include millions of other family members: siblings, spouses, children, aunts, uncles, cousins, grandparents, and great-grandparents. It's estimated that the number of people in America directly affected by the institution of adoption is over forty million.

Adoption doesn't end when papers are filed and documents are sealed. Adoption's influence, as evidenced throughout this book, is lifelong. Ultimately, curiosity about the past, about one's heritage and one's roots, can take over.

Today tens of thousands of adoptees and birthparents each year are deciding to seek out their roots. What happens when an adoptee decides to locate a birthparent or a birth-parent wants to find the child given up long ago? How does one search for people whose names may not even be known? What kind of an impact does a search have on the searcher's family? And what happens if a reunion occurs? Does every-one's life change? How are existing relationships affected? A searcher travels through unknown waters, and to many that may seem a careless, even dangerous, journey to make.

As little as twenty years ago, it was rare to hear about an adoptee engaged in a search, or a birthfamily being re-united. It just wasn't done. The few individuals who under-took such an endeavor were labeled "maladjusted" and "disloyal." They were slapping their parents in the face, go-ing against a system meant to protect the privacy of birth-parents and adoptive families.

The need to find one's roots was misinterpreted. Many assumed that searchers were looking for their "real parents"—that they were dissatisfied with their lives. No one seemed willing to accept that this connection might be nec-essary for healthy individuals. It was firmly believed adoptees were better off not knowing about their natural origins. Cer-tainly few championed the idea that adoptees had a *right* to know about their roots. Searchers were asked, "Why? Why on earth are you doing this? Don't you know all you're going to do is hurt your parents, not to mention people you don't even know?"

If society frowned upon adoptees who searched, it fre-quently vilified those birthparents who sought their off-spring. As birthmother Susan Darke once said, "Even criminals get paroled. But birthmothers receive a lifelong sentence of shame and anonymity." Birthmothers were fre-quently characterized as oversexed teenagers, or poor, un-educated single women. They couldn't be the girl next door or the housewife down the street. Such stereotyping encouraged many in society to deal with the birthmother as a nonentity.

To search in the fifties, sixties, and seventies took great courage. Despite strong opposition, a handful of adoptees and birthparents went against the system, fought the odds, and discovered their birthfamilies. They told their stories, and others began to follow in their footsteps. Organizations were formed to help searchers. Battles were waged to open sealed records. The search pioneers spawned a movement, both political and social, which began to reexamine the institution of adoption.

Now, only a few years later, not a day goes by without a reunion occurring somewhere in the country. Such events have become commonplace. We see them on the evening news and on syndicated talk shows. The media have embarked upon a feeding frenzy of reunion stories. From daytime to prime time, audiences tune in to see fantasies fulfilled, as people reunite after decades apart, watching romanticized fairy tales of the lost baby being found, the "true" parent being discovered.

But even if searches and reunions now seem commonplace experiences, they are not. Nor are they fantasies. They are unique, real-life passages, causing as much trauma and upheaval in lives as the death of loved ones. What happens after that initial reunion is over and all the excitement dies down? For some successful searchers (and people found), the aftermath of a reunion can be a difficult and confusing time.

Scant attention has been paid by the media as to what happens after the initial reunion. It is the fantasy that reunions represent that interests most people. The underlying reasons why searches are undertaken have been avoided. Reunions are fascinating, but society, as a whole, does not want to acknowledge that the system of adoption could be imperfect.

Why was confidentiality and secrecy incorporated into adoption practices? Although adoption was an open process at the turn of the century, being adopted was not a badge of honor. Children born out of wedlock were considered "dirty products of dirty relationships." It was this stigma, this notion of tainted blood, that triggered changes.

Beginning with the Minnesota Act in 1917, state laws were enacted to seal records. The reason confidentiality was established is discussed by birthmother Barbara Gonyo and social worker Kenneth Watson in "Searching in Adoption."[1] "The Minnesota law was not intended to maintain anonymity between the participants in an adoption, but rather to protect adopted children from the stigma of illegitimacy or 'bad blood' by removing such information from open court records." Thus the first sealed-records law was not created with the intent of hiding adoptive families and birthfamilies from each other, but rather to protect both from outsiders.

Minnesota sought to protect the child from the burden of the label of illegitimacy, but in a way sealing the records made the stigma of being adopted even worse. The message the Minnesota Act gave was that an adoptee's origins were too despicable to be known.

Gonyo and Watson explain that social workers supported the sealing of records for a number of reasons. "They believed that adoption should be a private matter and that children would *attach* to their adoptive parents more firmly if they were completely cut off from their original family. It was also felt that adoptive parents would more fully accept children whose ties to their previous family had been totally severed, and that birthparents could best be helped by making a clean break with the children they relinquished."[2]

Along with social workers and lawmakers, society also endorsed the notion of confidentiality. Being an unwed mother was something to be hidden. Sealed records would guarantee privacy. Unwed pregnant girls and women could be spirited away, have their babies in seclusion, and return home as if nothing had happened. Confidentiality would protect them.

Confidentiality would also protect the adoptive family. Agencies guaranteed adoptive parents that no birthmother would ever come knocking on their door. Curiously, the adoptee's needs were left out of the equation. That an adoptee could need to know about his or her birthfamily and might want to seek it out seemed preposterous. In fact, it was felt that if such a thing occurred it would mean there was either something wrong with the adoptee or the adoptive parents had failed.

These are several of the assumptions upon which the decision to seal records were based. In hindsight, it is easy to see how misguided many of these efforts to protect individuals and families were. It is interesting that society created this veil of secrecy rather than change the way children born out of wedlock were viewed. The concept that the circumstances of conception taint a child for life was endorsed by the adoption laws written in this century.

By the end of World War II, all adoption records were sealed, with the notable exceptions of those in Alaska, Kansas, and Alabama. Birthparents and adoptive families were protected. Adoptees would thrive, shielded from their pasts.

It all sounded good on paper. But the system had obvious flaws. Most birthmothers did not go home and forget about the babies they gave away. They buried the shame and guilt of their pasts in the backs of their minds, and tried to get on with their lives; but decades later, even after raising families of their own, they still couldn't forget the children they gave away. Moreover, they had never been allowed to deal with the trauma they endured during the tumultuous period of pregnancy, birth, and relinquishment. For many, this enforced denial caused ongoing, unresolved patterns of self-destruction.

Adoptive parents were affected. Placed under tremendous scrutiny by agencies, they lived under the constant pressure of high expectations. They felt required to be perfect parents. And although they were recognized as parents in the legal sense, they were never looked upon emotionally as the children's "real" parents.

And many adoptees grew up feeling somehow incomplete, but afraid to ask questions: Where did I come from? Who were my birthparents? What were they like? Why was I given up? The questions were natural, but to ask seemed disloyal, an act of betrayal. Yet the reality is that adoptees from loving, nurturing homes, with parents who loved them unconditionally, still felt something was missing. They had no knowledge of their origins. Profound connections, both primal and historical, were severed and denied.

By some measures, modern adoption worked. It provided countless children with loving homes, created the opportunity for childless couples to have families, and gave an option to birthparents to provide lives for children whom, for a variety of reasons, they were unable to support. Adoption's predominant failing was in its foundation of secrecy. The truth was avoided, hidden, obscured. Information was withheld from the very people for whom it was most vital.

Today, adoption issues are complicated and controversial. The legalization of abortion and an increasing acceptance of young unwed mothers who keep and raise their children has reduced the number of children available. It is estimated that one million couples are seeking to adopt, most of whom prefer healthy white infants—and there are fewer than 25,000 available each year.[3] This has caused an interesting shift in adoption's purpose. Because fewer babies are available, the focus is no longer on finding homes for babies, but instead on finding babies for childless couples.

Where will this shift in emphasis lead? The majority of adoptions are now facilitated by "baby brokers," and a great deal of money is changing hands. Who is adoption supposed to serve, the child who needs a home or the infertile couple who seeks a child? No doubt the babies adopted today, through international agencies, independent baby brokers, black-market channels, or resulting from artificial insemination or surrogate parents will face their own problems and challenges in the decades ahead.

Like any social institution, adoption will continue to evolve. The flaws in the current system will hopefully be addressed and new conditions set in place. But even as the laws and policies governing adoption change, they affect only the future generation. For twentieth-century adoptees, birthparents, and adoptive parents, the need to reconnect may be realized only through individual effort.

Sadly, the need to locate family members is no longer a task peculiar only to those individuals affected by adoption. In a nation where half of all marriages end in divorce, severed relationships are becoming more common. Search and support groups report increasing numbers of nontraditional adult searchers who, separated since childhood from family members by divorce or for other reasons, are now embarking on searches. Their need to locate people from the past can be equally compelling.

This book is a guide through the relatively uncharted seas of search and reunion. It is written not just for adoptees, birthparents, and adoptive parents, but for anyone seeking to connect with people long lost.

PART I: SEARCH

"... Behold, we know not anything:
I can but trust that good shall fall
At last—far off—at last, to all,
And every winter change to spring.

So runs my dream: but what am I?
An infant crying in the night:
An infant crying for the light:
And with no language but a cry."

—ALFRED, LORD TENNYSON
"Oh Yet We Trust"

~ 1 ~

MY SEARCH

WHEN I WAS SEARCHING FOR MY birthfamily, I had an insatiable appetite for reading about other people's searches and reunions. These stories were my inspiration on days when my own search seemed an impossible quest. In no small measure, my ultimate success was due to many strangers who shared their experiences in print. They gave me reason to hope, reason to try just one more thing.

Several people have generously shared narratives of their own searches and reunions for this book. Their stories give life to the pages that follow. Search techniques and discussions of reunions are just words on a page; they become animated and viable when connected with real-life experiences.

In that vein, it seems too impersonal not to share my own story.

JULY 20, 1988

It was a hot and humid night. We had just turned up the air conditioner and were getting ready for bed when the phone rang. My husband, Jon, handed me the receiver, and my life was forever changed.

"Jean, it's Sheila Klopper. You'd better sit down. I've found your birthmother."

Sheila was a private investigator I had hired several months earlier, but I had really given up hope of ever completing my search for my natural parents. Now, as adrenaline surged through me, all I could think of to say was "Wow!"

It is the moment all adoptees who choose to search dream about. I'd beaten the odds. After five years of following ambiguous clues, I now knew for certain the name of the woman who had given birth to me thirty-three years earlier. And there was more. Not only had Sheila found my birthmother, but she had learned I had several half-siblings as well.

Sheila gave me the phone number and address that would connect me with all of them. All that remained was to decide what to do next. Should I call? Write? Have someone act as an intermediary on my behalf to contact my birthmother?

Old questions ran through my mind. Why dig up the past? Why did I have to do this—need to do this? What right did I have to disturb other people's lives?

In 1955 I was Case Number 250 of my county's Social Service Department. Three days after I was born my birthmother relinquished me for adoption and I was placed in foster care.

Twenty miles away in Lafayette lived Betty and Lou Sacconaghi. They very much wanted a daughter. The day I turned three months old the Social Service Department contacted the Sacconaghis. On that very same afternoon, my adoptive parents picked me up and took me home. I can imagine the moment the social worker placed me in my mother's arms: it was like a nurse handing an infant to its mother in the delivery room. I was hers and she was mine. Forever.

The randomness of adoption fascinates me. A child's destiny is irrevocably changed when papers are signed. The person an adoptee would have been will no longer be. Who shapes that child's future? Whoever happens to be at the top of the list, whoever makes for a good match on paper. A decision is made by external sources and will affect all parties involved for the rest of their lives. It is, in a way, like playing God. Or roulette.

There are adoptees who never feel they fit into their selected families, but I always felt I belonged, wholly and completely. The fact that I was not "born" of Betty and Lou seemed to be of no significance to me. I never found them lacking as parents because we didn't share the same DNA codes. They were my parents and I was their daughter.

From the beginning I was told I was adopted. I have a memory of being slightly confused about the concept of adoption when I was about five. We had just seen the film *Dumbo* and I was inquiring how a stork could be strong enough to carry a baby elephant. This led to a discussion about where babies come from.

"No, storks don't really bring babies." My mother was impeccably honest.

"Well, where do they come from?"

"Puppies come from dogs, kittens come from cats, and babies come from people."

"What people?"

"Mommies and daddies."

"How do *they* get them?" At this point, I think she suggested I get washed up for dinner, but I insisted upon an answer.

"Basically, mommies and daddies make a baby, and the baby grows inside the mommy until it's ready to be born."

"So I grew inside of you?"

"No. Remember when we talked about adoption? You were born and your mother loved you very much, but she couldn't keep you. And Daddy and I wanted a little girl so much, and we found out about you and brought you home."

"Oh. Why couldn't I have grown inside of you?"

"I wish you could have, but Daddy and I couldn't make a baby."

"Oh. How do you make babies?"

". . . Ask your father."

My parents tried to say all the right things. I never consciously felt abandoned or rejected by my birthmother. I always took being adopted to mean that I was wanted. Planned. And I was.

My dad was a second-generation Italian-American, a Vince Lombardi look-alike with a smile that made anyone's day. Everyone loved my father. I was only nine years old when he died.

Death cheats a child of fully knowing a parent. I have only childhood visions of watching him clean his pipe, of falling asleep in his arms at a campfire, of riding on his back across a mountain stream, of building a kite with him just a few days before he died. I didn't get to know him as an adult. I don't know how he would have felt about my decision far down the road to search for my origins.

When I was sixteen, I became curious about my birthparents. Who were they? What did they look like? What did they do? Where were they now? One night at the dinner table I blurted out my curiosity to my mom. She didn't blink.

"We were told only a few things about them. Your mother was about twenty and was a secretary. Your father was in his mid-twenties and was a law student. They weren't married. It was very hard for your mother to give you up but she wanted to do what was best for you. I wish I had pictures of them for you but the agency didn't pass things like that along."

After dinner, Mom brought me a manila folder she kept in the family safe. "Here," she said, handing me the file. "This is all the information we were given. Maybe it'll help answer any questions you have." She hesitated, then smiled and left the room.

I scoured all the pages and was fascinated by a new piece of information. A name. My name at birth had been Cecelia Anne Porter. I remember trying it out, the way a bride-to-be tries out her new name. Cecelia. Cecelia Sacconaghi. It didn't fit.

My adoptive mother was a remarkable parent. She satisfied my curiosity by sharing as much as she knew with me. She made me feel this information was mine. She respected my right to know about my past. To hold me with such open arms could not have been easy. She was very wise. The bonds of our mother-daughter relationship were never strained by the insecure feelings adoptive parents must feel when dealing with the reality of the existence of birthparents. I returned the papers to my mother for safekeeping, and went on with my life, comfortable with the sense that I knew as much as was possible.

My mother might have been completely open with me,

but society was not. As an adult, I grew to believe that I had a right to know where I came from. My natural heritage was an important piece of my identity. That it was withheld, I felt, denied me the opportunity for complete self-knowledge.

Why did I feel I had to search? If I was so comfortable with my parents and with my childhood, why would I pursue such a quest? The reality for me was that I was never looking for parents. I was looking for answers. There was an empty chamber in my mind full of question marks. My curiosity changed as I grew older, until I no longer just *wanted* to know about my origins, I had to and *needed* to find answers.

What changed me? When did I go from idle curiosity to *having* to know? For me the moment came when I listened to a birthfather talk about his futile efforts to locate his birthdaughter. It was the first time I realized birthparents might not mind being found. His story ignited my dormant desire to know my roots.

At the time I felt that I was searching for three reasons: I was curious, and believed my origins were my business— my birthright. I wanted to learn my medical history. And lastly, I felt a strong urge to contact the woman who had given birth to me. I felt she deserved to know I had survived childhood, to know I was happy and doing well. I wanted her to know she had done the right thing. Somehow, I was sure she needed to know that.

How would I start to search? I had no idea. When I decided to begin this long paper chase, I removed the manila folder from my mom's safe. The documents inside were my starting point.

Oddly, I didn't share with my mom the decision to search. Even though she had been open with me about what she knew, she had never said, "If you're ever interested in finding out more, let me know. I'll help you look." I decided

I would tell her only if and when I found some answers. I wasn't comfortable with this deception, but I was even less comfortable with the possibility that my desire to search might hurt my mom. Realistically, my search might end unsolved, as so many do. My rationale was why have her worry over nothing?

Searching was almost like a game. I began with a mere handful of clues. I knew my name had been Cecelia Anne Porter. I knew from the papers in my mother's safe that my birthmother was born in August of 1934, in Portland, Oregon. I knew that she was five feet four inches tall, with light brown hair and blue eyes, that she had been a secretary, and that her father was a poultryman, her mother a housewife. I knew that my birthfather was in his twenties at the time of my birth, that he was six feet tall, had brown eyes, and was a law student.

That was all I had to go on. I was perplexed as to where to begin. I felt, as many adoptees do, that what I was planning to do was in some way illegal.

A journalism professor at the University of Southern California finally got me started on my path of "crime." John Riley was a former reporter for *Life* magazine. I wrote an essay in his journalism course about my desire to search. After class one day, he asked me if I had had any luck. Embarrassed, I told him I hadn't even begun, and had no idea even where to start. He asked if he could borrow the manila folder that contained all my documents. I dropped it by his office.

The next week, after class, Riley returned the file and handed me a single sheet of paper. "Here."

"What's this?" I curiously looked at the typed page.

"It's the address and phone number of the doctor who delivered you."

"What?" I was dumbfounded. How had Riley found him, and why?

"His name was on your amended birth certificate."

"But how did you get his address?"

"Simply by writing to Sacramento to the Medical Quality Assurance Board. They keep records on all doctors that practice in the state."

"But can you do that?"

"Sure. Why not?" Riley didn't share my fear that this was all somehow illicit.

"But what good does finding him do?" I was admittedly a little dense at the beginning of my search.

"Think. Doctors have private practices. They keep their own records. If he has your medical record, it will have your birthmother's name."

Light bulbs finally went on. I went home and wrote out how I would relate my story to Dr. "Smith" and then immediately called him up on the phone.

"Hello? You don't know me but twenty-nine years ago you delivered me and . . ."

My first step taken, my first lead followed. It led nowhere. Dr. "Smith" was wonderfully nice, but he had been a resident when he delivered me. Thus, he had no records, nor any recollection of my particular birth. This was a dead end but also a beginning.

Next, I wrote to the agency that handled my adoption and asked for as much information as they could give me. I received a background sheet reiterating all the information I already had—with some monumental additions. The last paragraph read:

> You were relinquished when you were 3 days old. We received a letter from your mother 5 years later; she

wanted to be sure you had been placed with a Catholic family. She also said she was married and had four children. We have heard nothing further from her.

This paragraph was the inspiration for the rest of my search. It told me that my birthmother wanted to know what had happened to me. My locating her might not be an intrusion.

But even more heart-stopping: she had four other children—brothers and sisters. The possibility of locating siblings had never fully entered my mind before. Somewhere out there these people existed. I became gripped by a desire to find them.

The background sheet held one other piece of information I had not known: my birthmother was also adopted. I had already tried to find birth records of a baby girl Porter born in Portland in August of 1934. Now I knew why I had not been successful. Her records were as closed as my own. Suddenly, one of the strongest clues I had became useless.

Disappointment and frustration are basic components of searching. Nothing stimulates one's emotions more than having a door slammed in one's face, even figuratively. Probably every searching adoptee has an incident that makes him or her feel an inch high.

I had written to the hospital where I was born requesting the medical records of myself and my birthmother. When I didn't hear from the hospital in ten days, I decided to go in person.

The County Hospital was a small facility, yet it was not easy to find the records office. After making my way through a maze of corridors and stairs, I finally found the office and, taking a deep breath, walked inside.

I was so nervous. If the young woman sitting across the

desk from me had been a customs agent, I'm sure she would have checked all of my bags for contraband. I was projecting that much anxiety.

I explained that I had sent a request for records ten days earlier and had heard nothing. Since I happened to be in the area, I wondered if I could just pick up the records. The young receptionist was very nice. She said my name rang a bell and turned to a set of shelves nearby, where she reached for two files.

"Ah, these are the records you requested right here." She placed the files neatly on her desk, one on top of the other. "Just a moment," she said politely. "If I remember, there was something unusual about your request. Hang on while I check with my supervisor."

With that, the young woman rose from her desk, walked three steps away, and began talking with another woman, her back toward me. I stared at the files in front of me. The one on top was for Cecelia Anne Porter: my given name at birth. That meant the one on the bottom had to have the name I wanted. The identity of my birthmother was right there, a few feet in front of me.

Probably a total of thirty seconds elapsed. "Grab them!" my brain was screaming. "Pick them up and run!" Yet I sat frozen in my chair while a flurry of other thoughts raced through my mind.

"That would be illegal."

"So what!"

"It was confusing enough finding this office. I'd probably get lost or trapped trying to escape."

"Quit being a coward. Grab them!"

"What if I got arrested? Who would I call to bail me out? My mom?"

A moment of hesitation. An opportunity lost. If only I

had had the presence of mind just to stand up, reach over, and slide the two files apart. I might have gotten the name. But the young receptionist quickly returned with a stern-looking woman. The supervisor. The look in her eyes made me shrivel in my chair.

"We have not sent your records yet because your records show you were adopted." She picked up the files and glared down at me. "You have no right to any of this information."

I sat there turning red, feeling both angry and embarrassed, and a bit like a criminal. My voice was shakier than I would have liked. "I understood that by law I have a right to any medical records concerning me."

"These records are sealed." Her sharp answer didn't leave much room for debate. The nice young receptionist was now peering at me suspiciously, and other workers in the office were glancing our direction.

"There isn't anything that I can see?" By then, I was standing, wishing I *had* taken the files and run. It would have been no more humiliating than this.

"All we could do is send you a copy of your record. But every piece of identifying information will be blocked out."

"All right." I began to sit back down. "I'll wait for that much at least."

"No." Her voice was taunting. "We couldn't possibly do this today. We'll have to mail it to you. Doing what you request takes a lot of work. We can't afford to make any mistakes by doing it too fast." Her last remark hung in the air, a stinging accusation.

Of course, I knew her concerns were real. I wasn't nearly as interested in the medical information as in anything identifying I might have found on the forms. Yet, as I retreated from the hospital, I didn't feel embarrassment or shame as much as anger and indignation. After all, I was merely a person trying to find out things about myself. Did that make me a pariah, deserving of that kind of treatment?

My motives for searching were not far removed from the forces that drive people to do genealogical research. Genealogists find people from the present as well as from the past. They do so to learn more about their origins. Long-lost cousins are reunited to form family trees. People view genealogy as an interesting hobby. By contrast, the search for my roots was seen, at least by some, as a heinous pursuit in violation of the highest moral codes of our society.

What happened in that hospital made me angry. It made me realize for the first time in my life that I was somehow different—branded "ADOPTED!" I was not to be accorded the same rights as other people—the ability to access information about myself. It was a subtle form of prejudice, yet I had seen it in the eyes of that supervisor. She viewed me as inferior.

My search continued. Every new idea I pursued resulted in a dead end. At times, I felt emotionally exhausted. I kept thinking, this is ridiculous. It shouldn't have to be this hard. Why isn't there an easier way to find answers?

Other times I felt apprehensive. I remember once, when I asked for my original birth certificate, pangs of guilt haunted me. Inside me was such a contradiction of emotions: this steadfast belief that I had a right to do what I was doing, yet this queasy fear that I would get caught. Caught doing what? Asking for my own birth certificate? I constantly sensed that hospital supervisor smirking over my shoulder. "You have no legal right to information about yourself."

Robert Lasnik writes in *A Parent's Guide to Adoption* that adult adoptees feel that in society's eyes they never outgrow the label of "adopted child."[1] They are forever regarded as children, and our legal system continues to treat them as such even after they have reached middle and old age. The sealed-records laws do not take into consideration that children become adults. Why? Are adoptees presumed more irresponsible? Unable to handle the truth? I was in concurrence with Lasnik. I frequently did feel treated as a child during my search. I hated having some bureaucrat or a blank piece of paper tell me "No!" After all, why should information about my birthfamily and my origins be known to some clerk in an office and not to me?

My quest continued. I pursued every lead I could think of. But without a name to go on, I was looking for the proverbial needle in a haystack. Surprisingly, I found the needle.

I didn't even notice it at first. I had gotten a copy of the City Directory of Portland, Oregon, from 1955, with the intent of locating my maternal grandfather. My background data had indicated that he was a poultryman. Discouraged at not finding a single Porter with such an occupation, I filed the directory sheets away. I never thought to look for my birthmother who was a secretary.

A month later I was going through all my paperwork, trying to see if there was anything I'd missed, when I came across the directory sheets and thought to check for any secretary with the last name of Porter. There were no secretaries but there was one stenographer.

Lee C. Porter. Could the "C" stand for Cecelia? But it was her place of business that made my heart stop. She was a stenographer at a law school. My birthfather was supposedly a law student. Had I at last found the name of my birthmother?

It would take four more years to answer that question. I tried to get records from the law school. I tried to get marriage records from the state of Oregon. I even drove by the apartment house where Lee C. Porter lived in 1955. All to no avail.

In 1985, I married and moved to the East Coast. My search slowed down. I was busy with a new life, and finding answers seemed less important. Then something happened that made me stop searching altogether. Something I hadn't anticipated.

My mother died.

I wrote in my journal:

Friday, February 13, 1987
3:00 A.M.

It's late but I can't fall asleep. I lie upon this hospital roll-away cot and watch you breathing softly in the bed a body's length away. The cancer that is devouring you has made you thin. So thin in just ten weeks.

I know you'll die soon. Maybe today. Maybe tonight after Jon arrives. You have been so brave. But that's always been your way, your emotions in check, never burdening others with your own pain or fear. No questions of "why me?" or claims that "it's not fair." We've laughed and we've hugged and we've been stoic. Tonight I feel curiously passive as I watch you let go. Away. Forever.

I need you now more than ever with the baby on the way. Last week when you said you wouldn't have been much help to me in the coming months because you had never given birth you surprised me. I never before heard you voice that you felt somehow "incomplete" as a mother because you hadn't gone through the birth process. I don't think you have to go through labor to teach someone about being a mother. . . .

I can only hope I will be as wonderful a mother as you have been. I wish I were your birthdaughter, if only because it would have been one more thing we could have shared together.

My mom lived through that day and the next. I think, even though she was in a coma, she knew Jon and I were going out for a Valentine's Day dinner. I had told her we were. Knowing her, she wouldn't have wanted to spoil it.

Mom died Sunday, February 15, at three in the morning. I was out of her room, at her home, asleep with Jon. She waited until the time was right and I was safe in someone else's arms. Because that's what mothers do.

My desire to search died for a long time. I grieved. I had my first child. I got on with my life. Then, in April of the following year, Jon and I were talking one night after dinner.

"You know," I said, "I think I can accept that I'll never find my birthparents."

"You ought to give it one more try." Jon had always encouraged my efforts.

"It's too hard to do anything from this long distance."

"Then hire a private investigator." Jon had suggested this more than once. As a last resort, I decided it would be worth a try.

A friend of mine from California gave me Sheila Klopper's name and phone number in Mountain View. Sheila was a private investigator and also an adoptee. She seemed like the perfect choice. But when I called her and relayed all the information I had, she gave me little hope.

"This is not the kind of thing I normally do," she explained. "It seems to me the only lead really worth following is on this Lee C. Porter. But I've got to be honest with you.

She married right after you were born. She's been living under a different name probably ever since. Even if Lee Porter is who you're looking for, she won't be that easy to find through normal channels."

"Aren't there other ways to get information?"

"Like what?"

"I don't know. Borrowing files without permission?"

"We don't do that kind of thing. That only happens in the movies."

I was disappointed. I had this fantasy of private investigators covertly retrieving documents I was unable to access. Like Magnum, P.I., they would sneak in the dead of night into the County Hospital and get the medical records of my birthmother so we would know her name for sure. Going through normal channels was something I'd been doing for years.

For the first time in five years, I gave up. In my heart, I was sure I would never locate either birthparent.

JULY 20, 1988

It seems that whenever I finally let go of something, it comes back to me on its own. I had no expectation of ever hearing from Sheila Klopper, outside of getting a bill. Now here she was, turning my life upside down.

How had she done it? How had she located Lee? How was she sure this was my birthmother?

Sheila had requested marriage records from the State of Oregon. A search (through normal channels) was initiated for any marriages occurring between April of 1955 and December of 1956 for a woman named Lee C. Porter. A copy of the actual marriage certificate was mailed to Sheila, and it contained all the information we needed to know.

Lee C. Porter's full name was Lee *Cecelia* Porter. She was born in August 1934. There was no doubt in my mind that we had found, on the slimmest of leads, the right person.

But where was Lee now? On June 7, 1955, only seven weeks after I was born, she married Louis Iacarella. Lou was born (according to the marriage certificate) in Minneapolis, Minnesota. After checking Oregon telephone listings without finding a single Iacarella, Sheila tried a Minneapolis information operator. There were twenty-six Iacarellas listed. Sheila called the first one on the list, a woman who was a cousin of Lou's. After a short conversation, the woman told Sheila that Lee and Lou had divorced, and that Lou had died a few years ago. Lee now lived in a town in Washington. Along with Lee's phone number and address, she gave Sheila the names of Mike, Sue, Jim, Cathy, Bob, and Charles, Lee's children.

How would I go about contacting Lee Porter? Now that I finally knew where she was, what did I want to say? I spent years looking, but little time thinking about what I would do if I was successful.

Sensitive to the shock my first contact might bring, Sheila, Jon, and I worked out the best plan. Knowing that Lee was devoutly Catholic (from information provided by my adoption agency), I called the parish priest in the town where she lived. The priest knew Lee and, after I explained the situation, he agreed to call her to break the news, and determine how she felt about any contact. He would then call me back.

Within two minutes my phone rang. The priest was very matter of fact.

"Call her," he said. "She's been looking for you for years."

Suddenly, my five-year-long search was ending too fast. My mind was a blank. What was I going to say? All my energies had been focused on *how* to find my birthmother, not on *what* to do when I found her.

I picked up the phone and dialed the number. A woman answered; her voice was shaky.

"Hello?"

"Is this Lee Porter Iacarella?"

"Cecelia?"

With those words, my long search ended. A new odyssey was beginning, one of a reunion and its often confusing and complex aftermath.

~ 2 ~

THE FIRST STEPS

HOW DOES ONE FIND PEOPLE LONG lost? The first step of the journey is making the initial decision to search. This decision is extraordinarily personal. No one can, or should, make it for you.

Annette Baran, coauthor of *The Adoption Triangle*, states that people who search belong to a broad category of "risk-takers." She feels that the vast majority of people *don't* search because they're not willing to "stir the broth."[1] Searches take hard work, patience, money, and energy, not to mention the high emotional risks of facing an unknown situation.

It's important to acknowledge that not everyone chooses to search. When I was searching, every so often someone would ask me, "Why do you have to find these people?" I couldn't understand the question. How could I not look? How could I leave those blanks unfilled? Forever was too long for me. But, while I expected people to understand and respect my motives and needs, at the same time I greatly respected those who chose not to search. A search is not something to undertake on a whim, or because someone else wants you to.

Why do some adoptees choose not to search? I asked a few people to contribute their personal insights. I began within my own family. My cousin Larry, three years older than I, was adopted as an infant. He is like a brother to me and was a major participant in, and supporter of, my own reunion. Yet he has never wanted to search for his own birth relatives, even though his mother has offered her help. I asked him why, and here is his answer:

> All my life I've known I was adopted. My parents wanted me to know that I was "chosen," and that I was loved very much. My only sibling is my sister, who is their natural child and six years older than I. My parents made it very obvious that they felt I was as much a child of theirs as my sister. They were very careful about treating my sister and me as equally as possible.
>
> There was a lot of love in our house when I was young. Since I've always known how much my parents loved me and never questioned the sincerity of their love, I never felt compelled to search for my birthparents.
>
> Over the years I've wondered what my birthparents were like. My mom has given me the few documents my adoption agency gave her that highlighted scant details about my birthfamily. I've seriously thought about finding out what my birthparents were like, but I've never wanted to meet them. Knowing what they look

like and learning about their personalities and what they've done in their lives is all I've ever wanted to know.

I don't feel any special kinship to them. I'm grateful to my birthmother for going through the process of carrying me to term, and I know that every July 30th she thinks of me, but I can honestly say that every July 30th I haven't thought of her. Instead, I've thought of the wonderful parents who adopted me and raised me. They are my "true" parents, even though we don't share any DNA.

Adoptees need to know their birthparents' health histories, what they looked like, and understand a little bit about their backgrounds. Knowing those details, I personally believe there isn't a need for me to know any more. The reasons a child is given up for adoption are extremely personal and I'm sure that some birthmothers never want to "meet their past." Indeed, that is their right.

Examining my situation more closely, I realize that I've never wanted to run the risk of seeking out my birthmother only to discover that she didn't want to be contacted. The rejection would be overwhelming. Perhaps if my birthmother ever left a hint that she would permit my seeking her out when I reached adulthood, I might have given it a try. But I'm content with the fact that she loved me enough to let me go, knowing that I'd be raised in a loving and supportive family that would give me every opportunity they could.

Larry's sentiments are echoed by ice skater and Olympic gold medalist Scott Hamilton. Scott, now in his thirties, has had no desire to seek out his birth family.

My parents were so giving and wonderful, and sacrificed so much for me. They are my parents. I feel that any search for a stranger who gave birth to me would be cruel to the people who raised me and gave me all the love and support I needed when I was growing up.

People have natural curiosities and I can understand that. Some people feel this bond, or this need to find and know their biological parents. But I really have no curiosity at all. I don't feel I missed out or that there's an emptiness or void in my life. To me it would be very bizarre to look for people who are really strangers. It wouldn't accomplish anything. I'd just be meeting more people (I do enough of that already!).

Edith Wagner, founder and publisher of *Reunions—the Magazine*, is also an adoptee. I've always been intrigued that Edith founded a magazine designed, in part, to assist people in their searches, yet she has had no desire to reconnect with her own birthfamily.

Writing about why I don't search is almost like trying to prove innocence. I consider myself insatiably curious and this wouldn't stand the test. "Aren't you curious?" people always ask, to which I respond, "Very, but not about this."

At the meeting to settle our parents' estate, my sister and I were told our birthmothers' names. It had never occurred to me to wonder. I've always known I was adopted. I've always known I was relinquished by someone who did so out of love and concern that I would have every possible advantage in life. My birthparents made a wise and loving decision. And it succeeded.

I was raised in a loving family. I feel connected to my adopted family and never recall feeling empty as I've heard others suggest. I also have a very good sense and confidence of who I am. I've enjoyed good health and don't need hereditary diseases to worry about. While I am a very curious person, I don't wonder much about my birthparents—which seems to be what starts a lot of searchers.

Just because people have chosen *not* to search doesn't mean they won't, at some point, change their minds. Many people who, well into adulthood, have no interest in searching ultimately decide to search. Often there are catalysts involved—a parent dies, a child is born.

In many ways, society inhibits the ability of an adoptee to make the choice to search. Issues of divided loyalty come into play. Adoptees are rarely encouraged to remember or feel any tie to their birthfamily. The idea that an adoptee has *two* sets of parents has never been acknowledged and, in fact, is a concept that makes many people uncomfortable. This is a paradox, considering society's commitment to ensuring ties to both sets of parents and extended families for children whose parents have divorced. In divorce, the need for a child to have equal access is supported by our judicial system, and severing family ties is only done in the most extreme circumstances. Maintaining those relationships is seen as a sacred and necessary right. Why should an adopted person's ties to their birthfamilies be viewed differently?

In spite of these enigmas and despite the difficulties of searching when records are sealed and information is withheld, more and more members of the adoption triad (adoptees, birthparents, and adopted parents) are undertaking searches. For some, the decision to search is an easy choice.

Driven by a strong desire to learn about a birth heritage, or to find a birthchild, they jump into a search without hesitation. Others, however, may agonize over the decision for years. Plagued by doubt or guilt, they ponder questions. How will this affect their parents? What if their birthparents don't want to be found? What if the birthchild was never told he was adopted? What right do they have to disrupt other people's lives? What if they find out something horrible at the end of the search? Until the need to know overcomes their fears, until it is too painful *not* to search, many triad members are not ready to begin.

Whichever way the decision is ultimately arrived at, one characteristic is common among searchers: they *must* know. It is this drive that sustains them throughout their quest. One searcher recalls:

> I started my search calmly. I'd thought casually about searching for years, and finally one day I decided to start. But once I began to look I was overcome by this strong need to find these people. I'm not an obsessive person, but I suddenly felt obsessed. Maybe I had suppressed these feelings before. They surprised me. Suddenly, I *had* to know my past. Nothing else in my life mattered. I really think it was this overpowering need to know which kept me from ever giving up during my search.

Of course, the initial decision to search is only the beginning. Once the decision is made, most searchers are confronted by a perplexing question: Now what? Where and how does one begin to look?

There are many places and sources to begin your investigation. Before you start actively searching, it is wise to spend time getting prepared. This involves planning, research, anticipation, and introspection.

HAVE A PLAN

Like most adoptees, when I began to search, I had no idea what to do. I was able to retrieve all the records my parents had kept about my adoption, but I didn't know how to use the information. If John Riley hadn't helped me, it might have taken me four decades to find my birthmother instead of four years.

Yet, even with outside help, my initial investigation was haphazard and turbulent. I rode an emotional roller coaster. I went from high every time I found a new piece of information to low every time a door was closed in my face. I was putting so much pressure on each information source that I actually impeded my investigation. Like a rookie detective, I was nervous. I'd never done anything like this before. But my desperate attitude worked against me.

For example, when I went to the hospital to try to retrieve my records, I was afraid it was my last chance to find my birthmother's name. I was searching "one step at a time," and I put undue pressure on myself to succeed. More importantly, I hadn't thought ahead of time about what could happen in that office. I walked into the hospital without a clear mind. I had no *plan*. An opportunity presented itself while I was there, and I might have gotten my birthmother's name. But I wasn't prepared. Consequently, I was an ineffective sleuth.

Eventually I realized I was pursuing each lead as if my entire search hinged upon it. To hope to succeed, I had to change the way I approached searching. I needed a game plan—something that would shift my focus away from *what* I was seeking to the process of *how* I was seeking it.

I began to research how others succeeded in their search efforts. Finally, I began to organize what I was doing, and divided my search into two parts: gathering and cross-referencing. Creating a methodology to follow changed my whole attitude. It enabled me to have a sense of control. I began to *think* instead of *feel*.

I encourage everyone to approach his or her own search with a strategy. You'll still have highs and lows, but you'll also have specific goals to focus your energies on. Devise a method that will empower and support you throughout your search. The plan I developed is simple.

In the first phase, the "gathering" phase, the goal is to amass as much background information as possible. There are seven major sources used for research in this phase. These sources are the organizations and individuals who were involved in the events of birth and adoption. They include your adoptive *parents*, the delivery *physician*, the *hospital* where you were born, the adoption *agency*, the *attorney* who represented your parents, the *courts*, and *vital-statistics* offices that recorded your birth.

The "gathering" phase is done first. "Cross-referencing" occurs later, after you've compiled as much background information as possible. This second phase demonstrates your true genius as you take the information you've gathered and cross-match clues. Numerous resources can be utilized, from local libraries to government agencies to private individuals. Cross-referencing is like piecing together a jigsaw puzzle. As each piece fits into place, the picture becomes clearer.

Structuring a search is helpful in many ways. Discouragement will still occur, but the next step to take will already be in your mind. As you read this book and others, formulate your own road map for searching. When you have a map to follow, it's always easier to find your way.

READ!

If there were only one single thing I could recommend to every searcher it would be to *read*. There are many books available on search techniques and reunion experiences. They can be the foundation to success and the key to understanding. Rather than reinventing the wheel, you can benefit from the experience and insight of others. In the back of this book is a detailed bibliography of books that may be difficult to find at your local bookstore or library, but invaluable to own. Most are available directly from their publishers for a modest cost, and it will be money well spent.

Create your own search library. Then *use* it. Read everything from cover to cover. There is no one "right" way to search, no one single author who has all the answers. Each book will offer unique perspectives, different approaches, and new pieces of wisdom, leads, ideas, and suggestions.

The more you know about what you're doing, the better your chances will be for success. And even more important, the more you learn, the more compassion and understanding you will have for every member of the adoption triad, including yourself.

THE SEARCH JOURNAL

The first thing to do to begin your search is to get organized. You'll need to create your own personal system for cataloging information. From day one, you need to keep meticulous track of all the information you gather. Whether in a binder, a journal, or a shoebox, every piece of paper, every fact you learn, should be recorded and kept together.

Create a system that works for you. Some people use a computer, storing all their information on floppy discs. Others use three-by-five cards and a filing system. I used a big binder with two dozen dividers. What works for one person won't necessarily work for another. Our brains all have individualized logic. Determine what method will best enable you to maintain records and to see the big picture as you search while locating the minutest details.

The issue is not what cataloging system you use. Documenting your search is. The tiniest clue found early may be the one that leads to the end of your search years down the road. Take care to record every lead that you follow. Write down synopses of telephone conversations and meetings. Xerox everything. Something seemingly insignificant may become the keystone of your efforts.

That was certainly the case for me. If I hadn't carefully kept track of every piece of paper that I accumulated in my search, I might have lost track of the city-directory page with Lee C. Porter's name on it. Remember, I didn't even notice the clue the first time I looked at that directory. It wasn't until weeks later when I was browsing through my search journal that I stumbled upon the one piece of information that led me to my birthmother. If I had kept my research scattered around the house, or worse, if I had thrown away pages that seemed of no value, I might never have found her.

Be sure to keep copies not only of what you have received and gathered but also of what you yourself have *sent*. This will help you recall *whom* you contacted, *how* you worded your request, and *when* it was sent. Such records are valuable for future correspondence and for tracking your investigation.

I recommend that you also make a place to record your thoughts and feelings. Use your journal as a "friend," a sounding board, a place to record all the emotions you're experiencing. A search can be a roller-coaster ride. You may feel ecstatic, depressed, obsessive, brilliant, excited, angry, and scared all in the same week. It can be cathartic to write it all down.

How to Ask for Information

Some people are born investigators. They ask for information without batting an eye and are cool, calm, and collected in every situation. Able to think quickly on their feet, they charm or finesse information out of sources seemingly without effort.

Unfortunately, such characteristics are not in everyone's repertoire. Many searchers are hyper, unsure, and revealing in their dealings with sources. I was certainly that way in face-to-face encounters in the early stages of my search.

What can be done to be more effective in requesting information? Here are a few suggestions for you to consider as you begin your search.

1. *Believe in your right to know* about your origins. Your attitude will inspire confidence in others, particularly sources.

2. *Always be friendly and courteous*—even when someone does not respond in kind. There's no sense burning bridges for yourself or for those searchers who follow in your footsteps.

3. In a polite way, *never take "no" for an answer.* Keep calling back, keep trying. Don't be neurotic. Calmly

convince people that your need for information is not an idle request.

4. *Be prepared*. Always think through ahead of time how you're going to approach someone. Write it out and even practice in front of a mirror.

5. Whenever possible, *write to request information* instead of going in person. You may not get the information as rapidly, but you may have a better chance for success.

KNOW YOUR RIGHTS AND KNOW THE LAW

It's important to know what the laws are regarding adoption records and access to information in the state where you're searching. Your local library may (and certainly a law library will) have current legal texts that can enlighten you about your legal rights in your state. It's wise to check periodically to see if your state has changed its policies regarding sealed records. Many states have amended their procedures over the past decade. Some now maintain state registries to facilitate reunions. Learn what services are available to you. Talk with other searchers in your area to get an idea of their personal experiences.

PROFILING

As you acquire bits of information about the people you seek, begin to *profile* them.

Who are they? Where are they from? What do they look like? What interests do they have? What do they do for a living?

THE PROFILE CHART

Name: _____

Birthdate: _____ Birthplace: _____

Age at Your Birth: _____ Last Known Address: _____

Marital Status: _____

Height: _____ Weight: _____

Eye Color: _____ Hair Color: _____

Religion: _____ Race: _____

Citizenship: _____

Nationality(s): _____ _____

Educational Background: _____

Medical History: _____

Military Service: _____

Background History: _____

_____

_____

It can help to organize all the facts about each person on a single page. Here's an example of a profile chart (page 33). Create a chart on each individual, and then keep the charts in your search journal. Make charts for each person about whom you have information, including birth grandparents, aunts, uncles, siblings, etc. Refer to these charts frequently throughout your search. Use them to try to envision in your mind the people you're looking for and what paths they may have followed since your birth.

ARE YOU READY TO SEARCH?

What do you expect from your search? What do you think you might find? How do you hope that will make you feel?

We all have conscious or subconscious fantasies about our roots. Part of preparing for a search is to address those desires, needs, fears, and assumptions, and place them in perspective with the uncertain outcome ahead.

When I was searching, I tried to think ahead to what the possible outcome of my search would be. I tried to prepare myself for rejection. I sat down and made a list of all the possible scenarios that I could envision.

This was the most important exercise I did to prepare, not only for searching, but for finding. It made me think about what I was feeling, to discover what my hopes and fears were, and to ready myself for the uncertainty ahead. It also made me focus on the people I sought, and to try to anticipate what their own needs and fears might be. I was looking for human beings, not encyclopedias. It was important to try to put myself in their shoes. I had no desire to hurt anyone.

Use the following list of questions as a framework to help you examine your feelings and needs periodically throughout your search.[2]

QUESTIONS FOR SEARCHERS

How long have you been wanting to search?

What has happened that precipitates your desire to do it now?

What are you looking for?

What do you want to find? (Your conscious expectations.)

What are your fantasies? (Your subconscious imaginings.)

What are your fears?

What do you want from these people when you find them?

How little will you accept?

If you are a birthparent, how much information are you going to be willing to share with your birthchild?

Are you angry? If so, whom are you angry at?

If you were the one being found, how would you want the search and first contact handled?

Who can you talk with about your search?

If you find something horrible, will you accept that you searched because you needed to, not because of what you might find?

These are important questions to consider throughout your search. The more of an assessment you can take of your innermost feelings, the better prepared you'll be to search. No matter what anyone else says, you have to listen most to yourself.

There's no bible that can tell you exactly what's going to happen or what you should do. Each individual's situation is unique. A search is a journey into the unknown. The only "known" that you have the ability to control is yourself. The more you examine your own feelings, the more awareness you'll have of what you think you might find—the more prepared you will be both to undertake your search and to handle a reunion.

Once you've taken time to get organized and to plan your search, it's time to begin. But remember this as you start your quest: No matter what you listed as possible outcomes of your search, no matter what you've determined are your innermost hopes, the reality is there is only *one* thing that you can truly hope and expect to find in your search: *knowledge.*

Knowledge about your origins is your birthright.

~ 3 ~

PHASE I: YOUR SEARCH BEGINS

YOU'VE DECIDED YOU MUST SEARCH. YOU'VE analyzed your motives. Emotionally you feel ready for the journey ahead. You've decided how you're going to organize all the information you gather. Now your search begins.

As you begin to search, it's important to consider what principals will guide your efforts. Follow your own sense of ethics. Be true to yourself and don't let others deter you from your goal. I found the following ten rules helpful to me throughout the years that I was searching.

10 RULES FOR A SEARCH

1. Try to stand in the shoes of the people you seek.

2. Ask the right questions.

3. Keep records of everything.

4. Be patient. Don't jump to hasty conclusions.

5. Repetition of information helps establish facts.

6. Leave no stone unturned.

7. Assume anything you've been told could be wrong.

8. Never assume you are seeking people who don't want to be found. Your birthparents didn't seal your records—society did.

9. Think. Use your own creativity. *You* are the most motivated searcher you can hire.

10. Remember—you are not alone. There are many people who care about you who will support your effort.

The first phase of the search is targeted at defining precisely *whom* you're looking for. To know whom you're looking for, you need to know a number of facts. Most importantly, you need a name.

AMENDED BIRTH CERTIFICATES

Your first objective is an easy one: your amended birth certificate. A copy of this piece of paper was given to your parents when your adoption was made final. Your original birth certificate (which contained the names of your birthparents) was then sealed.

Perhaps you have had this document in your possession all your life, yet never realized it holds clues that can help you learn your original identity. Certain obvious changes were made on the amended certificate: the names of your birthparents, their ages and states of birth were removed and replaced with your adoptive parents' names, etc. The name you were given at birth was also changed. But the rest of the information is usually intact. Your birthdate, the exact time of your birth, the hospital or location where you were born, the city and county, and the name of the physician who delivered you are generally listed. These clues will help lead you into your past.

Most searchers start out without knowing their given names at birth, or the names of their birthparents. There are seven resources that you can initially turn to as you begin to try to find them:

> Adoptive parents
> The adoption agency
> The attorney of record
> The delivery physician
> Vital-statistics agencies
> The delivery hospital
> The state courts

ADOPTIVE PARENTS

The first people to consider approaching are, for many adoptees, the most difficult: their adoptive parents. There are some parents who open the door before an adoptee ever has to ask, offering their assistance in search efforts. A few go so far as to initiate a search themselves, sensing the information they find is important to their child. But other parents hesitate to discuss even the fact that their children are adopted (in fact, some adoptees never learn until adulthood that they were adopted). Obviously, there's a wide range of scenarios between these two extremes.

Whether you choose to include your parents will depend

upon your circumstances. But there are a number of reasons why it's helpful to discuss the search with them. To begin with, chances are they have documents and memories that can help you get started. They can also provide tremendous support. But asking for that information and help is not always an easy proposition.

I know this from personal experience, having chosen not to include my mother in my search because I thought I was protecting her. Afraid she might misunderstand my motives and assume that I was searching to find better parents or a better life, I worried about causing her grief. But I must also admit that beneath my altruistic concern about hurting her was an enormous fear. As close as my mother and I were, as much as I knew she loved me, subconsciously I was afraid she might reject me—abandon me—if I pursued my search. Nothing in our mother-daughter relationship gave any credence to this fear, but it seemed logical to me. A mother had "abandoned" me once before.

For an adoptee, that step of including parents in the decision to search can be the ultimate test of the love and experiences that bond them to each other. Certainly nowadays, with so many searches and reunions being covered by the media, most adoptive parents must ask themselves at some point how they will respond if their children choose to search. They may hesitate, however, to bring up the subject. Many parents simply decide to wait until their children ask.

Even though both parents and adoptees may be reluctant or afraid to broach the topic, once it's out in the open it can be a relief. Virgil Klunder writes that he was concerned he might hurt his adoptive mother when he decided to search. But when he finally chose to confide in her she was, to his surprise, delighted. "She wondered why I had never asked earlier, gave me all the information she had, and proved to be a great help!"[1]

If your parents are willing to help in your search, ask them to gather all the documents they have from your adoption. Their paperwork may include your background history from the adoption agency (unless your adoption was handled independently through an attorney). They may have forms from a foster parent who was responsible for your care before placement. And, most importantly, they will probably have the final decree of adoption.

The *final decree* is the document issued by the court that grants parents permanent custody of the adopted child. This is issued at the end of a probationary period and legally finalizes the adoption. Most parents keep a copy of this document because it proves the adopted child is legally theirs.

The decree is important to you as a searcher because it should tell you *your original name.*

Unless you were abandoned and your birthparents were never located (in which case you might be listed as "Baby Jane Doe"), you were probably given at least a first or last name when you were relinquished. Many birthmothers gave their children complete names.

Names can carry hidden clues. Your first name or middle name may have been the name of one of your birthparents, or the name of a grandparent. Having the last name alone is a great coup. If you can learn what the marital status of your birthmother was at the time you were born, it may indicate whether the last name you were given was hers or your birthfather's (single mothers almost always give the child their own last name).

Another document your parents may have is the *petition to adopt.* This legal paper is the formal request to the court by your parents that they be granted adoption. Like the final decree, this document should have your original name, birth-date, and birthplace. It also may contain your birthmother's full name and address. Parents are less likely to have received a copy of the petition, but sometimes they do. You won't know unless you ask.

If for some reason your parents no longer have a copy of either the petition to adopt or the final decree, the attorney who represented your parents in the adoption may have a copy on file. The attorney's office might not be willing to release a copy to you, but they should to their clients—your parents.

ADOPTION AGENCIES

Many adoption agencies will provide information to adult adoptees, except names and addresses. In fact, some agencies, with the consent of all three parties of the adoption triangle (or sometimes only two parties) will assist in facilitating a reunion. Social workers may even (on behalf of an adoptee) initiate contact with a birthparent to see if he or she is willing to be reunited with the birthchild.

In recent years, many agencies have become more sensitive to the strong needs of adoptees to connect with their roots. They generally try to complete as much of the picture as they can for the adoptee. But, as a rule, most will not release any identifying information. Some social workers feel honor-bound not to do so. Others are restricted by law.

The agency that handled your adoption may have provided your parents with a background history of you at the time of your adoption. This report can include:

A physical description
Age
Birthdate and/or birthplace of birthparents
Nationalities
Religion
Occupation
Education

Most agencies also try to provide as complete a medical history of the birthparents as possible, though most birthparents are young and healthy. The report may include a synopsis of the events surrounding your conception and birth. Sometimes this information may have been informally relayed to your parents through a conversation with a social worker. Ask your parents to try to remember specific facts they were told by the agency.

If your parents have the background report, should you still attempt to contact the adoption agency? By all means. More information might be divulged—either facts omitted from the report at the time of your adoption or events that have occurred since.

For example, I already had a background report from my parents, but I contacted the agency anyway. The agency's response that my birthmother had contacted them when I was five and that she had other children gave me both confidence that she wanted to know what had happened to me and inspiration that I had half-siblings to find as well. And the agency's repetition of the information my parents had been given further substantiated what I already knew about myself.

Give the agency as much information about yourself as possible so that they will be able to locate your file: your birthdate, your social-service case number (from agency paperwork your parents may have), the court-order number (from the final decree), and your parents' names and address at the time of your adoption. Follow up this information with every question you can think of:

Are there photographs of your birthparents on file?
If not, is there any written description of them?
How old were your birthparents at the time of your birth?
Were they married? Divorced?
Where were they born?
Where were their families from originally?
Had they gone to high school? College?
What were their personalities like?
Did they have special talents? Hobbies? Interests?
What did they do for a living?
Is anything known about your natural grandparents?
How about other blood relatives? Aunts? Uncles?
Is there any medical information you should be aware of?
Do you have any known siblings?
What were your birthparents' religions?
What were the circumstances of your relinquishment?

Think up as many questions as you hope they have answers for, and also ask questions about things you may already know. Redundancy of information helps establish the facts.

It's advisable to make the initial contact with the agency through the mail. Call the agency first and ask where to direct your inquiry. This saves time and makes sure the right person receives your request. Except in rare instances, agencies will answer such inquiries.

Follow up the agency's response with a thank-you letter. Try to establish a rapport with the social worker. Use this opportunity to ask about the possibility of a reunion.

You will find that agencies and individuals are more supportive if you have your parents' support. One document that will be quite helpful to you throughout your search is a *waiver of confidentiality*. Many adoption agencies have their own waiver forms, and state departments of social services may have waivers that you can use.

If possible, ask your parents to sign a waiver. Carry this with you whenever you meet with someone in connection with your search. Most people are much more comfortable in assisting your efforts if they understand you have the blessing of your parents.

Make sure you give a copy to the agency and the lawyer who handled your adoption. On the outside chance that your birthmother or birthfather is trying to locate you, the agency will need a waiver from you on file to make a reunion possible. Some states, like California, no longer require a waiver from the adoptive parents. There, reunions can be facilitated by agencies if a birthparent and an adoptee sign waivers—as long as the adoptee is of majority age.

In your follow-up letter to the agency, ask if they can assist you with any further information. Would they be willing to try to contact your birthmother to see if she is interested in a reunion? More and more agencies are willing to try to help with reunions. Generally, however, they will *control* the process. They will not reveal any identifying information but instead will act as intermediaries on your behalf. Many people are surprised to hear that most of the individuals in the open-records movement don't support this move toward agency and state mediation of reunions. Why not?

Jean Paton, who many consider the "mother of the

search movement," because forty years ago she was the first adoptee to publish works documenting the need of adoptees to know more about their origins, explained her concerns in an essay on intermediaries. In it, she questions why intervention of any kind is necessary.

> A social worker wants to be, and is rapidly becoming, an intermediary between an adoptee and his birth family. But exactly what training and poise does the social worker bring to this task, and why is an adopted adult unable to make this move by himself? . . . [Social workers] are not trained in any way to make these encounters. They have never done any follow-up contacts with birthmothers. Why do they insist on getting the law to give them this opportunity? . . . They are asking for intermediary power with the same sure organized hand they used to get records sealed.[2]

One cannot ignore, however, that an agency has the ability to solve your puzzle. And many social workers can be a tremendous help. Rather than acting as intermediaries, they can provide empowering assistance to the searching adoptee. It depends upon how enlightened and how knowledgeable they are about the process of search and reunion.

Many social workers have made a great effort in the last decade to learn from the adoptees and birthparents who have come to them seeking information and help with reuniting. Their increased understanding has often led to a more cooperative attitude and changes in agency policy.

Contact the agency again to let them know the reasons you want to locate your birthparents. Can they tell you your birthparents' first names? After all, how could someone's first name be considered "identifying information"? At the very least, could they tell you their initials?

Always use your intuition. Has the agency seemed helpful so far? Can you couch your request in such a way that they might respond more readily? Should you wait longer, establish a better contact, before asking the agency for help?

Knowing someone is holding all the information you want and need right before him or her, and then having it withheld from *you* can be extraordinarily frustrating. Every adoptee who searches probably feels that frustration at some point or another. When it happens, try to maintain your composure. *Always be courteous and appreciative.* That keeps the door open for another day, not only for you but also for others searching.

Whatever the outcome with the adoption agency, you are likely to have new information to add to the profiles of the people you seek. You may not have names—yet. But any information you acquire about them can help you find their names elsewhere.

THE ATTORNEY OF RECORD

The amount of involvement of an attorney in your adoption depended upon whether your adoption was handled through an agency or independently. Your parents were the clients that the attorney served and, if at all possible, they should be included in any attempt to retrieve information from the law office. At the very least, bring along a signed waiver of confidentiality if you can. Make an appointment with the attorney and offer to pay for his time. This approach makes your request formal and professional.

Whenever you have contact with an individual, your potential success in gaining information will rest somewhat on that individual's personal value system. Even though there may be no law restricting attorneys from providing information about adoptions, if they personally disagree with an adoptee's right to search, the adoptee has no power to force them to cooperate. Hopefully, the law firm will share with you (or your parents) the documents maintained in their files.

THE DELIVERY PHYSICIAN

Odds are you were delivered by a physician in a hospital. Locating the person who delivered you can be the key to solving your mystery. Even if a delivery physician doesn't remember your birthmother (and chances are he won't), he may have *medical records* on file that will have your birthmother's name and an old address.

Doctors are easy to find. The first place to look, obviously, is the hospital where you were born. If the doctor no longer works there, the hospital administration may know where he or she is currently practicing. Also, try your local library for a copy of the *AMA Medical Directory* in the reference section. These list almost every licensed physician in the country, and will give you current addresses.

If you strike out at the library, contact the Medical Quality Assurance Board or the Board of Medical Examiners in the state of your birth—usually located in the state capital. Call or write them and ask for your doctor's license number and a copy of his license file. Midwives are also licensed by the state, so if your birth was attended by a midwife and not a physician, the board may help you to locate her.

Vital-Statistics Agencies

Sometimes records remain unsealed. It is not unknown for an adoptee to receive a copy of the original birth certificate simply by writing to the state Bureau of Vital Statistics and requesting it.

The key to receiving an original birth certificate is using your original name. Most states require the following information: your original name, your date of birth, the city where you were born, and both your mother's and father's names.

Write a short letter to the Bureau of Vital Statistics, and use only the facts you know. Your birthdate and time, the county and hospital, and the attending physician are all things you already know. By now, you may know your original name. If you know either birthparent's name, include that. Find out what fees are necessary, and mail your request in with a *money order*. Don't use a personal check—it has the wrong name.

The Delivery Hospital

Although my delivery hospital sent me little information that was useful, I remember how just seeing my birthmother's smudged thumbprint next to my baby footprint on the hospital record made me feel a strange sense of connection. It wasn't a picture or a name, but it was *her* thumbprint. In a sea of many dead ends, this felt like a small victory.

Hospitals usually keep files on both you and your birthmother. There will be a record of your birthmother's admittance to the hospital, which will have her name and address. There may be a certificate of live birth and a newborn record on file, both of which might list vital information like your birthmother's name and signature.

Call the hospital records department and learn what procedures are necessary to obtain a copy of your medical file. You may need to know your original name. It might be helpful to have your personal physician make this request for you. While a clerk may hesitate to respond to your personal request for records, he will not question such a request from a doctor.

STATE COURTS

If you've had no luck receiving information from any of the above sources, then there is another avenue to try: appeal to the state courts to open your records.

One professional searcher advised me to put this step at the top of the list of things to do. She feels that many people avoid this path to open their records because they are intimidated by the idea of going to court. Because of this, judges only see people come into their courtrooms as a last resort.

Most adoptees don't realize that judges have the most power in the system. Definition of "good cause" for opening an individual's records is totally at a judge's discretion. In many ways, a judge is more powerful than a legislator. More than any other group of individuals, judges can help effect changes in the sealed-records system. It's crucial that they become aware of how many adoptees and birthparents want to and *need* to see their records.

Learn what decisions have been made by the courts in your state regarding opening adoptee records. Are records opened only when a medical emergency warrants it? Or are there other instances when records are unsealed? Are there circumstances like yours? Could there be? Is there a specific form that must be filed in your petition to open records? You can shortcut your legal research by talking with local search groups or searchers who are already familiar with codes and recent legal interpretations.

Some adoptees have had success contacting a judge informally before filing a petition. Some judges are sympathetic to an adoptee's impassioned plea to learn about his or her roots. Explain why you need to learn about your birthfamily. If your parents have signed a waiver of confidentiality, include that as a part of your plea. If you are unsuccessful in either a written or in-person plea with a judge, then hire a lawyer and file a formal petition with the courts.

Gathering as much information as you can from these seven sources completes the first phase of your search. Depending upon your own circumstances, you by now have either a lot of information or seemingly little. But even without that all-important original birth name, you may have enough information to profile your birthparents:

Who were they? Where were they from? What did they look like: height, weight, hair and eye color? What interests did they have? What did they do for a living?

The adoption agency nonidentifying information is frequently key to creating this "sketch." Create a profile chart on both your birthmother and birthfather. Make charts on other birth relatives as well if you have been able to learn anything about them. Review every piece of information that you have cataloged in your search journal. Reread each line, each word, for possible clues. Is there anything you might have missed? Fill in as many blanks as you can.

Now look carefully at your birthmother's chart. If you have her name or an old address, you have a lot to go on. But perhaps the opposite is true in your case. You don't have much. Let's say you only know her physical description and a few other meager clues. Your profile chart has blank spaces.

Don't despair! I *never* knew an exact name. All I had was a description, an occupation, and a birthdate. And I was able to find my birthmother. It happens!

If you feel you have been clever to date in your search, you're right. But now your search becomes truly creative. You will use your own genius to cross-reference clues and solve more of your puzzle.

Armed with whatever information you now have, you're ready to cross-reference. Now you are searching for a person.

Where do you look next? Take your search journal and your wits and make haste to your local library.

～ 4 ～

PHASE II:
CROSS-REFERENCING

FACT: THE PEOPLE YOU ARE SEEKING have their names in print somewhere. All you have to do is find them through a process of elimination.

Whether in phone books, newspapers, directories, class lists, or drivers' licenses, everybody appears somewhere on paper. As you move forward in your search, try to zero in on a specific person, cross-referencing clues to piece your puzzle together.

Trips to the library may not have excited you in the past. That's about to change. Your whole mystery can be unlocked within a library's stacks. There are vast resources at your disposal, and no one at a library is ever going to say, "No, you can't see that."

A good central library will have all the reference materials you need to begin. If you're not familiar with how to use a library or how to find specific information, just ask. Librarians can be the most helpful people on earth. You may find yourself working in tandem with a librarian in your hometown and a librarian a thousand miles away in the home county of your birthmother. Doing research long distance through interlibrary loan is entirely plausible, effective, and practical.

To me, the key to being a successful searcher is to ask the right questions. Asking, "How am I ever going to find anyone?" or "Where on earth do I begin?" is never going to move you forward. Set small goals and objectives, and ask questions that will help you solve them. The ultimate destination may seem impossible, but each little task you accomplish will get you closer. Empower yourself. Focus on one step at a time.

Regional Connections

You can begin Phase II of your search by asking, "What was the town where I was born like in the year of my birth?" What is it like today? What about the area where your birthmother or your birthfather was from?

Profiling a town or region won't necessarily give you specific clues—although it can. It *will* definitely give you a sense of time, place, and circumstance. Use it to broaden your knowledge of your past and an understanding of the people to whom you're biologically related.

Use the many resources available in libraries and elsewhere to develop profiles of those regions where you and your birthparents originated.

What industry exists?
What's the population of the area?

What schools, churches, and hospitals are there?
What are the people from the region like?
Are they predominantly middle class?
Catholic, Jewish, Protestant? Liberal or conservative?

You *can* find the answers to these questions. Knowing more about where you're looking serves two purposes: it enhances your knowledge of your own roots and provides insight into where to look.

Being able to visualize the area you're looking in can also be extremely helpful. Get maps of the town where you were born, the places where your birthparents were born, and the place you believe they might be in today.

If you are lucky enough to have old addresses or places of employment, locate the street your birthmother lived on. Are former neighbors still living there who might remember her? Could they know where she moved? If she married, do they know her new name?

When divers do an underwater search, they begin where they expect to find an object and anchor a rope in that spot. Then they slowly and meticulously swim a spiral out from the center until they locate the object of their search. This saves time and energy and keeps them from missing what they seek.

Searching for a person can be done in a similar fashion. Begin where you started, and in the regions that your birthparents were from, and spiral out, checking surrounding towns and counties for contacts and records.

CITY DIRECTORIES

Do you have a possible last name for a birthparent (from your own original name), but no *first* name to know exactly whom you're looking for? Or do you have an old address or phone number as a clue, but no name?

Most cities publish, or have published, city or crisscross directories. These marvelous resources list residents in three ways: by name, phone number, and street address.

A city directory can tell you:

Resident's name
Address
Whether the resident owns or rents
Telephone number
Marital status
Occupation
Place of business

Directories may also give forwarding addresses of residents who have moved in the previous year. This is invaluable for tracking someone to a new location.

How can you use a directory to cross-reference information and lead you to a person?

Let's say you know your original birthname from your final decree. If you know a location—a town—where your birthmother may have resided, begin by looking in directories for the appropriate years. Perhaps your birthmother was too young to be employed, but you know that your maternal grandfather was a clockmaker. Armed with a directory for the year *before* your birth, look under the heading for your original last name. Can you find any individuals who were clockmakers? If so, you may have located your birthgrandfather. Obviously, if your birthmother or birthfather had an occupation, you would also check them in this way.

To verify if you're on the right track, follow individuals listed in city directories forward and backward through different years. For example, if you locate an individual with the same last name and occupation as your birthmother in a directory a year or two before your birth, does she disappear the year of your birth? Does she reappear a few years later? Did she exist five or ten years before your birth? Would this match the description of your birthmother? Let's say your birthmother was twenty-one when you were born and you were told she was a dental hygienist, and you find a dental hygienist with the same last name in the city directory. But cross-referencing backward you find the person was also listed in the city directory ten years before your birth (when your birthmother would have been eleven). Obviously, the hygienist in the directory couldn't be your birthmother.

Directories can help you narrow a list of names down to a single person. Note where she lived. Can you tell if she owned or rented the residence?

Using the directory section that indexes by *addresses*, determine who her neighbors were in the year of your birth. Do they still live there? You can locate them through current directories and phone books.

Are there other people you can locate who may have known this woman? A landlord perhaps? Is her place of employment listed? Does the company still exist? Does anyone working there remember your birthmother? Do personnel records exist?

It goes without saying that discretion is necessary when contacting other people in order to locate birthfamily members. Say you're trying to locate an old friend of the family. Respect each individual's privacy as much as possible.

If you think you've found a potential match, track that person through subsequent years. Did she move? Did she suddenly disappear? Could that mean she married? Check marriage records and announcements for those years.

A word of caution about city directories. They are wonderful resources, but be aware that it can take time for data to be updated. Information on an individual isn't always complete in each publication. Check a span of years instead of just one single year to avoid missing a key listing.

NEWSPAPER BIRTH ANNOUNCEMENTS

When you were born, your arrival was probably not listed in the birth-announcement section of the newspaper. But when your birthparents were born, unless they were also adopted, it's possible their births were announced in a local paper. If you know approximately *when* and *where* your birthparents were born, or if you have an exact date but no name, newspaper birth announcements are a great resource.

What can a birth announcement tell you? The baby's name and birthdate, the parents' names and sometimes their address. That's a lot!

Once you know which newspaper you want, all you have to do is get microfilm copies—most are available through interlibrary loan.

There are three main records that newspapers keep: birth and marriage announcements and obituaries. They all tend to be in the same section. Some papers announce births only once a week. See if your paper follows any such pattern—it will save you time.

When looking for birth announcements in newspapers, realize it can take months for an announcement to appear. You should check several months after the date you are trying to confirm. Let's say you know from the background information your adoption agency supplied you that your birthmother was born on September 2, 1937, in Philadelphia, but you don't know her name. You would want to make a list of all baby girls you can find that were born on

September 2 in Philadelphia. To be safe, check for announcements at least six months after that date.

With that list of names, check a city directory of the area where you believe your birthmother lived when you were conceived or born. Do any names match up? For example, if there are fifty baby girls born in Philadelphia on September 2, 1937, and you know you were born in Seattle, Washington, do any of those fifty names, or the baby's parents' names, show up in the Seattle city directory or phone book in the years near your birth?

Another way to use birth announcements from newspapers would be if you don't have a birthdate for your birthmother but you know your original last name from your final decree. Let's say it was *Dutton*. You also know from your adoption agency that your birthmother was born in Topeka, Kansas, and that she was twenty-four years old when you were born. If you were born in May of 1950, that would mean your birthmother would have to have been born between May of 1926 and May of 1928. Check Topeka papers for a two-and-a-half-year period from May of 1926 through December of 1928 looking for the announcement of any baby girl Dutton.

Again, be sure to write down *any* names you find for your search journal. Then begin cross-referencing with other sources. Remember, birthmothers often give their birthchildren first and middle names that have meaning. Whether it is her own name, or the name of a relative, your original first and middle name could be significant clues.

MARRIAGE ANNOUNCEMENTS AND CERTIFICATES

Newspaper marriage announcements and obituaries are also useful. For example, knowing your birthmother's maiden name is helpful, but unfortunately it might not leave a trail you can follow very far. She may have married at least once between your birth and now. If you have an idea where she grew up, check old newspapers from that area for her marriage announcement.

Marriage announcements give significant information: parents' names and addresses, and most importantly, the last name of the groom. Also, announcements frequently include a picture of the bride and groom.

Checking county marriage records can also yield results. Marriage certificates can tell you:

Names of bride and groom
Birthdates
Birthplaces
Parents
Addresses

Marriage certificates also give you names of three other people who may help you locate the people you're seeking: the minister who married the couple and the two witnesses. The name of the church may be on the license, which will help you locate the minister. Witnesses frequently list their addresses.

OBITUARIES, DEATH RECORDS, AND CEMETERIES

Obituaries are another valuable resource, although one that searchers seem to avoid. Death records generally contain a short biography of the deceased *and* a list of next of kin.

If you have traced a birth grandparent, for example, through city directories and then that grandparent disappears, one of two things may have happened: the grandparent either moved or died.

Check the obituaries of the local paper for a five-year period (city directories may take a year or two to catch up on current information). Let's say you are lucky and find a birth grandparent's obituary. Your birthmother's maiden name was Lois Smithe. You have never been able to discover her married name. A typical obituary will give it to you as "Jonas Smithe is survived by two daughters, Pauline Smithe of Belmont, and Lois Greer of Las Cruces, New Mexico." Obviously this sentence could lead you straight to your birthmother.

Another way to use the obituaries is by starting in a cemetery. If you know your original last name and the town your birthparents or birth grandparents came from, check the local cemeteries to see if you can locate individuals with that name who've died. Record the date of death from the gravestone of anyone who seems to be a possible relative. Then look up the obituaries for that date.

There are investigative companies around the United States that have copies of the "Master Death File" from the Social Security Administration. This data base contains the records of the majority of deaths that have occurred in the U.S. since 1962—over 46 million names. Each record contains the name, birthdate, and date of death of the deceased and the zip code of the place of death. These pieces of information can prove very valuable in locating next of kin of the deceased.

One company that has this data base at very reasonable fees is:

Cambridge Statistical Research Associates, Inc.
23 Rocky Knoll
Irvine, California 92715
714–509–9900

High Schools and Colleges

Your birthparents probably attended high school. It's possible that they went to college. If you have an idea where they might have attended school, you may be able to locate them.

High schools, both public and private, generally publish annual yearbooks. These often include pictures, not just of the graduating seniors but of every attending student.

Can you guess by what you know of either birthparent *where* he or she may have attended school and *when* he or she should have graduated? Remember to take into account the details of your birth. For example, if your birthmother was seventeen when you were born, she may not have graduated with her class or finished high school at all. Look for her as a freshman or sophomore.

If possible, visit the school you believe your birthparents may have attended. Old yearbooks are often housed either in school libraries or in administrative offices. It's wise to call the school before making a special trip to be sure old copies still exist of the yearbook you seek.

Be sure to check the year before and the year after because some students skip grades, others are held back. I know of a young woman who located her birthparents on the first day of her search simply by looking them up in a college yearbook. Obviously it helped that she knew their names.

Name Derivations

There are ways to use school yearbooks to locate people even if you don't know their names. Let's say you know from background information that the adoption agency supplied you with that your birthmother was of Czechoslovakian descent but you don't know her last name. Let's say you also know from the agency that she was from Madera, Missouri. You learn there's only one high school in Madera. On the chance that she attended Madera High, you could go through the high school yearbook for the year(s) your birthmother may have attended school and write down the names of any girls with Slavic sounding surnames. How can you find out what the national origin of a surname is?

Books like *A Dictionary of Surnames* can help sort out which names are Czechoslovakian versus Yugoslavian, which names are English versus Irish, which are Russian versus Polish.

Identifying the national origin of a surname can be very helpful in confirming a possible name or in narrowing down a list of names. If you know a physical description of your birthparent, the photographs of each student in the annual can help narrow down the list even more. And remember, you may greatly resemble the person you seek.

I know one adoptee who knew her birthfather attended a specific college and also knew he was of Norwegian descent but didn't know his name. Simply by going through the school annual and using a book of surname derivations, the adoptee was able to narrow down the list of possibilities to one specific individual.

Also, local newspapers frequently print pictures and names of graduating high school and college seniors, sometimes indicating the student's plans. This is another way to use newspapers to help you "follow the trail" that your birthparents left behind.

High school classes usually have reunions after ten and twenty-five years, with a reunion chair for each class. The administrative office of the school (or the school district if

the school no longer exists) should be able to help you establish contact with the reunion chair. Ask for an updated
address list of the entire class. This can be an extraordinary
find. Even if your birthparent's name is not on the current
list, you may be able to locate someone who knew him or
her. Again remember to exercise discretion. No one needs
to know *why* you're trying to contact this individual. Tell
them you're seeking an old friend of the family that you've
lost touch with. Doing this protects your birthparent's (or
birthchild's) privacy.

CHURCH RECORDS

Depending upon their denomination, churches can provide
significant information to searchers through birth, baptismal,
marriage, divorce, and death records. Churches are used to
receiving requests from people for genealogical research, and
will frequently open their records. Events are generally cataloged by sacrament, and then by date. If you know the
denomination of your birthparents, and the area they may
have been living in when they were born or married, a local
church may provide the key to locating birth relatives.

Also seek out your own records. For example, if you are
Catholic, check the Catholic church in the immediate vicinity
of the hospital where you were born to locate original baptismal records. Many parents baptized their children as
quickly as possible, lest the infant be doomed to an eternity
in limbo.

One adoptee discovered his birthmother's name simply
by visiting a church near where he was adopted. He had only
visited the church to see if a priest there could enlighten him
as to more information about the local orphanage, which had
been closed years before. But while he was there, the priest

allowed him to see the parish baptismal records. There was the adoptee's birthmother's name, right next to his own, in the record book. The adoptee left the church in shock. It was the first day of his search.

SEARCH AND SUPPORT GROUPS AND REGISTRIES

Any experienced searcher reading through this book is by now shouting, "Hey, what about search and support groups and registries!!" I haven't excluded them, but felt that first I needed to devote an entire chapter to the organizations and private individuals that provide search and reunion support. Chapter 5 details many of the options available.

ADVERTISE

It can pay to advertise. By placing an ad in the classified section of a newspaper from your search area, you may be able to have immediate and direct contact. An ad might read:

BIRTHMOTHER: DO YOU KNOW ME?
BABY GIRL SIMMONS
Born: SEPTEMBER 9, 1948
County Hospital, Elmora, Virginia
Please reply: P.O. Box 1, New York, NY 10000

Where should you place an ad? In any newspaper of a locality where you believe your birthmother or other birth relatives might reside. When? The best time might be around the time of your birthday every year. You can try at any time, of course, but many birthmothers indicate that they think about birthchildren on their birthdays. An ad may be more likely to catch a birthmother's eye during this time.

There are also specialty magazines in which it might be useful to place an ad. Periodicals like *Reunions* have a section specifically for people searching. Advertising there might facilitate a reunion.

Reunions—the Magazine
P.O. Box 11727, Milwaukee, WI 53211
414–263–4567

Another excellent specialty magazine, which always has interesting stories of reunions as well as essays by adoption-reform specialists on topical issues is:

AdoptNet
P.O. Box 50514
Palo Alto, CA 94303–0514
415–949–4370

PRIVATE INVESTIGATORS

Contrary to what I'd hoped and imagined, when I hired a private investigator she didn't sneak into agencies to retrieve the information I needed. But hiring an investigator *did* lead me to my birthmother. An investigator brings special methods to aid in your search.

However, unless money is no object, I recommend that you pursue every angle on your own first before using the services of an individual or organization. Why?

Two reasons: an investigator's time is expensive. Searches can easily run several thousand dollars, particularly if you've done no footwork ahead of time. If an investigator is starting from scratch, piecing together your whole puzzle

might take hundreds of hours (or one hour). It depends on the specific circumstances of your case.

The second reason is that I believe the *act* of searching is very empowering. Certainly it carries its frustrations and emotional ups and downs. But it can also be cathartic. You are taking charge of your own destiny.

After an extended period of time, however, you may run out of ideas and into dead ends. At that point, the right investigator can be a tremendous help. If you do use an investigator, be sure to understand before you begin the fees to be charged and what services will be performed. Request that the investigator provide you with a step-by-step synopsis of their efforts for your records so you'll know exactly what has been done, and whom they have contacted.

MILITARY RECORDS

Could your birthparents or grandparents have been in the armed forces? If you have their names, request their records from:

> The National Personnel Records Center
> 9700 Page Boulevard
> St. Louis, MO 63132

There is a wonderful comprehensive guide that is useful if you believe that anyone you're related to might have served in the U.S. Armed Forces. I highly recommend you purchase *How to Locate Anyone Who Is or Has Been in the Military*, by Lieutenant Colonel Richard S. Johnson. For information call: 800–937–2133.

Phone Books

Many libraries have phone books from around the country. If you have a name and location, you can simply look them up. If the name you are looking for is Jane Johnson and you're looking in New York City, you may have pages of names to copy. On the other hand, if you're looking for Zelda Kurzgowicz, your job will be much easier.

Let's say you don't know a location, but you *do* have a very unusual last name like the one above. There are national phone books on CDs, which list over 90 million names. You can purchase one yourself. You'll need a CD-ROM drive to hook up to your computer, and a minimum of 120 megabytes on your hard disc to run the program. There are also companies that provide this service. One is:

Josh Butler and Company
SEARCHLIGHT DIVISION
P.O. Box 259
New Middletown, OH 44442–0259

Many search organizations now have CD-ROM National Phone Books as an integral part of their service. Also, check your local public library to see if phone discs are available there.

Voter Registration

If you know a city or town where a birth relative might live or have lived, you can use voter-registration records to try to find them. Voter records are generally kept at the county courthouse and are open to the public. Large cities some-

times keep voter-registration lists in their central library. Depending on the state you live in these rolls may contain:

Name
Address
Date of Birth
Physical Description

Voter-registration lists can be a good tool for confirming information about someone before making the first contact.

INTERNATIONAL SEARCHES

There are many resources available for someone wishing to search in a foreign country. Both the AAC and CERA (see Chapter 5) have referral information for international adoptees. A computer network in New York called Kin-Quest-BBS can also assist with referrals, including modem access to lists of independent search consultants worldwide. For information call: 718–998–6306.

Using these methods of cross-referencing information and piecing together different clues, you will hopefully be able to add to the profile you began in the gathering phase and solve your puzzle. But what if you reach a dead end at every turn, or the trail disappears after years of gathering information? What if everything you try leads you nowhere?

There are many stories about adoptees who refuse to take no for an answer, continuing their search for decades until they finally locate their birthfamilies. I would encourage people not to give up, but certainly to take a break from searching when necessary. Searches are draining. Be good to yourself. Pamper yourself while you search.

Your own search may take a day, a year, or a decade. But the reality is some searchers are never able to locate anyone. If this is your fate, to search without ever locating your roots, try not to despair. Your search for the "holy grail"— your origins—has been a quest for self-knowledge, as well as a search for specific people. I believe if you try everything suggested in this book, you will learn something about your roots. You will at least know part of the story. This enhancement of self-knowledge, while incomplete, is worth every moment you have devoted to your search. And perhaps the fact that you have tried against all odds to pursue this quest tells you as much about yourself as anything you will ever find.

~ 5 ~

SEARCH AND
SUPPORT GROUPS

NOT LONG AGO I ATTENDED A support-group meeting. A wide mix of folks were in attendance: people thinking about searching, people in the middle of searches, and searchers who still hadn't given up after years of effort. Then there were those who had been reunited: adoptees, birthparents (birthmothers mostly), and a couple of adoptive parents.

I sat in the back—just listening. The meeting lasted three hours but the people in that room could have talked for days. As always, every person's story was touching. One woman had just met her brother; they were separated for fifty-five years. There was an adoptee who, after an extensive search, located her birthmother living in a shelter for the homeless.

While the value of search and support groups is enormous to those contemplating or actively searching, telling your story and listening to others after a reunion can be even more important. Dirck Brown writes that "the *telling* of one's story is at the heart of the search and support experience. . . . There is a powerful healing effect simply from the telling of one's story."[1]

Support groups provide a safe environment, a place where feelings can be validated and compared. Group discussion can "give permission" to those new to a search. Joining a search group is not always an easy step to take. Dirck calls it a "coming-out" experience for each new member. "For many, it takes courage to attend the first meeting for there is so often a tendency to minimize or deny the significance of adoption in one's life."[2] This was certainly the case for Paul, an adoptee, at his first Adoption Connection meeting.

I shall never forget the first meeting when I was introduced to the rest of the group. I stated my name and said I was there in hopes of finding my birthmom after being separated for fifty years. This was a very emotional moment for me. It was difficult just to try to get that statement out of my mouth.

Perhaps the biggest value of the support-group experience is learning to stand in someone else's shoes. For an adoptee to listen to a birthmother is to hear and begin to understand a completely different perspective on the lifelong effects of adoption. For the birthmother, hearing of an adoptee's ambivalence toward his own birthmother can help her understand that a similar reaction by her own birthchild is both normal and common. And for adoptive parents, listening to the stories of birthparents and adoptees can assist them in accepting both the need for reconnection and the reality that their child was born to someone else.

An adoptive mother remembers the epiphany she experienced when she first attended an adoption support meeting. "Adult adoptees, adoptive parents, and birthparents spoke of search and sorrow, big time news to me. . . . The woman seated next to me, with just a hint of pain filtering through her smile, held out a snapshot of the son she had lost through adoption. Forgive me, I thought, thinking of my children's other mothers."[3] She had never before allowed herself even to think about her children's birthmothers, much less to consider the impact of the adoption on them.

Adoption search support exists in a multitude of forms today. There are national advocacy groups, professional and amateur searchers, registries, support groups, workshops, marches, and retreats. The addresses of several organizations are listed in Appendix B. Depending upon where you live, there may be numerous choices available to you for emotional and "technical" support.

As you look at the options available to you, it's important to look at what services each organization does and does *not* provide. There is a difference between search *assistance* and search *support*. Assistance means that someone else primarily *performs the search* for you. Support means that the organization *provides only emotional encouragement* for your search effort.

REGISTRIES

There are two different types of registries: public and private. Public registries are run by state or county agencies. Several states now have registries, and the rules governing them differ.

Some state registries are "passive." The way they work is that an adoptee or birthparent will contact the state registry indicating they would like to be reunited. Their request is then filed. If the person sought then also *contacts* the registry indicating they wish to be reunited, the state registry coordinates a reunion between the two parties. In a passive registry, the state will *not* actively seek out birthfamily members.

Other state registries are "active," meaning that when an adoptee or birthparent requests a reunion, the state registry actively seeks out the birth relative to ascertain if they also desire a reunion. If the birth relative indicates an interest in reuniting, the state registry assists in bringing the two together.

The downside of such registries is that once again outsiders are in control of information and can actually impede a reunion. Some public registries require that the adoptee or birthparent who registers must sign a document stating that they will *not* do any active searching on their own. Obviously many searchers are reluctant to relinquish that right.

You can find out what services the state(s) where you were born and adopted provides by contacting either the State Registrar of Vital Statistics or the Department of Human Resources. Recheck the situation periodically to see if postadoption services have changed.

Private registries are not governed by laws or state codes. Some large organizations maintain their own registries. Other private registries crop up from time to time. But in my estimation, the most important registry by far is the International Soundex Reunion Registry (ISRR). Known to most people simply as "Soundex," this privately run registry is the single most important vehicle that currently exists to help facilitate reunions. Every individual who is interested in being reunited with birthfamily members should register. Soundex is a marvelous, free, and humane way for birthfamilies to reconnect. Adoptees, birthparents, adoptive parents, siblings—anyone can apply. Soundex exists to help people locate each other. Even if adoption records were opened tomorrow, there would still be a need for this national registry.

There is no doubt that Soundex, founded in 1975 by the late Emma May Vilardi, will survive in perpetuity. A board of directors oversees it, and highly committed private donors sustain it. The number of people registered is quite large, and untold numbers of reunions have occurred.

To register is quite simple. Send a request for registration to:

International Soundex Reunion Registry (ISRR)
P.O. Box 2312
Carson City, Nevada 89702–2312

The registry is completely confidential. The way it works is that when an individual registers, vital information is computerized (birthdate of adoptee, place of birth, time of birth, etc.). If data between two individuals (an adoptee and birthparent) matches and the ISRR registrar determines a relationship exists, both parties are notified immediately and told how to reach each other. Soundex does *not* act as an intermediary between individuals—to do so is unnecessary, for obviously both sides desire to be contacted if they have registered.

There is no fee for this service, so be sure to at least include the stamp to help defray the costs. Soundex will *not* send you a confirmation that it has received your registration, so if you want an acknowledgment, include a stamped postcard, which can be dropped in the mail to you.

I cannot emphasize strongly enough the need for every searching individual to register. The more people in the system, the better the chances are for more matches to occur.

NATIONAL ADOPTION REFORM

Ensuring equal access to information is at the root of several of the national adoption-reform organizations. There has been a strong movement and political battle in recent years to open adoption records. At the forefront of that movement is the American Adoption Congress (AAC). But while the AAC has its roots in adoption reform and education, it is also a valuable organization for anyone contemplating a search.

The AAC has a variety of services, which it extends to searchers, and the breadth of those services is ever increasing. The AAC offers a free search referral service, connecting searchers to organizations and individuals who can help them. Referral information is available for both domestic *and* international searching. All one need do is call: 800–274–OPEN.

The AAC also operates a bookstore catalog, with several guides on searching and reunions, as well as other related topics. Another "service" available to members and non-members is the AAC's annual conference. Spanning several days, and held at different locations each year, this conference allows individuals to explore many postadoption and postreunion issues relating to all three sides of the adoption triad. Past conference topics have run the gamut from "Including Adoptive Parents in the Search" to "Post-Traumatic Stress in Birthparents."

Another adoption-reform group, which has taken a significant lead in the past few years, is the Council for Equal

Rights in Adoption (CERA). CERA is responsible for an annual March on Washington, which attempts to galvanize national attention on the need for open records and adoption reform. While CERA, like the AAC, has its roots in political reform, it is also an organization that provides support services to individual searchers. CERA sponsors adoption-related conferences and mental-health retreats. The organization also has a private registry, and maintains the largest search and support network in the world. Members receive CERA's quarterly newsletter, and are entitled to search referral assistance. CERA does *not* actively perform searches, instead providing a large umbrella of 240 search and support organizations in eight countries. One phone call to CERA, just like a single phone call to any of the organizations listed in this chapter, links any searcher to a network of organizations.

SEARCH ORGANIZATIONS

Two of the largest search support organizations are ALMA and CUB. Each has its own orientation and each provides different services.

The *Adoptees' Liberty Movement Association (ALMA)* was founded in 1973 by Florence Fisher. Florence, an adoptee whose book *The Search for Anna Fisher* recounts the twenty-year search for her birthmother, started ALMA to assist other adoptees who wanted to search. Today, more than two decades later, ALMA has local chapters throughout the country, and has provided support for countless searches. Dues for membership cover the cost of a search guidebook, a newsletter, and registration in ALMA's registry. Local groups typically meet once a month, and the highlight of each meeting is presentations by members who have recently been reunited.

While ALMA certainly provides *support* for searchers, for the most part the organization does not *assist* directly in member's searches. There are volunteer "mentors" and staff who can give advice, but the active searching is generally done by members on their own. ALMA does offer a network of search assistants. If you live in Florida but need to do research in Oklahoma, ALMA can match you with a search buddy to help.

ALMA members give the organization mixed reviews. Many feel the organization is too controlling, and that the organization's structure perpetuates secrecy (only the leaders are privy to special search methods). But others feel strongly loyal, and indebted to the organization for its support during their search. I would not discourage anyone from considering ALMA as a choice for a support group, but it is no longer the only show in town. Today, many options are available to searchers. I encourage everyone to locate a support group that best suits his or her own individual needs. Both CERA and the AAC have lists of organizations available in each state.

Concerned United Birthparents (CUB) is a nonprofit organization that was created to provide mutual support for birthparents. The organization now includes members from throughout the triad, as well as professionals in the field of adoption.

CUB provides a lot of emotional support to its members. Since the majority are birthmothers, CUB can create a secure arena for birthmothers to discuss their own specific issues. CUB not only provides emotional support during the search but encourages vitally important postreunion support. The organization's system of "soft shoulders"—a hotline of individuals who are available at all hours to lend support and empathy—is a symbol of CUB's dedication to postreunion support.

The Adoption Connection (TAC) is a (barely) for-profit organization, which provides a wide range of services. Where ALMA and CUB only help to point their members in the right direction during their searches, TAC actually performs the searches. The fee for this service can run as high as a few hundred dollars, which is not exorbitant in light of the number of staff hours involved.

TAC's success rate is high, and the care with which the staff deals with clients is quite special. Phone calls are frequent throughout a search to keep the client abreast of each development. When an individual is located, TAC does not initiate the contact, but instead counsels the searcher on the best way to approach birthfamily members for the first time. Susan Darke, founder and president of TAC, developed a highly sensitive letter to be sent to the located birthfamily member. The letter is so vague that only the birthparent or adoptee will know who the letter is from. This gentle introduction protects the person who's been found, and allows her or him some space to control the pace of the reunion.

TAC also provides a marvelous network of support-group meetings to extend pre- and postreunion support for clients. Of all the groups I spoke with, TAC members seem to stay involved with the organization longest—for months, sometimes years, after their reunions occurred. This continuity of support seems to have been quite beneficial for members.

TRY (Today Reunites Yesterday) is an example of a regional support organization, serving western and central Massachusetts. TRY's mission is essentially education and support. The basic membership fee entitles members to the

TRY newsletter, free use of the extensive resource center, and an unlimited listing in the "Try to Connect" column of the newsletter. Monthly meetings are held, and TRY's extensive library and bookstore are valuable resources available to all members and the general public.

TRY does not perform searches for members as a basic part of the membership, but private search consulting is available. TRY also provides postreunion support.

Better than 50 percent of the members stay in any support group after they have been reunited; at monthly meetings, long-standing members offer insights and support.

There are hundreds of local and regional organizations like TRY throughout the country.

Professional and Independent Searchers

My own search lasted almost five years. I was discouraged a great deal of the time, and probably would have benefited from membership in a support group. Yet, even without utilizing the cadre of search support now available, I was able to learn a great deal on my own. Ultimately, however, I reached a point where I could go no further. That's when I decided to enlist a private investigator. The person I hired did not have specific expertise in adoptee searches, but was a professional who worked for a large company. At the time, I was unaware of the large number of private searchers specifically trained to do adoption-related searches.

There are numerous options for you to consider. I'm going to list only two. Do not consider these exclusively. Be a good shopper. Check around. And by all means know exactly what's going to be done. Insist upon a contract that spells out what services are to be performed.

This much said, Independent Search Consultants (ISC)

is a good place to begin. ISC qualified consultants have expertise in most states and in many foreign countries. For information, write to:

Independent Search Consultants
P.O. Box 10192
Costa Mesa, CA 92627

Another organization is PURE, Inc., also based in California. For a very modest fee, PURE will perform a basic search review of the information that you have gathered, and then make specific recommendations on how to proceed and who can best help. PURE also offers a more comprehensive service called Searchelp, which provides search assistance for one year. Your case is analyzed, the practices and policies of the agencies and courts involved are researched, and the most expedient avenues to take for your search are identified. For information contact:

PURE, Inc.
Triadoption Services
P.O. Box 638
Westminster, CA 92684

Before you hire any organization to do your search, ask:

1. What kinds of searches has it performed in the past, and how many were successful? Check its track record.

2. What kinds of services will be performed, and what fees will be charged?

3. What fees will be returned if the search is unsuccessful?

4. What kind of accreditation does it have?

5. Will it provide a step-by-step synopsis of its efforts, as a record for you?

Check with a number of individuals and professional agencies until you find the one that seems to fit your needs and pocketbook best. Independent searchers may either charge by the hour or assess a flat fee regardless of how long the search takes. Some may be willing to negotiate the price, others are firm in what they charge. Some may charge fees that seem extremely high, but they may have a record of success that backs that up. As one birthfather told me, he didn't mind paying thousands of dollars for some search assistance. He could afford it, and the information he had spent years seeking was in his hands within days of hiring a professional.

My one major reservation about spending thousands of dollars on a search is that, for some people, that kind of investment can create a higher level of expectation. Upon locating a birthparent or birthchild a person can feel, "Hey —I spent several thousands of dollars finding you—you owe me a relationship!" Obviously not everyone is going to place that kind of expectation on someone they've found, but I've talked to people who have. However much time or money a searcher spends, he or she must understand that the outcome of a reunion will still have no guarantees.

This issue becomes evident whenever someone attends a support-group meeting. The knowledge—the truth about one's origins—is very healing. But the relationships (or lack thereof) following a reunion are a struggle for many people.

The single best place to deal with that struggle is within a support group. Within the understanding circle of other triad members, people are able to bare their souls, expose their rawest emotions, talk about feelings and events they may never have revealed to others. There you will find a tribe that understands you. There you will begin to understand what your journey is all about.

~ 6 ~

BIRTHPARENTS AND THE SEARCH

IT CAN BE MORE DIFFICULT FOR birthparents to search than it is for adoptees. Unless they have access to the legal documents finalizing the adoption, which list the adoptive parents' names, they must solve a more complex puzzle.

Certainly one thing that birthparents *can* do is leave a trail. Use this book, and others like it, to know where to leave clues in case your birthchild is looking for *you*. Contact the adoption agency, the lawyer, the delivery hospital, and let them know that you would welcome a reunion. Inquire whether or not they will keep your signed waiver of confidentiality on file.

Keep your eye out for ads in appropriate newspapers that may have been placed by your birthchild. Check especially around holidays, or your birthchild's birthday. Place your own ads, wherever it seems prudent to do so. Advertise in specialty magazines like *Reunions*.

Register with Soundex (ISRR) immediately. Many reunions occur overnight simply through a registry match. An obvious advantage to this way of locating each other is the knowledge that both sides want to be found.

Make sure you're listed in phone books and city directories. If you're a birthmother, and you've married or moved away, you can still have your maiden name listed in the phone directory of your hometown, or the town where you gave birth to your child. If you're a birthfather, you'll be easier to find unless you've changed your name. Be sure you're listed in your local phone book. If you want to be found, you can't have an unlisted phone number. List as complete a name as possible that might help your birthchild know that you're the person he's seeking. If your birthchild has your name, a search through a national phone directory might lead him right to you.

Tell the courts you want to be reunited. Talk to judges. They may or may not help open your records, but if thousands of birthparents make their needs to be reunited known, people within the legal system will become more aware of the strong need for reconnection. At the very least, the court may retain a waiver of confidentiality on your behalf should your birthchild file a motion to unseal the records.

If the adoption was handled privately, contact the attorney who handled the case and ask to see copies of the adoption files. The final decree should be one of the documents on file, and this would have the child's amended name and the names of the adoptive parents.

Check old newspapers to see if the adopted parents placed an announcement about the arrival of their baby.

Was the baby baptized before being formally adopted? If so, the baptismal record might contain both the birthparents' and the adoptive parents' names once the adoption was finalized. If you know, or can surmise, the church where the baby was baptized, check the baptismal records.

Approach the adoption agency the same way that an adoptee would. Ask as many questions as you can.

What were the adoptive parents like?

Were they well educated?

Did they graduate from high school? College?

Were they professionals?

What were their occupations?

Was either of them in the military?

Was your child adopted immediately, or was there a period of foster care?

If there was foster care, how long did it last?

How many homes did your child have before he or she was placed?

Were the adoptive parents from the local area?

If not, where were they from?

What did they look like?

Did they have other children?

Why had they chosen to adopt?

Has there been any subsequent contact from them?

Any indication from them how your child has been?

How long had the adoptive parents been married when your child was placed with them?

Had either of them ever been divorced?

What was their religion?

Was your child baptized?

Again, *the way to find answers is to ask questions.* Don't ask broad questions like "What can you tell me about the adoptive family?" Ask specific questions. Use the above list to plan your search. Focus on learning specific pieces of information.

Once the agency responds to your initial request for nonidentifying background information, follow up with a new set of questions.

If you sign a waiver of confidentiality, will the agency keep it in the adoptee's file?

Would the agency assist in effecting a reunion if both the adoptee and the birthparent request one?

Can you write a letter to the adoptee to be kept in the agency's file?

Can they tell you what the adoptive parents have named the child? Would they give just the first name, so that any letter you write won't seem impersonal? (How could someone consider a first name by itself a piece of identifying information?)

What if you are writing your will, and want to be able to leave something to your birthchild? You will need some way to identify the child.

What is the best way for birthparents to begin to search? Many join search and support groups. With help from organizations like CUB, ISC, TAC, and hundreds of other search and support organizations, they are often able to ultimately connect with their birthchildren.

Specific facts that most birthparents know can help them get started:

The child's sex

Birthdate

Time of birth

Birthplace

A birthparent may also know the name of the delivery physician, the hospital, and possibly the attorneys who were involved.

But sometimes a birthparent knows almost nothing about the birthchild. One of the more interesting search stories I came across was from Robert, a birthfather. I thought I had had little to go on in my search, but Robert basically had *nothing*. All he knew was the birthmother's name. Yet his search for his birthchild took less than two years.

I was a pretty wild guy when I was in college in the late sixties. A heavy drinker. Played guitar for a rock band. School was an afterthought. I met a bright pretty girl named Julie and we fell in love.

We'd been dating heavily for about a year when she got pregnant. She wanted to have an abortion. I was against it. I wouldn't pay for it. By the time I realized how much I wanted to marry her, she didn't want anything to do with me. At the eleventh hour when she needed me most I misread her signals—when she said she wanted an abortion, I now think she really wanted me to stand up to the situation and come get her. I let her down.

So we split up. The last time I spoke with her, she said she was going to have an abortion, so I was surprised when I got a call from her three or four months later. She was still pregnant, angry, wanting financial help. She had decided she was going to put the baby up for adoption. She wouldn't see me or talk to me. She wouldn't tell me where she was. She just wanted help. I didn't even know how far along she was.

I paid for the doctor bills through a family friend —an attorney. I wasn't even sure where Julie was. I wasn't told when the baby was born. I never even knew if she had a boy or a girl.

I remember many times crying myself to sleep thinking about Julie. I knew there was a child out there somewhere. I always wondered what happened. I always felt what happened was for the best, but things sometimes haunted me. But I went on with my life. I married and my wife, Elyse, and our two teenage boys and I have a good life.

Everybody in my family knew about this child. I was content to live my life without knowing what had happened. But there was nothing I'd rather do than to have Julie in front of me so I could apologize to her. I hoped that the child was adopted by a nice family. I never considered a search. I thought I had no right to look.

Then, two years ago on Father's Day, an article appeared in our newspaper about a man who'd searched for his child. His daughter was searching, too, and she found him. They were absolutely thrilled to have found each other. They said being reunited made them whole.

It suddenly occurred to me that if my child was looking for me, I'd be hard to find. What if that birth-child was looking? Thinking of the child put a whole different light on it. I thought, "I wouldn't at all mind being found." Eventually I decided to search.

The people at the search organization I joined must have thought I was crazy when I registered because I didn't know anything. I didn't know the birthdate or the birthplace. I didn't even know if it was a boy or a girl.

I was urged to find and contact Julie. I had to do a *lot* of soul searching before I did this. I didn't want to intrude in her life. All I wanted was the birthday and sex of the child. Surely Julie had reconciled the situation after twenty-five years. The interests of the child seemed to outweigh any further pain Julie might suffer. I felt I, we, ought to leave a trail for this child to follow if he or she was in need of finding us.

Julie was the only person who had information I needed, but when I contacted her she refused to tell me anything.

Now it got interesting. I was looking for a child I still knew absolutely nothing about. I spent some time going back over all the events from 1966 and 1967. I hoped the attorney who had acted as a liaison could remember at least the place where Julie had given birth, or the month. By the time I contacted him, though, he was quite old. He wasn't able to remember much. He couldn't remember where Julie had gone or even the time of year. I asked my stepdad if he could remember anything from that time. He recollected that the birth had been in Dallas.

I tried to remember dates. When had Julie first told me? February? She'd called me four months later. . . . I decided the baby must have been born sometime in the fall, probably in late September of 1967.

I began to have a little fight in me. I was going to find this kid.

I learned that if Julie had given birth in Dallas the baby would have been born at a specific hospital where unwed mothers were sent. I contacted the hospital, but they were not very helpful. I asked if I signed a waiver of confidentiality, would that help? Finally a person at the hospital suggested that if I sent in a letter with a waiver, one of two things would happen. I would receive an acknowledgment back, or I would receive a letter saying there was no such file. I sent the waiver and letter for the file. When I followed up later by phone, I learned that my information had been placed in the file. The baby *was* born there!!

If the adoption also occurred in Dallas, one of two courts would have handled it: the city court or the county court. The one fact I did know about the baby was the birthmother's name. Since Julie's last name was somewhat unusual, it was at least a place to begin. I wrote to both courts asking, "Did you handle the adoption of a baby born in the fall of 1967 to Julie. . . ."

Unbeknownst to me, at the time the baby was born in 1967, that hospital had a horrible thing happen: babies born in the unwed-mother ward began to get sick, and some died for no known reason. The hospital was using a new disinfectant cleanser, but no one attributed the problem to this chemical at first. The hospital moved all the babies out of the ward, thinking that a virus was involved. The ward was scrubbed down thor-

oughly with even more of this cleanser. They then returned the babies and they again became ill. A few died.
While the babies were out of the ward, they had been
fine. It was finally ascertained that this disinfectant they
were using was the culprit.

The year I was searching, a young woman who had
been an infant in that ward filed a lawsuit because she
had leukemia, which she felt was a direct result from the
exposure to this cleaning agent. After the case, the judge
who presided decreed that all the birthmothers and babies who had been in that ward in 1967 should be notified of the potential problem.

The city court became responsible for contacting
all the individuals involved, and a list was compiled from
all agencies who'd handled adoptions of babies from
that ward. This list had only recently been put together
and its purpose for existence ceased as soon as all were
notified. Julie's name was on that list.

I had not yet received a response from either court,
so I called the city court and spoke to a clerk. Had my
letter been received? Had they handled the adoption?
The clerk said that she had sent a letter saying that the
city court hadn't handled any such adoption for Julie.
. . . Hadn't I received the letter? Disheartened, I said
that I was pretty sure the baby had been born in this
specific hospital. There was a pause. I could hear her
moving papers. Then all of a sudden she asked, "Was
the young woman's middle name Phyllis? . . . Oh, then
you're talking about the baby boy born on such-and-
such a day in June? . . . That was handled through Catholic Charities."

Simply by chance, this list with such a short life was
on the desk of the woman I called. This woman was the
one responsible for contacting the individuals born in

that hospital in 1967. This was a very emotional moment for me. By accident, and sheer luck, I'd learned the baby's birthdate (I was way off in my calculations) and confirmed that the baby was a boy. My son. I hung up the phone and cried.

The next day I got a letter from the city court saying they hadn't handled the adoption. If it had come a day earlier, I never would have made that phone call. I had called the wrong court, the wrong person, but by chance she had that list on her desk that day. There are times when you feel like a "higher power" is involved.

I contacted Catholic Charities. It turned out that Julie *had* listed me as the birthfather. The agency was willing to give me some nonidentifying information about the adoptive family.

I finally had some information people could use. I contacted a private investigator. Within days, my son was located. His name was Mark. They gave me his phone number. I waited until Elyse came home. I needed her with me. We joined hands and said the Lord's Prayer together. . . . Then I picked up the phone.

Robert's ultimate reunion with his birthson (which follows in Chapter 13) was made possible by his tenacity and perseverance. But not all searches are this difficult. Ruth's search was very different from Robert's. Her story is important because it illustrates that, while search agencies and organizations can be enormously helpful, so can adoption agencies. Birthparents frequently avoid recontacting the agency that handled the adoption for obvious reasons. Many had a bad experience with the adoption bureaucracy. With justification, many birthparents resent the power that social workers wielded over them. Some (but certainly not all) social-service agencies have changed their views. Depending upon the individual, a social worker might provide a great deal of support and help.

This was true for Ruth. While many argue against the social worker's acting as mediator between the birthparent and adoptee, Ruth did not view the agency worker who assisted her as intrusive.

When I first talked to the agency that handled the adoption, they had no file on my birthdaughter. The agency had moved, and some files were lost. This was not a scenario I had thought of in advance. . . .

The man at the agency assigned to help me was from the personnel division. He was helpful in the extreme, and extended himself to try to find more information. He was able to track down the social worker who had handled my case over two decades earlier. This social worker remembered everything! She remembered the adoptive family's name, their address, everything. I found this retention amazing because the social worker was blind.

The agency mediator called my birthdaughter's family. Immediately after speaking with them, he called me. There were no obstacles. Not on the part of the agency nor on the part of her parents.

Our first meeting took place at the agency. The man who had helped me introduced us and led us to a conference room. Then he left us alone. I didn't mind having him involved as a third party. To me he seemed very empathetic, not controlling. He went out of his way to help facilitate our reunion.

It is perhaps important to address the opposite side of a birthparent's search. What if you're a birthparent and you *don't* want to be found?

If you desire no contact, why not leave a personal letter with the adoption agency explaining why you would prefer not to be located. Use this as an opportunity to "validate" your birthchild. Maybe leave a picture of yourself. You don't have to use your name, or tell your whereabouts or disclose anything about your private life. But you could help a lot by filling in the blanks. What are you willing to reveal about your ancestry? Your ethnic background? What would you be comfortable telling about yourself?

The more information you provide, the better off your birthchild will be. I *know* that if my adoption agency had responded to my request for more background information on me by sending me a personal letter from my birthmother or birthfather explaining that they would prefer I not seek them out, I would have honored their wishes. I would have respected their message, because a part of that message would have been, "I know you may have needs, and I care enough about you to fulfill them to the best of my ability." If a face-to-face meeting isn't possible, then at least the adoptee is being acknowledged.

Part of preparing for a reunion is accepting that you must respect each other's needs. If a birthparent wants no contact, or isn't ready for a reunion, that must be respected. It's a bitter pill, but it's easier to swallow if the birthparent takes time to explain why. "Talking" to your birthchild through a letter will help. And leaving behind a photograph of yourself—even an old one—will provide a powerful, and much needed, connection.

The gesture of the letter is respect. Courtesy is contagious. If the adoptee is treated humanely, with understanding, the odds are high that the adoptee will reciprocate.

~ 7 ~

ADOPTIVE PARENTS
AND THE SEARCH

WHAT *DO* ADOPTIVE PARENTS FEEL WHEN their children search? Do the search and reunion have to be viewed by everyone as a competition between one set of parents and another?

The media focus so much attention on adoptees and birthparents, and their search and reunion experiences, that adoptive parents appear as an afterthought in most television programs and magazine articles. Sometimes adoptive parents are portrayed as "bad guys." Sometimes they are portrayed as victims. Rarely are they, or their situation, ever portrayed in an accurate way.

To begin a discussion of how the search affects adoptive parents, we must start at the beginning of their journey as parents. Because of limited space, *Birthright* focuses solely on parents for whom adoption provides the *only* chance for having a family.

How do these adoptive parents feel about their child's desires to seek out his or her roots? Equally important, how do they feel about *themselves*? The ability of adoptive parents to cope with the inevitable questions about birthparents depends upon how well they have resolved their own sense of loss at not being able to procreate. Infertility is not a simple issue, easily brushed aside. Our society is beginning to recognize the loss, grieving, and pain that adoption can cause to adoptees and birthparents. But most people don't realize that adoptive parents have also had to contend with loss and grief.

For many couples, not being able to conceive a child is a terrible blow. They feel like failures—second-class citizens, detached from the human race. They feel vulnerable and unworthy. As Thomas Shannon states in his book *Surrogate Motherhood*, "The desire—and quest—for a child is a powerful one. Many know individuals with infertility problems and have suffered with them to some extent. Studies of such couples reveal tremendous frustration and feelings of inferiority. . . . For some, the meaning of marriage and self-identity hinges on this reproductive ability."[1]

Certainly, Marilyn and her husband, Steve, experienced a wide range of these emotions when they had trouble conceiving. For Marilyn, infertility was something she had never even considered.

The neighborhoods I grew up in were full of kids. Most families had six to sixteen children. My mom had eight. I took pregnancy for granted. It was *not* getting pregnant I had been taught to worry about. Three of my sisters produced twins. We're talking about a very fertile family. So when I didn't get pregnant right away, I was bewildered. It didn't make sense.

When I walked into the infertility specialist's waiting room for the first time, I was smug. The others were there for "major overhauls." I could see it in their eyes. I was sure I was just there for a "jump start."

My gradual realization of the severity of our infertility shook me to the very core. It caused me to question everything: Who am I? What am I doing here? and even "what's the use of having these wide hips?" (the neighbors used to deflect family comments about my generous posterior by noting that they'd love me in the "old country" . . . my wide-body status assured I was good for making babies).

My husband, Steve, and I invested over three years in trying to produce a biological child. My contributions to the problem were premature ovulation, insufficient luteal phase, endometriosis, and a tendency to knock Steve's sperm out at the pass (a hostile cervix?). Steve's semen stubbornly refused to "liquefy," forcing his sperm to exhaust themselves trying to swim through the muck.

We went through the usual pokes, jabs, scrapes, and intrusive attention to our sex life that all infertiles are tortured with. I willingly altered my moods and body with up to four different regimens of medication each month. Bimonthly I overfilled my bladder so as to observe (via sonogram) one to three (inevitably inadequate) eggs develop and detach themselves from my ovaries. I dutifully recorded my temperature every morning, along with a description of our sexual activity.

We became obsessed with pregnancy. Every month I anticipated ovulation with excited hopefulness. Part of me felt pregnant for the last two weeks of each cycle. Part of me "lost a baby" with each menstruation. Steve always knew I got my period before I told him. I looked stricken. He held me. I cried. We would grieve for two weeks. Then I'd "get pregnant" again at ovulation, "lose a baby" at menstruation, cry in Steve's arms. . . .

There came a time when parenthood became more important to us than reproduction. What we wanted was a child of our own that we didn't have to give back when the weekend was over (nieces and nephews visited frequently). It dawned on us that we didn't have to make our child. We decided to adopt our child.

Marilyn spent a lot of time educating herself about adoption and adoptees before she and Steve adopted their daughter. Marilyn felt that part of preparing for adoption was resolving her feelings about her infertility. But for some adoptive parents the feelings that infertility creates may not be conscious ones. Adoptive parents may never have allowed themselves to grieve the babies that were never born. It ultimately comes down to an acknowledgment of their loss. Many people are afraid to admit: "I can't have a child of my own, and that makes me sad and angry and hurt." Parents who deny this won't be as secure in their role as mother and father.

"Ironically," psychologist Dirck Brown states, "parents who are supportive of their child's search have a much better chance of getting what they want—which is that they [the adoptive parents] are number one to their children." He cites two examples, case studies from his own practice. In the first one, a daughter located her birthmother after a long search. Though they had a good relationship with their grown daughter, the adoptive parents were petrified, even angry. The daughter and birthmother went on to become friends, but when the birthmother asked to meet the adoptive parents, they refused. Their fear and subsequent rejection of the birthmother created an awkward situation for their daughter. Ultimately, it became a divisive wedge between them as a family.

The second case history is of a family in which the daughter was quite alienated from her parents and was drifting into a self-destructive lifestyle. When she decided to search for her birthparents, she was shocked by her adoptive father's support. He went so far as to go to the courts to petition to open her records. His assistance helped his daughter locate her birthmother, and the entire family participated in their reunion. This experience changed the whole pattern of the family's relationships, and brought them all together in a way they had not experienced before.

Dirck explains: "The parents in the first example had tremendous fears. It's sad when you think about it. This insecurity was something they lived with for decades. Their story finally had a 'happy ending.' Eight years later they finally agreed to meet the birthmother."[2]

Since, until quite recently, the idea of adoptees' needing to connect with birthfamilies was considered preposterous, most adoptive parents need some time to adjust to the idea. They have been conditioned to view adoption in a specific frame, in which adoption "ends" when the papers are all signed. They have been encouraged to view adoption as a single, legal event, not a lifelong experience. Agencies have encouraged adoptive parents to go home and make the adopted child their own. Information about the birthfamily was seen as unimportant and irrelevant: there would be no difference between this adopted child and a child they had given birth to. Whether the idea was stated or not, the adoptive child was supposed to erase their infertility. The birthparents were supposed to be out of the picture. The idea of a reunion would seem to place the stability of the adoptive family in question.

James Gritter, social worker and author of *Adoption Without Fear*, acknowledges that "There were so many games built into the process that there were actually books written for adoptive parents instructing them how to play the game well."[3]

My own parents were given one of these books by their adoption agency. In it, adoptive parents were counseled: "A child adopted very young has no real picture of his biological parents, and no idea of what they were like. . . . He therefore has no real kinship with them." The child might ask questions about the birthparents on occasion, but this should be no cause for concern. "It is essential to recognize that the child adopted as a baby has no tie to the biological parents." It was recognized that the adoptive parents could be vulnerable to a child's questions about where his biological parents are now. Adoptive parents might mistake these questions and "think that their child is yearning for his biological parents. This is false in every case."[4]

Interestingly, the book, and I must assume the verbal advice as well, never addressed the adoptive parents' personal feelings. That their own issues of infertility and loss were ignored is further evidence of society's inability to look at adoption in completely realistic terms. Romance and fantasy guided interpretation, and hence people and policy-makers never recognized the loss suffered on all sides of adoption. Why should parents mourn over the babies they were never able to have? Someone else's baby could easily take the place of their own child. A baby was a baby.

A valorous picture was painted for the adoptive parents. They were rescuing this child from a horrible fate. Adoptive parents were told that what they were doing was heroic.

The family that consists of an unmarried mother and her child is disapproved of. . . . People are apt to be overly critical of the child who is raised by an unmarried mother, without the guidance of a father. It is always a problem for a child to be subjected to excessive criticism. The possibility that such problems might arise are erased when a child is adopted by a married couple.[5]

James Gritter confirms this universal view of unwed mothers' being unfit to parent when he recalls how he viewed adoption when he was a rookie social worker, fresh out of graduate school in 1974.

> I presumed the professional prescription for appropriate adoption practices had been well thought through and I mindlessly accepted. Adoption was that happy bit of social work by which "unwanted" children were placed with highly deserving, infertile, middle-class couples. . . . Professional wisdom, at the time, held that [birthparents] were a pathological client group. Pregnancy out of wedlock was automatically viewed as a manifestation of unconscious hostility. Conventional wisdom held that birthparents were uncaring, wild, reckless, promiscuous, and usually from the wrong side of the tracks. As such, they were considered highly unstable; there could be no doubt that their children were better off without them.[6]

It should be no surprise that many adoptive parents feel extremely threatened by the search. They have been conditioned to believe that the birthparents were unnecessary to the child's well-being. Because of the way they were encouraged to view adoption, the need of their child to know his or her birthparents could easily be interpreted as a failure on their part. If they had done a better job, their child would not need this connection. This summation is a natural outgrowth of the "education" about adoption given to adoptive parents by agencies.

When an adoptive parent feels threatened by the search, a situation is created that can be very difficult for the adoptee: the natural desire to seek out the birthfamily is interpreted as a disloyal act. They are hurting their adoptive parents. The reunion is seen as a competition, with one set of parents taking on the role of "the bad parents" and one set of parents being "the good parents." The reunion can feel like an enormous risk. Notwithstanding the threat of rejection by the unknown birthfamily, the adoptee must also wonder whether his adoptive parents will also reject him.

It is therefore understandable why some adoptees search in secrecy, afraid both of hurting their parents and of risking their love. Ironically, the adoptive parents and the adoptee frequently fear the same thing: that the search and reunion will alter their relationship, perhaps damaging it irreversibly.

The search accomplishes many things for the adoptive family. One of those is the testing of the bonds of the adoptee and adoptive parents. Are the bonds of their love truly unconditional?

Accepting and dealing with the birthfamily means confronting a reality the adoptive parents have long been encouraged to ignore—this child is not completely their own. His or her roots *are* different. The heritage through the adoptive family is experiential and social, not physical. Yet, while the adoptee and the birthparent can begin to resolve their loss and pain through being reunited, the adoptive parents have no real ability to resolve their own loss and pain. There exists no "search" for them. They can confront their pain and learn to accept their losses and hopefully have an even stronger bond with their adoptive children through the reunion process. But they cannot change that there is no one for them to "search" for. The unborn children they may grieve do not exist.

A reunion can be a catalyst for examining relationships and can encourage communication about the significant effects adoption has had on everyone's life. This openness can create new awareness and closeness. Perhaps only through search can adoptive parents know without a doubt where they stand with their child. It all comes down to trust—trust in the bonds that time and love and common experience make. If the adoptive parents can allow their children the freedom to explore this part of themselves, search and reunion has the potential of being one of the healthiest, most bonding experiences that adoptive parents and their children can share.

This was certainly the case for Jane, an adoptive mother. She was forced to face something she believed would never happen: her child's birthmother came looking for *him*. How Jane dealt with her and how Jane ultimately confronted her own fears, changed the course of all their lives forever.

When our son David was thirteen years old, my husband, Dave, and I received a letter from his birthmother, Barbara. She said that she was writing us because she thought that, since David was approaching adolescence, he'd like to know about his genetic background. It was a very nice letter, thoughtfully worded. I later found out she had labored over that letter for months.

This was in 1980. Searches were not in the public spotlight very much back then. There were no reunions on talk shows, especially not of minors and their birthparents. I hadn't expected this at all. After I read the letter, I sat down and cried. My first thought was:

"How wonderful. David has another family." Then fear set in. I imagined this younger, beautiful woman. I thought: "She's going to take him away from me." My third thought was: "How did she find us?" She was supposed to have forgotten about him. I was scared. Dave read the letter and stared at me. "Can she take him away from us?" Not legally, I thought, but what about emotionally?

We gave her letter a great deal of thought. David was just about to start high school. We were concerned that introducing him to his birthmother at this time would be too much for him to handle. In my soul, I worried it was too much for *me* to handle too. Dave and I wrote her back. We told her we would tell David about her when he was eighteen. We thought she would just go away. But three months later we got a phone call from an intermediary, a college professor, calling on her behalf. He filled in more of the blanks. Barbara had married David's birthfather three years after he was born. They had no other children. The intermediary convinced us that we should at least talk to her. A conference call was set up between the intermediary, Barbara, and us.

When I heard Barbara speak, she suddenly became real. Her voice was low and friendly as she suggested that we meet. After the call I sent her some baby pictures of David. I sent her mostly pictures of David alone or David with our daughter Karen. I didn't send her lots of pictures of David with Dave and me. I tried to put myself in her shoes.

Just because I was accommodating her needs, though, didn't mean I was happy and comfortable about any of this. I was scared to death. In hindsight, I don't know why I was so frightened. It's just that—it was so unknown to me. I had never even considered the thought of meeting a birthmother before. I saw an ad in a local newspaper about a meeting of an adoption support group, where a birthmother was to be the guest speaker. I went to the meeting just to see what birthmothers and their families looked like.

I felt like I was on an island. There was nobody there to help me with any of this. I went to the library and found two books on postadoption issues: Betty Jean Lifton's *Lost and Found* and Annette Baran, Reuben Pannor, and Arthur Sorosky's *The Adoption Triangle*. Reading them helped a great deal. I talked to the minister of our church. He encouraged us to think of David, and how he would feel when he was eighteen if we had not trusted him with this information earlier. I spoke with the group of social workers who knew us. They told me that they could see how upset and worried I was, but that once I told David, everything was going to be all right. The major advice I got was: Trust in the relationship that you have with your child. No one can change it.

Dave and I decided it was time to include David in all of this. Dave came home early from work, and we both waited in the living room of our house for David to come home from school. When David walked in and saw us sitting there, he thought something horrible had happened, that we were getting a divorce or that someone had died. As I read him the letter from Barbara, I cried. When I was done, David said, "Is that all? I thought something was wrong. This is wonderful. This is a gift!"

He wanted to meet her, so I wrote Barbara a letter,

and we agreed to rendezvous at a hotel near the local airport. Before the meeting, I got sick. I never get sick. I knew it was psychosomatic. We were under so much stress.

The day we were to meet, the weather was horrendous. It was pouring down sheets of rain as we arrived at the hotel. I was soaking wet, and headed for the ladies' room to get cleaned up. As I walked into the bathroom, David saw a woman come out. He knew it was Barbara. She saw him too. I was oblivious.

"David?"

"Barbara?"

They shook hands. By the time I came out, they were well into a conversation. I had been petrified the entire time leading up to this, but the moment I saw Barbara, and saw that she was a real human being, all my fears went away. I knew everything was going to be fine.

We've had many meetings since, and David has benefited greatly from being reunited. It increased his self-confidence, and gave him an opportunity to talk about his feelings about being adopted. He's now finishing his Ph.D. at Penn State, and is considering doing his dissertation on an aspect of adoption.

I went from being a parent, frightened by the changes a birthparent might cause, to an advocate that reunions were vital events for every adoptee. When our daughter Karen turned sixteen, I decided to do a search for her birthparents. She was not averse to my doing a search, but did not want to do it on her own. My only concern was the unknown: what if her birthmother rejected her? When we finally located her birthmother (whose name is also Barbara) she was so happy, and glad to have been found. She immediately wanted to meet Karen.

Talk about clones. Karen and Barbara are so alike it's scary. They first met about five years ago. To this day, they still get together once a week or so for lunch. They've had their moments when they don't like each other. But being reconnected has been good for both of them. It's been good for all of us. The reunions caused us all to look hard at our relationships with each other, and to appreciate each other more. They have caused us to communicate more openly.

Nowadays, reunions are certainly a lot more commonplace, and more and more adoptive parents are themselves "coming out of the closet," wanting to search to help their children. But I do know that, no matter whether the adoptive parents have helped in the search or not, right before the reunion they're scared. It isn't until you see that birthparent that the fantasies and fears go away. It isn't until you face the unknown that it is no longer a threat.

Certainly David's birthmother helped make the reunion a success by including Jane from the beginning, and by respecting Jane's role as David's mother. Jane admits that "If either birthmother had ever gone behind my back to meet one of my children, and not included me, I would have turned into a tiger. To leave me out of one of the most important events in my child's life would not only be dishonest, but unforgivable."

Jane was ahead of her time when she decided to face the unknown. Ultimately, she made all her decisions based on what she felt was in the best interests of her children.

It's when adoptive parents aren't open to their child's

needs, when they feel threatened and positive that there's nothing in this experience that could benefit them personally, that reunions are particularly difficult for them. Adoptee Robert Andersen reflected in his book *Second Choice: Growing Up Adopted*: "Searching usually strengthens adoptive relationships. It made mine worse. The rule probably reads: Searching strengthens good relationships and weakens bad ones."[7]

When adoptive parents have the best interests of the child in mind, there is a greater chance that everything will ultimately work out. Obviously, this can be easy to say, yet difficult to do. It can be hard to focus on the best interests of the child when you're dealing with your own pain.

PART II: REUNION

You never really understand a person
until you consider things from his
point of view . . . until you climb
into his skin and walk around in it.

—HARPER LEE, *To Kill A Mockingbird*

~ 8 ~

ANTICIPATING
REUNIONS

TRY TO PICTURE THIS DAY. YOU have a telephone number in your hand. It belongs to your birthmother or your birthchild. What will you do with it? Have you considered the way in which you will first establish contact?

Preparing for a reunion is something you need to do throughout your search. What do you anticipate from your reunion? What do you want to have happen? Equally important, how do you think your contact will affect the people you seek? What do you think it would be like to stand in their shoes?

Nothing can completely prepare you for the moment when the solution to your puzzle is at hand. Steve, an adoptee, remarked, "The thing that you never expect is that your life is going to change forever." I could relate to his comment. The entire time I searched, I viewed the reunion as a singular event—the end of my search. The climax. That's how it happens in the movies.

But the reunion is not the *end* of something. It is the *beginning* of another lifelong journey. The search ends the moment you learn the phone number, the address. Everything that happens afterward, every decision you make, is part of a new experience: reunion.

Anticipation helps. Searchers can attempt to prepare themselves for the moment they confront the unknown by trying to envision a wide range of possible conclusions. They can try to gauge what to expect based upon the experience of others.

What, in reality, do people find at the end of their searches? There are as many answers to that question as there are adoptees and birthparents who have sought and found each other. The spectrum of outcomes is illuminating. Try as one might, it would be difficult to anticipate some of the reunions that people have experienced.

For example, an eighteen-year-old located her birthmother and learned that all those she is genetically related to—mother, father, and siblings—are alcoholics and drug addicts.

Another adoptee found out that her birthmother and birthfather had had a twenty-year love affair. The father was married. The mother was not. The adoptee learned that her birthmother had become pregnant and, shortly after the birth, placed her for adoption. Not an unusual story, but it didn't end there. She dug deeper and learned that she was not the only child born to this couple. She uncovered that she was one of eleven children her birthmother had borne this married man. All of these children were put up for adoption.

Faith Daniels, a TV talk-show host, learned during her

reunion that she was conceived by rape when her birth-mother told her that she got "Me and a black eye in the same night. I knew what that meant."[1]

The harsh realities these adoptees faced are not common, but they are possibilities. Knowing what others have experienced helps prepare one for "opening that door."

People experience happy endings. Yet even positive stories carry hidden consequences that people didn't anticipate. I consider that my own reunion was very positive. But I was completely unprepared for the feelings I would encounter that were a natural part of the process.

In advance, I tried to picture all the possible scenarios. I was prepared for rejection—or worse, that the people I sought might be dead. I considered the gamut of possibilities, or so I thought. But when my search ended, and I had this wonderful family and a thrilling reunion, I found myself knocked askew. I had never considered being totally accepted. Wanted. *Needed*. I could not have anticipated how this would make me feel. It surprised many people, including me, that being needed and wanted in this instance didn't feel good. It felt wrong. It felt disloyal.

Strong emotions descended upon me: guilt, anger, repulsion, fear. The early months following our reunion were a very confusing time for everyone involved. I learned there is a significant difference between searching and finding—wanting and having.

The early stages of a reunion *are* a rather awesome experience. It would be surprising if they were not, in some ways, traumatic. Time is needed to adjust. To absorb. To establish new relationships.

Is it possible to prepare for a reunion? Yes, to a certain extent. One of the best ways to prepare is to continually ask yourself a number of questions. Keep a journal. Asking questions and recording your thoughts can help you achieve self-awareness, and give you a focus while you spin in an emotional maelstrom.

What kinds of questions? Ask, "What is it you want to find?" "What are your fantasies?" "What are your fears?" These are not simple questions to answer. What you consciously think you want to find may be quite different from what you subconsciously hope to find.

One thing is certain. What a birthmother desires to find will probably be different from what an adoptee wants to find. Those differing needs and dreams are at the crux of the awkward emotions that can occur in reunions.

A birthmother consciously remembers the child she lost. She may never have seen her baby's face, but she remembers carrying that baby for nine months. She is connected to that infant in a way stronger than any social worker could imagine. One birthmother spoke for the vast majority of birthmothers when she said, "I never mentioned my child for over twenty years to anyone . . . but forgetting her was impossible, no matter how I tried. . . . I never forgot her and never will. She is just as special in my heart now as she was the day she was born. Take my word for it, birthparents *never* forget!"[2]

What did this woman hope for in reuniting with her birthdaughter? I can only conjecture. I believe she needed to tell her daughter that she loved her and that she hadn't wanted to give her up. I believe she wanted her pain to go away.

Do those emotions lessen for birthparents after they are reunited with their children? Not necessarily. Some birthparents only begin to face such emotions during a reunion. After our first phone call, my birthmother recalls she felt transported back to the year I was born, reliving all the difficult and intense emotions she felt at that time.

What do adoptees want from a reunion? Most adoptees I've encountered say that they searched because they felt incomplete. They wanted to meet their birthparents. They were curious about them. What did they look like? What were they like? Who *were* the people they were related to?

They are seeking the truth. Knowledge. The basic foundation of their identity is built upon a lack of information. The incomplete descriptions, half-truths, and sometimes outright lies that are a part of closed adoption are not solid mortar with which to build a strong sense of self. Discovering information is often at the core of the search.

Are adoptees also looking for acceptance? Validation? Probably. Are they looking for love? Maybe—or maybe not. Feelings of being disloyal to their adoptive parents and family can make this less likely. Ambivalence is a more common emotion for adoptees to feel toward their birthparents, at least initially. Are adoptees looking for guidance and a parental relationship with their birthparents? If they've had a strong relationship with their adoptive parents, probably not. In *Being Adopted*, David Brodzinsky, Marshall Schechter, and Robin Henig say, "The compulsion to search usually says little about the adoptee's satisfaction or dissatisfaction with the adoptive family. Classically, the searcher is *looking for a relation, not a relationship*; he already has a mother and father."[3]

What do you want to have happen? Adoptees and birthparents can have very different answers to that question. How much do you know about the birthparent experience if you're an adoptee? How much do you understand of what adoptees go through in a reunion if you're a birthparent? What are the adoptive parents going to feel? How much can everyone empathize with each other?

Trying to stand in the shoes of the people you seek is perhaps the single most important task in preparing for a reunion. There are two simple ways to accomplish this: read and listen. Read as much as you can about what others have to say about their reunions. Seek out other triad members and ask them to tell you their stories. Understanding their experiences will make you more empathetic and prepared for what lies ahead.

As in preparing to search, it is valuable to ask questions as you prepare to reunite.[4]

QUESTIONS FOR THOSE ON THE VERGE OF REUNION

What do *you* want to find?

What might the people *you seek* want?

How long has it taken you to be ready to search? Months? Years? A decade? How long might it take them to be ready to meet you after you first contact them?

You may have taken years to begin your search. Are you willing to allow your birth relatives an equal length of time to prepare for a reunion?

How little will you accept?

If you are a birthparent, how much information are you going to be willing to share with your birthchild?

If you are uncomfortable sharing information completely with your birthchild, who are you protecting?

If you were the one being found, how would you want the search and first contact made?

How do you anticipate the reunion may affect your life?

How do the other people in your life feel about the upcoming reunion?

Are there people you can turn to for support?

Are there people you can find, books you can read, that will help you to anticipate the reunion process?

Are you making time to "talk" to yourself? Are you listening to your inner dialogue?

If you find something horrible, will you accept that you searched because you needed to, not because of what you might find?

Are you ready for this contact right now?

Do you expect that the reunion will solve problems that you have? Is this a realistic expectation?

What kind of relationships do you anticipate might occur?

What else can one foresee about a reunion? Expect it could be traumatic. When someone close to us dies, we anticipate a lengthy period of adjustment. We know we won't feel better tomorrow, next week, or next month. Friends and family will gather around, advising us that it might take months, even years, to get back on our feet. Our culture acknowledges and approves of this need to process a major loss in our lives.

But most searchers are unprepared for the fact that the reunion will cause a similar, lengthy upheaval. Emotions will surface that have been shoved aside for a lifetime. Everyone directly involved will have personal issues to work through.

Part of what reunions are all about is reconciling the losses necessarily inherent in adoption. The adoptee has been disconnected from his original family. The birthparent has lost a child. The adoptive parents grieve children never born, and fear losing their family created by adoption. These losses aren't worked out and resolved in a day. Expect to need some time to process these long-dormant emotions.

I believe reunions can have five phases: fantasy, first encounters, the morning after, limbo, and reconciliation. If one breaks down the process, realizing that there *are* different stages, hopefully reunions can be less painful or, at the very least, less confusing.

FANTASY

For the adoptee, the first part of the process—fantasy— probably begins at a very young age. To be honest, I don't ever remember daydreaming that I was the daughter of royalty or movie stars nor did I envision my birthparents were destitute. But looking back, I can see that I did assume that my birth had little or no long-lasting effect on my birthmother. I figured she'd gotten on with her life and that she'd appreciate knowing how terrific my parents were. As subtle and benign as those assumptions appear, they were fantasies that would affect my reunion with my birthmother.

Fantasies are hard to avoid when one has little or no information with which to establish reality. And not all fantasies are positive. Robert Andersen, in his book *Second Choice: Growing Up Adopted*, discusses at length how his inability to learn about his origins created fantasies that were difficult to avoid. Andersen, obtained by his adoptive parents through a black-market adoption, has had no luck in his search for his birthparents. A member of his search group told him about an article she'd read in *Reader's Digest* that stated that most black-market babies came from prostitutes. Andersen writes:

For those of you who have never had to consider whether your mother walked the streets, let me tell you that the issue assumes some importance. . . . Issues such as this do not easily integrate. I may not have been born to a hooker, but the possibility existed. . . .[5]

How did this possibility make him feel?

Does it matter if one's birthmother was a harlot instead of a nurse? I think so. . . . What do people mean by the phrases: Blood is thicker than water; chip off the old block; like father, like son; it's in the blood?. . . . I did not like the implications associated with trying on the identity of a prostitute's son. . . . What did this say about who could have been my father?[6]

What's important to recognize in Andersen's dilemma is that *he doesn't know*. The fact that his origins have been hidden from him creates a field where fantasies grow. What if his fantasy came true? What if he was finally able to locate his birthmother, and learned she was, in fact, a prostitute. I believe he'd figure out a way to incorporate that information into his life. Lots of adoptees find tough realities at the ends of their searches, and interestingly, rather than causing them problems, this knowledge seems to give them a sense of peace. It's the *not* knowing that's unbearable for adoptees like Robert Andersen.

Fantasies will range from lofty dreams to nightmares. Thus the shadowy birthmother is either a starlet or a prostitute. The birthfather is either a hero or a rapist. Neither extreme provides a healthy grounding in which to root one's identity.

Fantasies are, of course, not limited to the adoptee.

Birthparents and their families can have fantasies too. I remember one of the first things one of my birth siblings said to me was "We're so glad to just know you're alive. Every time we saw a program about an adoptee that had been murdered or abused by their parents . . . well, we just hoped you were all right." So the adoptive parents can be seen in fantastical terms by the birthfamily. They can be a rich, brilliant couple who helped that birthchild into Harvard, or they can be manipulative, abusive people, capable of murder. How is the birthmother to know? How can she reconcile the loss of her child without knowing his or her destiny?

Conscious awareness of one's fantasies may be limited. The realization of what one's true fantasies were may not actually occur until long after a reunion happens. But conscious or not, those fantasies are forever replaced and altered by the realities triad members encounter in phase two: the first encounters.

FIRST ENCOUNTERS

Every first encounter is different. Some adoptees make that first phone call only to be shunned or lied to. Some never receive an answer to the letter they send. Others are welcomed openly.

For those individuals who face rejection, the first encounter can be a devastating experience. Time may ultimately change the feelings of a birthfamily member who "slams the door" in the searcher's face. But the days, months, or years between rejection and reconciliation can be difficult.

Fortunately, the majority of reunions are civil, many even joyous. For these, the phase of first encounters is an exciting, highly charged time, dominated by information sharing. A thousand questions can finally be asked and answered. The mystery is solved. One feels omnipotent.

Photographs, long letters, and phone calls fill the time before a physical reunion takes place. First encounters can be so exciting that reunited members ride on a high for days or weeks. It's not unlike falling in love.

But eventually, when all the questions have been answered and things begin to return to normal, new questions arise. Who are we to each other? How do we incorporate these new relationships into our lives? The third phase of a reunion begins with these kinds of questions.

THE MORNING AFTER

Calling this stage "the morning after" is not meant as some kind of joke. Frequently that is how it feels. First encounters can be very intimate. Information is shared freely. Feelings and emotions long contained are suddenly expressed. But when the dust settles, birthfamily members can find themselves reeling, as if they've just slept with a stranger.

If we equate a reunion to a roller-coaster ride, phase three is the big drop right after you've gone to the very top where you can see everything. All of a sudden you come crashing down. It can be unexpected. Everything was so high, so good, so happy. Then *crash!* Who are we to each other?

The reality is that even though birthfamily members are intimately connected, socially and experientially they are strangers. The people being sought, in a way, no longer exist. That baby is an adult. That young birthmother may be a great grandmother. Although there may be exciting similarities between the adoptee and birthfamily members, there can also be notable differences. The adoptee has been raised in a different family, with a different background, different memories, and quite possibly different values and beliefs. As the reunion progresses, these differences can become more and more obvious.

The morning after can be a shock to many searchers and people being found. They have waited so long to find birthfamily members, to be reunited with them, see them, touch them, that they haven't given much thought to what happens next. Each reunion will have varying lengths of this phase. Some reunited birthfamilies figure out quickly what bonds they want to make. But most struggle for a long time, months, even years, not only with defining these new relationships but in coping with a multitude of emotions they haven't anticipated. Many adoptees and birthparents describe complicated and unexpected feelings postreunion.

When these feelings become too strong, too painful, or too confusing to deal with, individuals frequently put up walls and back away. Thus begins phase four of the reunion: limbo.

LIMBO

During this phase, an interesting phenomenon occurs. One side pulls away to reside in limbo, leaving the other side treading on eggs. Sometimes it is the birthmother who must deal with the eggs. She may have different needs from the reunion. She may have been waiting to welcome her baby back. But that baby is now an adult, who the birthmother may feel has treated her as if she were an encyclopedia, then simply "put the book down." As the adoptee backs away, perhaps being overwhelmed by feelings of divided loyalty between birthparents and adoptive parents, the birthmother is hurt. She is terrified that the door might be shut once more and that she will again be out of the picture. She finds herself fearful that anything she says or does might destroy any chance she has at a relationship. She begins to stifle her emotions, afraid to be herself. These insecurities then feed on each other, creating more problems.

Sometimes it is the adoptee who must wait while a birthparent asks for more space or decides to avoid any further contact. The interesting thing is that it seems rare for both sides to feel exactly the same way during this phase. Almost always, one side wants something more and the other side wants something less.

What is happening to the person who chooses limbo? Processing. So many issues may come to the forefront all at once that everyone gets pushed away. The person in limbo needs to be alone to figure out what all these new emotions mean, and what he or she wants to have happen. Demands for a greater relationship may only serve to widen the gap. Overwhelmed, the person in limbo may choose to ignore the "new" birth relatives entirely for a while.

Distancing occurs as birthfamily members retreat to establish boundaries and define relationships. Who are we to each other? What kind of permanent connections do we want to have? These questions are at the root of this phase of the reunion.

RECONCILIATION

The final stage of reunions is reconciliation. There is no definitive starting point for this phase. At some point (possibly years into the experience), triad members individually decide to confront their losses, and get on with it. They begin to recognize the complexity of both the adoption and the reunion experience, and begin to make personal decisions about how they will assimilate the new person(s) in their lives. The choice may be to have an ongoing relationship. Or the choice may be to go forward alone. The difficulty comes when the two sides choose different paths.

In some ways, true resolution begins when both individuals decide that resolving their adoption losses is a solitary experience. The birthparent must heal without the adoptee. The adoptee must heal without the birthparent. Adoptive parents must work through their own issues.

The reconciliation phase is a time for setting goals. This phase is ongoing. Issues will crop up at different stages of one's life that relate to the adoption. The only constant in a reunion, as in life, is change.

Author and social worker Annette Baran suggests there are some major don'ts in a reunion:

1. Don't move into your birth relative's house during the reunion. Stay in a hotel—somewhere where you can have some space. The reunion is an intense time. Make moments for personal solitude.

2. Don't commit to feelings you don't feel. Don't tell a birth relative that you love them just because you don't want to hurt their feelings. Be kind but honest.

3. Don't expect a permanent relationship.

4. Don't expect that meeting and finding your birth relatives is going to solve your problems.

5. Don't press. Be sensitive. Go slowly, especially where other members of the extended family are concerned. They may not have your intensity.

Once the reunion takes place, it might be wise to take a deep breath and step back. This is such a heavy thing. Rest.

No matter what the ultimate result of a reunion is, whether or not strong bonds and lifelong relationships develop, the reunion is a powerful rite of passage. Fantasy is replaced by reality. Great effort is put into incorporating new relations and information into one's life. Integration of these myriad issues is not a simple task.

Do reunions change people? You bet they do.

Reunions force the opening of long-avoided and deeply buried wounds. Reunions remove the veil, making the wounds visible so that they can finally begin to heal.

Reunions are about facing and accepting reality. It is important to know ahead of time that whatever relationships are an outgrowth of the reunion are a gift, not a given.

The more one can comprehend about this journey in advance, the better the chances are for understanding throughout the process. The flight might still be turbulent, but at least you'll have your hands on the controls when you hit an air pocket.

~ 9 ~

MY REUNION

I felt numb. I kept thinking, "I should feel something." I sat on our bed holding the phone on my lap, staring into space. I was about to talk for the first time to the woman who gave birth to me and I had no idea what to say. Or what to feel. I'd waited five years, no, a lifetime to make that phone call, but now that it was really happening I didn't know what to do.

Words will come, I thought. Just pick up the phone and call her.

I wondered what my life would be like after I dialed that number. Would it change? Would *I* be different?

Even though I knew Lee, my birthmother, would be expecting my call, I felt apprehensive. This kind of thing was almost like a marriage proposal—something you get to do only once. I wanted to do it right.

"Hello?"

"Is this Lee Porter Iacarella?"

"Cecelia?!" The voice was shaky on the other end of the line, and full of emotion. What should I say?

"Yes. Well, Jean really. My parents named me Jean."

"My God. I don't believe this. I just called my daughter Sue and told her that you were going to call and she's so excited. You have lots of sisters and brothers—Mike, Sue, Jim, Cathy, Bob, and Charles. And they all know about you!"

"This is amazing" was all I could think of to say.

Over the next hour, both our stories came spilling out, like water rushing from a broken dam. I told her how I had come to find her and about my home and my parents. Then she openly told me her story: the story of how I had come into this world.

In tones hushed to show that she still knew she'd been a "bad girl," in words that showed she still desperately wanted to be accepted despite her sinfulness, she told me what had happened. Hers is a story tens of thousands of women share, women who were made to feel they had committed a crime because they bore a child.

Lee explained that I was the result of one date. She wasn't "that kind of girl," but it had just happened. She was four months along before she even knew she was pregnant.

"I wouldn't believe the doctor at first," she remembered. "I kept saying, I can't be pregnant. He finally X-rayed me to prove it. I'll never forget him saying to me, Lee, the baby's hand is four centimeters long."

For a single girl in the 1950s, getting pregnant was the ultimate crime. Lee lost everything. Her parents turned their backs on her, sent her away, and would always look upon her differently. The Catholic Church, deeply important to her soul, condemned her. She lost a job that she cherished, and a new boyfriend for whom she cared greatly. The man who had been responsible—my birthfather—responded by saying, "How do you know it was me?" She never heard from him again. She lost her self-esteem, and her hopes for the future were forever changed. Finally, all alone and a thousand miles from home, she gave birth to a baby girl, and was forced to lose her, too.

As I listened to her story, I felt both empathy and guilt. My mere existence had caused her great pain, and this had not disappeared upon my adoption. She was haunted by guilt and anger. This episode had affected her whole life and, indirectly, the lives of her husband and children. This was not easy for me to hear.

One reason I had searched for Lee was that I wanted to tell her she'd done the right thing. I always felt she deserved to know that. I proudly said it now on the phone, sure that this one sentence would make her feel good about her decision thirty-three years earlier to relinquish me for adoption. "You know, you did the right thing when you gave me up."

Her answer burst my hallucination. "I'll never believe that. I should never have let you go. I wish I had taken you and run. I looked for you in every one of my children."

I was taken aback. My fantasy had been that she would want to and need to know I was happy with my life, that I'd been given a good home with parents that I loved. But Lee didn't want to hear how terrific I thought my parents were. She wanted to erase thirty-three years and *be* my mother.

For an instant I felt uncomfortable. Had she wished I had been unhappy, needy, unloved?

No. The truth was I could not begin to comprehend what she was going through. With that phone call, Lee began a painful healing process. The child she had given up, whom she never thought she'd see again, had returned. The last time she'd seen me I was three days old. That's how she remembered me, and in a way that's who she was talking to in that first phone call.

"I want you to know that I have always loved you."

"I never doubted that," I said. "I never felt abandoned. My mom taught me that giving a child up for adoption is an act of love."

I cannot presume to know how any birthmother feels. Over the course of the next few weeks, Lee was in shock. My arrival caused her to enter a time warp, reliving the anger and anguish she had suffered in 1955.

Our conversation wound down. After agreeing to talk the next day, I promised that I would call her daughter Sue. My call to Sue led to a call to Charles and Bob. Then Cathy. Then Jim. By two in the morning I had talked to five brothers and sisters. It was one of the most exhilarating experiences I have ever had.

When I finally got off the phone, I had the oddest sensation. For the first time in my life I felt like a whole and complete person. It was strange. It wasn't as if I had sensed something missing before, but now I knew there had been. It was as if I never realized something was broken until it was fixed.

I lay back on our bed and stared at the ceiling for a long time. I felt great. I felt overwhelmed. My life *was* different than it had been three hours before.

We spoke again the next day, and I learned more of Lee's story. She had returned to her hometown just days after my birth, and quickly got the message that marriage was a way for her to atone for her sins. Her mother introduced her to a tall, handsome schoolteacher ten years her senior, Lou Iacarella. It was a union both jumped into. Just seven weeks after Lee left the maternity hospital she was walking down the aisle.

I felt an instant empathy with my newfound siblings. I wondered how much they paid for following so closely in the wake of my birth.

Lee's birthday is August 10, and she already had planned to visit her children in Minnesota from her home in Washington in mid-August. Within a day of our first phone call it was decided that we should all meet in Minneapolis. I would fly in from Massachusetts. Bob and Charles would come from Los Angeles. Our reunion was less than three weeks away.

Sue called with the pronouncement, "Did you hear what Charles is trying to do? Get us on *Donahue* or *Oprah!* I told him he better not do anything without talking to you first."

I thought about that. Did I want media involved in our reunion? I remembered all the times when I was searching and I would read of someone else's success. Those stories gave me hope and kept me from giving up. No, I wouldn't mind sharing our story. But what about all the Iacarellas? Did they really want this to be a public occasion? What about Lee? Surprisingly, they seemed to welcome the idea.

People magazine agreed to do an exclusive story on our reunion. Suddenly, our story was national news. The various emotions we were all experiencing were to be intensified by the microscope of a reporter and a photographer.

Such intensity caused introspection. I began to analyze my day-to-day feelings, and I realized something was happening. The initial rush and excitement after talking with Lee were wearing off and were being replaced by uncomfortable feelings. We had shared every shred of information that each of us needed from each other. What was supposed to happen next? What kind of relationship were we supposed to have? Certain words began to feel threatening. Words like "mother" and "daughter," "true bonds" and "love."

This *was* a new experience—one none of us had any preparation for. But I was surprised by how awkward and uncomfortable I was beginning to feel. I began to wonder, "What's happening to me? Why am I feeling this way?"

Almost too quickly, the tenth of August arrived.

I hadn't had more than eight hours' sleep in the entire five days before the trip. I had just learned that I was pregnant with my second child. My due date was my own birthday. Everything was beginning to feel like fiction.

Just before I left for the airport, I took my mom's wedding ring out of my jewelry box, and put it on the ring finger of my right hand. I'd never worn it before, but I put it on now. To me it was a symbol of my bond with her. I was taking Mom with me on this journey. I wore the ring almost as a married woman wears her wedding ring to show I "belonged" to someone else.

I sat on the plane, flanked by Mike Ryan and Mimi Cotter of *People* magazine, with my one-year-old son Kristoffer on my lap. Time seemed to be moving faster than normal. For the first time ever, I prayed that air traffic control would put us into a holding pattern.

Mike Ryan held out his tape recorder's microphone as we were about to land and asked me what my final thoughts were. I stared out the window, trying to think of an answer, but, as the first night I called Lee, I felt numb. My mind was blank.

There had to be a glitch, of course. The meeting had been too planned, too choreographed. Ryan and Cotter left the plane ahead of me to capture the first moment of reunion. I walked through the ramp from the plane, holding

Kristoffer, my heart pounding. But when I stepped into the airport, no one was there. Mike Ryan mirrored my perplexed look. He later compared my face at that moment to the face of a child coming downstairs at Christmas and finding out Santa Claus hadn't come.

It was a simple case of wrong flight numbers. The Iacarellas were all at a different gate. We finally located each other via white courtesy phones and agreed to meet at baggage claim. Mimi Cotter got her unique photo opportunity. Mike Ryan had his story. And I had a moment I will never forget.

I heard Sue yelling, "There she is! Jean! Hey, Jean!" And they all came running. Bob and Charles and Cathy and Jim and Sue and Mike. I was swept up by this wave, in the middle of a crush of brothers and sisters, trying to hug everybody at once. It was a moment of pure joy.

Then, as if they all remembered at once, the kids stepped back. And there was Lee.

Here was the woman who had given birth to me. Here was the person to whom I owed my physical existence. The person I'd begun my search for, to be able to meet her face to face, to be able to say "thanks."

But my emotions were confused and mixed. After we gave each other a hug, I stepped back. She was shaking with emotion and I was backing away. I felt like a jerk. An honest jerk, but a jerk just the same.

Why was I being so callous? So aloof? It would take me over a year to begin to understand the emotions I felt that day.

I turned back to her kids. They were all so beautiful. Mike, who had held back during the initial hugging session, now stepped forward and put out his hand. "Hi, I'm Mike." Something clicked right then. Immediate recognition? I felt as if I had known him before, that we were already good friends. How easy it would be to call him my brother.

I looked up at Bob and it was almost like looking into a mirror. He had tears in his eyes, and the look on his face at that moment touched me more than anything else during the days to come.

Now I was feeling really mixed up. Here I was wanting to distance myself from Lee, yet having wonderful feelings toward everybody else. I knew Lee wanted to be close, needed to feel accepted. But I couldn't respond. It didn't feel right. She was sending out motherly signals, and I did not want or need a mother. I never before felt like such a louse while so happily high at the same time.

That night, we all spruced up and took Lee out to an elegant restaurant. We had an inspired evening of frivolity. Surrounded by all these brothers and sisters, I found myself regressing, wanting to play. Bob and I embarrassed the rest of the family by having a food fight. In the midst of it all, a birthday cake arrived for Lee.

"I want to welcome Jean to the family," she said. "This is the happiest birthday of my life."

Then Jim stood up. Raising his wineglass, he said, "I want to wish Mother a happy birthday and I want to welcome our sister Jean to the Iacarellas. We are all grateful that you never gave up your search and for your finding us. Here's to Christmas at your house this year!"

There was a rousing chorus of "Here, here" as wineglasses were emptied. I looked around at this family, at these wonderful, warmhearted, handsome people. God, I was happy. What a perfect day. What a perfect time. The Iacarellas had given me a tremendous gift. They welcomed me to become one of them without paying any dues. And I was proud to be counted as part of the tribe.

But was I really one of them? There was a storm brewing inside of me, a rash of questions I had no answers for. Was I a reflection of what I had found? Would all of this change me?

I spent the first night of our reunion with Kristoffer alone in a Holiday Inn. It had been a perfect day, but I needed some time alone to sort out my feelings. Perhaps the Iacarellas did as well. What were *they* feeling? A myriad of emotions spun inside of me: utter happiness, confusion, guilt, and joy.

One event of that day I couldn't shake from my mind. Lee had suggested that I call her "Mom." Of course, I told her I couldn't. But I found myself actually angry that she would even suggest it. My adoptive mother was the only person I wanted to call Mom. But Lee seemed to wish my mom had never existed. She didn't want to hear about her.

Late in the afternoon, several of us were standing in the kitchen of Sue's house. I turned to respond to a question and said, "Well, your mom said . . . ." Lee never heard the word "your." She gasped and rushed to embrace me. I realized right away she thought I'd called her "Mom." I just stood there stiffly and said, "I didn't say 'Mom.' I said '*Your* mom.'" Lee ran from the room. I followed her and tried to explain again that I didn't mean to hurt her but I had to be honest and it just didn't feel right to use the word "Mom" for anyone but . . . my mom.

I knew Lee needed something from me, but I couldn't give back to her what she lost when she gave me up for adoption. Later, as I sat in my hotel room, I felt such a conflict of emotions.

I had assumed this would be easy, but it was not. Fantasy and reality clashed, leaving me in an emotional limbo. I watched myself put up walls and hold back. All of what I felt could be summed up in a single word: threatened.

I returned to my home three days later, my conflicting emotions unresolved. Weeks passed, but time and distance didn't help clarify any of what I was feeling. I couldn't envision what place my birthmother and her family should have in my life. I kept thinking that time would solve this—that eventually I would sort all this out.

In mid-September, Mike came to visit. My friendship and feelings for him were a continual surprise. The fantasy of connecting with a birth relative became a reality for me with Mike. It was so easy to be with him. I suppose part of our comfort and ease with each other was an outgrowth of similar interests. I liked having this brother.

Yet this conflicted with my attitude toward Lee. How could I want to disassociate myself from her, yet want to consider Mike as my brother? I felt like a hypocrite.

That same month, Jim and his wife, Cheryl, journeyed to visit us. With the complete fixings for an Italian dinner packed in one of their suitcases, they set up shop in our kitchen, concocting a magnificent feast. Afterward, we stayed up until four in the morning just talking. As with Mike, I found many similar interests with both Jim and Cheryl, and my affection for them continued to grow.

Later in the fall, Kathleen Dunn's radio show in Milwaukee, Wisconsin, asked to do a show with Lee and me. We each spoke from our respective homes via telephone, talking about searching and the reunion.

At one point Kathleen asked Lee, "Is there anything you would advise others who are hoping for a reunion?"

Lee responded, "I think I would tell them not to expect too much." It was an innocent observation, one that was meant in a positive way, but I felt immediately angry. "Don't expect too much or you might be disappointed like I was." Was that what she meant? Why disappointed? Didn't Lee get to know the truth? Didn't she get a chance to meet me, to know what had happened? What more did she have a *right* to expect? That I would look upon her as my mother?!

These angry feelings were so foreign to me. I didn't know how to deal with them. So I ignored them. They would go away, I kept thinking. Eventually I would understand all of this. But one thing I knew for certain. I was not going to be comfortable with Lee, even as a friend, until I had a handle on these emotions. I didn't want to hurt her, but for the life of me I couldn't seem to change how I felt.

Weeks passed. Then one night Lee called. In a hushed "don't kick me" voice she whispered, "I just wanted to know if you were still alive."

Yes, I was fine. I explained how busy we'd been, that I hadn't had time to write or call.

"I know you're busy," she said. "Mike says he can't keep up with you." There was pain in her voice. I knew I was causing it, but I didn't like her letting me know. I didn't like this drama.

When the call ended, I was furious. I hadn't searched to find this, I thought. I searched to learn about my origins. I searched to give a message, because I felt Lee deserved to know what happened. Instead, I felt I'd opened a Pandora's box full of expectations and responsibilities I had no desire to bear. Why? Why? My strong feelings of resentment continued to surprise me. I cringed at Lee's voice on the phone. Leave me alone, I wanted to say.

Threatened! That one word still captured my emotions best. Threatened by whom or what? The answer was simple. By my birthmother, and what so many people automatically assumed she would become for me: a mother.

Perhaps if my mom had not died less than two years before I met Lee, perhaps if Lee had never asked me to call her "Mom," none of these emotions would be hounding me. I didn't know. All I was sure of was that no one was going to replace my mom. No one!

In April I gave birth to my second son, Jonathon. He was born on the 19th. Jim and Cheryl also had a little boy, their third, on the 26th. I was ecstatic when Jim called to announce the news, enjoying the fact that my kids would have cousins close to their age. Yet again, my feelings seemed hypocritical. I was ambivalent at best toward Lee, yet felt a desire to have this family tie to her children.

I kept asking myself, What do I owe Lee? That spring, two different people had said to me, "This won't go away. You're ignoring it. But you owe Lee something. *You* found her. You intruded on her life."

I always held the advice of friends as wise counsel. But to this advice I said no. I didn't think they understood. Who could understand who had not gone through this?

I argued that knowing my past was my right. It was never my intention to interfere in the lives of those who created me, but the only way for me to answer the provoking questions about my past was through my biological parents. I didn't think I had a right to expect anything from them other than to know who they were and what I had genetically inherited. Conversely, I owed them no more than the knowledge of who I am and what happened to me.

If I owed Lee anything, I believed I had paid it. She had a right to know I was well cared for, that I was happy, that from my perspective she had done the right thing when she let go. She did not have a right to expect anything more from me. I could not be her daughter. Ever!

Over a year passed from our first reunion. My husband, Jon, and the kids and I stopped in Minnesota for four days on our way to Christmas in California. Things, emotions, had not changed. There was a closeness between some of us, but the tension between Lee and me affected my relationship with many in the family.

Cheryl and Sue had created a surprise for everyone for Christmas: all the old Iacarella family movies had been put on videotape with background music. It was an emotional moment for everyone because their dad, Lou, who had died only a few years earlier, featured prominently in the tape. In between watching their individual reactions to the video, I caught glimpses of my birthfamily growing up. As I watched Christmases past and summer vacations from long ago, I was witnessing a life that might have been—Cecelia's. The video made me feel closer to the family, made me feel I knew them better. This gave me an idea that I tucked away for the future.

After Christmas, Mike was at our cabin in California. One afternoon we drove around the top of our mountain so that I could introduce Mike to one of our neighbors. En route, we talked about how awkward certain moments of Christmas had been, and how I was still grappling with how to fit all these new relationships into my life. As we talked, I remarked that I felt being a family comes in large measure from shared experiences.

We pulled up a dirt driveway to a rugged mountain home. The front door opened and out came our neighbor holding on to the collar of his barking five-foot-tall Great Dane. I hopped out of the car. I had met both the dog and his owner before, and I reached out my hand toward the dog saying, "Hi, boy, remember me?" Before I finished my greeting, the Dane lunged from his owner's grip and sank his teeth through my right hand. I felt the bones crunch as I went down to the ground.

Our neighbor yanked his dog back, took me inside his house, and shoved my hand into his sink under cold water.

"Here you go. You'll be okay." Mike was standing in the doorway. "Hey, Jean—you all right?" I felt ready to pass out, but I didn't want to admit it.

"It doesn't look too bad," our neighbor said hopefully. I looked down and saw chunks of flesh hanging out of a hole in my hand. Mike stepped forward. "You don't look so good. Come on. I'm taking you to the hospital."

The nearest emergency room was a half hour away. I began to feel queasy and was glad that Mike was talking nonstop. At the stoplight at the bottom of the mountain, Mike turned to me and grinned. "Like you were saying earlier, it's experiences like this that will make us a family. Times like this will bond us together."

It was a much-needed joke at the moment. And Mike was right.

Sources of help come when you least expect them. It was over dinner at Stanford University with a college alumnus that I learned of psychologist Dirck Brown. One of the primary focuses of his practice was working with adoptees, birthparents, and adoptive parents, helping them through the reunion process.

I had not considered working on any of this outside of myself, but as soon as I heard about Dirck, I hoped he could help me. Perhaps that alone was the sign that I was ready to resolve my feelings. I wanted help figuring out what was going on.

Dirck lived on Long Island, and we talked a few times by phone. His approach for sorting out the emotions I was feeling was to get me to focus on goals. What did I want to have happen? What were some realistic goals to target? What would Lee have to do to make me comfortable with her?

We had just talked on the phone and I was sitting in my office, when it suddenly hit me. What would Lee have to do for me to be comfortable with her? It was so simple. She would have to acknowledge that Betty was my mom. That was it! If she could do that, and *mean* it, then that would mean she accepted me and my adoptive family and the reality of who I am.

Was that asking too much of a birthparent? Of course it was asking a lot. Maybe that was an acknowledgment within myself that Lee had a right to feel pain. Maybe it was okay for Lee to feel pain and anger and I didn't have to feel that it was my fault. Maybe I could separate the problems she had encountered in her life from my own existence.

During Christmas in Minneapolis I had been inspired by the Iacarella home movies. I decided to transfer my family's movies to tape, too, so I could share them with the Iacarellas. I undertook this project mainly for Sue. She had said more than once that it was impossible to get to know me if I didn't make a greater effort to stay in touch. I thought a video would be the best way to communicate my past. I created a mini-documentary with both home movies and a montage of snapshots chronicling most of my life.

I mailed copies off to both Sue and Mike. I was surprised by how anxious I was to hear what they felt once they saw the tape. Had I been so overwhelmed by their acceptance of me as one of them that I felt a strong need to show that I did have a past? That I had my own identity?

Whatever my inner drive was to create this production, I was surprised by the result. Contrary to my intent, Sue found it painful to watch. Instead of seeing it as a way to know me better, she said it only made her realize more what she'd missed by my being adopted. I felt bad. My effort to share my past seemed to have failed.

But then I received a phone call from Lee. "Your tape

was terrific," she said. "For the first time, I feel like I did the right thing. I can see that your parents loved you so much."

A huge pain lifted from inside of me. Just as I had needed Lee to acknowledge my parents, she had needed to *see* the past, visually see my parents, to be able to accept them.

It was a beginning.

Two years from the day when we all first met, I returned to Minneapolis to be reunited a third time with my birth-family. My feelings had changed enormously since the spring. The threat that Lee posed had been slowly melting away. Had time been the reason? Or the video? Or was it establishing goals? Probably all of the above.

Time had changed Lee, too. She finally seemed to have found peace for herself. She opened up with me, asking questions about my mom. To be able to share my mom with Lee erased the threat Lee posed to my mother's memory. I was growing comfortable about having Lee in my life.

We didn't call each other every other week or even every month to see what was going on. But we accepted each other. We stayed in touch. We were becoming friends.

The whole Iacarella family came to Minneapolis except for Charles. But we were not just meeting socially: there was an agenda. Sue had organized a three-hour marathon session with two psychologists to discuss some of the feelings family members had had since our first reunion.

Beforehand, I had enormous trepidation about the session. Even though Lee and I were growing more comfortable with each other, there was still tension within the family. I knew some members of the family had been unhappy since the reunion. There had been expectations left unfulfilled in the last two years, and I seemed to be at the center of them.

As I flew to Minnesota, I wondered if I was about to enter a lion's den.

I couldn't have been more wrong. The session was very productive. As I listened and watched, I began to realize that I was not the cause of great unhappiness. Instead, I had perhaps been a catalyst for change and growth within the family. Contrary to my expectation that I would be a target of anger, I was just one other person in the room, trying to sort out my feelings like everyone else.

The most important thing I walked away with was a clear sense of the situation. There were three dynamic relationships that existed between me and the Iacarella family: one between Lee and me, one between me and each of my brothers and sisters, and one between Lee and her kids. How each of those relationships worked was the business of no one but those within the equation. We were all crossing into inappropriate spaces. These boundaries provided a framework to help us build and understand our relationships.

Perhaps it was just me, but I sensed a release of tension after the session. Lee's kids, my siblings, were not responsible for seeing that she and I "worked." And she was separate from my relationship with them.

Lee and I have shared some unique experiences in our lives. Yet it took me two years to be comfortable with the idea of being close to her. Why?

There are many reasons.

Most certainly the timing of my mom's death in relation to my reunion with Lee contributed to many of the emotions I felt. But then I don't believe the emotions I felt were all that unusual. Other adoptees report experiencing similar feelings during their reunions.

Whether I wanted to admit it at the time, the reunion was overwhelming. Literally overnight, I had almost twenty new relatives. There were so many new people to get to know. Time was a problem. Since I had two very young children, my free time was a scarce and valuable commodity that I covetously divided between my husband and kids, my aunts, uncles and cousins of my adoptive family, and my friends. The time needed to get to know all the Iacarellas was difficult to budget.

The road from our initial reunion to a more relaxed situation seemed long. There was great discomfort on all sides at times, but major growth was, and continues, to take place. It would have been easy to walk away at any point and say, "This isn't worth it. It's too hard." Patience, and a desire on all sides to work it through, paid off. If there is any lesson to our story, it is that it can be worthwhile to stick with it. There's still work to be done, but at least now we can see the value of that effort. I know that we will get out of this journey what we put into it.

Where will we all be in twenty years? I wonder. Only time will bear witness to that future. I know only that we will never be quite the same people that we were before July 20, 1988. We cannot walk away from each other unchanged. And that makes us a certain kind of family.

~ 10 ~

ADOPTED MEN

THE EXPERIENCES THAT PEOPLE ENCOUNTER IN reunions are as varied as human beings themselves. Although each individual's story is unique, the knowledge of what others have experienced can be enormously helpful to those preparing for a reunion. As with any traumatic experience—and every reunion is traumatic, whether it's mutually desired or not—that linkage to and awareness of others traversing similar paths provides a base of understanding.

Several individuals have generously shared their own reunion stories for this book. I have separated the adoptee and birthparent chapters by gender, because there are some special issues that seem gender-related in reunions. Women frequently initiate searches when they begin to have their own children. One cannot escape thoughts of the birthmother during the experience of giving birth. Intuitively, a young mother senses the loss that her own birthmother suffered. For many, the search is an outgrowth of this awareness.

But a male adoptee is generally less tuned in to this loss. Subconsciously, he may view the relinquishment differently. The birthmother was the first woman who ever "rejected" him. The decision to look can take great courage, for the risk of rejection by the birthmother carries an enormous weight for a man. To search might place his ego, his sexuality, and his very being at risk. One middle-aged adoptee I spoke with told me that he'd had no interest in ever looking for his birthmother. "She gave me away. I viewed that as her rejecting me. I always felt totally disinterested in searching for her. In fact, I thought, 'To hell with her!' "

Sometimes an adoptee searches, but then never pursues a reunion at the conclusion of the search. The anticipated pain of the unknown acts as a barrier to taking that final step. This has been the case for James, who has had the ability to locate his birthmother for several years.

My absolute worst memory as a kid was when I was in the seventh grade at a Catholic school. The school was holding a special confirmation ceremony. A number of seventh-grade altar boys were chosen to participate. I was not one of them. I remember looking out at the church from a window of the school watching the other boys participate, and one of the nuns told me that I couldn't be a part of the service because I was an adoptee. To Catholics back then, and probably even today, people like me are the dirty by-product of a dirty relationship.

Somehow I have always felt flawed because I'm adopted. Friends who do not know my background have said things to me like "Adoption is like buying a pig in a poke" or "You never know what you're going to get when you adopt." This notion of feeling flawed is buttressed by the fact that my adoptive parents felt compelled to hide so much of the truth from me. My parents told me from the start that I was adopted, but that was the end of the story. Any questions regarding my roots or the details of the story were answered with "We weren't told much but don't worry. They were married." Somehow, this never made me feel better. If they were married then why did they give me up?

When I was in my midthirties, I read a newspaper story concerning searches for birthparents. I had never made an effort to find out about myself, in part because I never felt convinced that I needed to know or had a right to know. But, after reading that article and thinking about the fact that I was approaching middle age, I realized the longer I postponed my search the more difficult it would be. I went to the agency cited in the newspaper article, and they referred me to another agency, which had records from the Catholic Diocese near where I was born.

I learned there was a young priest assigned to the parish back in the late forties, and he had now returned to the parish in the eighties. I made an appointment to meet with him. It is ironic, my contacting him, because I only went to see him to find out what he knew about the home for unwed mothers that had existed. I had no idea he would have the answers I sought.

As we spoke, the priest asked me when I had been baptized. My mother always told the story of the drive home after they picked me up on Valentine's Day. It was a dark and icy night. They were driving a borrowed Hudson. She didn't think they would ever make it. She enslaved herself to Saint Anthony. She wore out her rosary beads. They lost their way. But in the end the Hudson pulled through and I was home.

This story made it fairly simple to determine the date of my baptism. Being good Catholics, my parents would have rushed me off to be baptized right away. Thus, I could easily figure an approximate date.

When I told this to the priest, he pulled out the parish's baptismal records, which dated back to the 1890s, turned to the volume from the year of my birth, and there it was—with a catch. The original listing identified my birthmother by name. Six months later, when the final decree came from the court, the listing was amended to include my adoptive parents' names.

Very little shocks me, but this did. My adoptive parents had *known* her name. I suddenly realized that this information had been within my grasp all these years, and I never knew.

I have now known my birthmother's name for seven and a half years, but I have made no effort to find her, and I do not know if I ever will. Part of me says do it, but a greater part wants to know how to strike up a conversation. Very little of me wants to know the details of how I was conceived.

Maybe things will change. I am reluctant to pursue this as long as my adoptive mother is alive, since I am sure that any knowledge of it would cause her extreme pain. I have never told her that I found the woman's name, and she has never admitted to knowing, as she must have, that it was in the church records from the start.

In some ways, I have always felt ashamed of being adopted. I never had a good relationship with my adoptive parents, and maybe that is one thing holding me back from reuniting with any birthfamily members. I won't set myself up for a fall. I don't want to deal with any more pain. I can't and won't face another rejection.

Every adoptee who searches must go on his or her gut instincts. I believe James is very wise. He isn't ready yet to handle whatever he may find. He may never be ready. And that's okay.

Wealth and fame are no buffers to the problems that an adoptee will face. In fact, having celebrity parents can compound the difficulties. Michael Reagan, in his book *On the Outside Looking In*, documented what it was like growing up as the adopted son of Jane Wyman and Ronald Reagan. The book was written shortly after Michael was reunited with his half-brother Barry, whose mother, Irene, was Michael's birthmother (she had died). I contacted Michael to see what had transpired in the years since.

Being adopted by celebrities is different. Hollywood is a town of perceptions, not of reality. I believe that a strong image that stars in the thirties and forties were supposed to portray was family. A lot of people back then in Hollywood, though they'll never admit to it, had children for image only, not for love. Therefore you find a lot of adoptees in families from that era. Why were these families so big on adoption? Did they all just wake up one morning and say out of the goodness of their hearts that they were going to go out and adopt a child? They may think they did it for all the right reasons, but I think the real reason was that they were under pressure to portray an image to the public that they had an All-American family.

I'm not the only Hollywood adoptee to feel this. A lot of kids from Hollywood from that time will say, "We were there for the pictures only." Once the pictures were taken, we were taken out of the building. We were props. Props to portray an image.

If I was talking to adoptive parents, I would tell them to get as much information on the birthparents as they can, because there is going to come a point in time when that child is going to ask where he came from. And answers like "that's none of your business" or "they gave you to us to raise because they couldn't raise you" are not going to satisfy that child for a lifetime. Show an openness with your child, a willingness to be caring, understanding, and accepting of their differences. Because there are differences. Adoptees have another set of parents, and it's natural for them to want to know about them. And don't *ever* introduce them as "my adopted child" or allow friends to say "that one's the adopted one."

My mom and I have never once discussed my reunion with my birthfamily. It's not something she wants to talk about or acknowledge. Even with my dad and Nancy, I don't feel a real freedom to open up and discuss my reunion. I will mention to them that I have talked to my brother, Barry. But it's not something we discuss in depth. I believe it's generational. As much as my dad may understand me today better than he ever has, I don't know if he or his generation understands everything that an adoptee goes through.

Nancy has thought a lot of this through. In her book *My Turn*, she was very kind to my birthmother, Irene, saying that, in this day and age where everyone sells their sensational stories to the tabloids, here was a woman who really had a sellable product, and who out of deference to her son and where he was in his life, never said anything. Nancy appreciated that through all those years Irene remained quiet. She died with that secret, never knowing that I would have loved to have had a chance to meet her.

Since writing the book, I've met my birthfather. He found Barry and me because of my book. He flew to San Diego to meet me, staying with me for a few days while I did my radio talk show. He's a big hulk of a guy, gruff, a hunter, fisherman, and outdoorsman. He has a daughter who I've enjoyed getting to know.

My reunion with my birthfather hasn't been entirely easy. He's looking for me to give more than I can. I think this is because I didn't really look for him. I wasn't dancing on clouds to meet my father. It was my mother whom I really needed to meet. I had to resolve that side of it. I feel I talk with my birthfather more to help him try to resolve some guilt he has, more than I'm trying to close a circle in my life by knowing him.

I told Nancy that I'd met him, but I've never told my dad. I've also never told my mom. I just sense they'd prefer not knowing. I'm not upset by this. Part of the problem in my situation may come from the fact that Nancy is adopted (by her stepfather), and my mom is also adopted. We're this piecemeal family. To sit down and discuss what I went through brings up too many unresolved memories in the people I would have to talk to. It's easier on everyone not to discuss it.

My children, Cameron and Ashley, have been a part of my healing process. I raise them and try to do everything right, as if to reverse how I was raised. But the way I was raised has been a problem of sorts for me. I find myself working too hard, at times, at having my kids accept me. Being adopted has affected my self-esteem. I go overboard with my kids because I have this need to have everyone accept me. If I can't give my kids everything I want (and I can't), then I feel this real guilt, as if I've let my kids down. There's a part of me that needs to be able to do everything for them that I feel wasn't done for me.

This past summer my birthmother's family had an enormous reunion. One hundred and eighty-seven people showed up. I balked at having a big reunion with my birthfamily for a long time. I still have this guilt. I've had it all my life. Other people have helped to create it by saying things like "the people who raised you are your family, how can you think of looking for the person who gave birth to you" and "how could you slap your parents in the face like that." So even now, I feel uncomfortable in some ways at being reunited with my birthfamily. Guilty.

If someone were to come up to me and tell me they were embarking on a search, I would tell them to listen to themselves. Don't listen to other people who are going to try and steer you in their own direction. Listen only to yourself. Make your own choices. Even if your search is unsuccessful, you need to know that you ultimately did something because *you* wanted to do it, not because you were trying to make someone else happy. Perhaps, for the first time in your life, you are working to make yourself happy.

I worry about other adoptees. I don't think I'm unique in the fact that I was sexually abused (by a camp counselor when I was 8 years old). I believe some adoptees can be more susceptible to abuse because they

are constantly looking for acceptance. In trying to resolve their initial sense of abandonment, they go overboard at trying to be accepted by everyone else they
encounter, and they get themselves into positions where
they are hit on by pedophiles and taken advantage of.

Writing the book was very cathartic for me. There
were so many things going on in my life that I had to
sort out. Meeting Barry and learning about Irene, my
birthmother, helped me close that door. It gave me the
power to know myself more completely. But it doesn't
just suddenly end. My adoption is something that has
affected my whole life. Society wants to hear that it's
over, that you get healed completely. Since I've talked
about it, written about it, gotten all this off my chest,
the assumption is that I should be fine. But there's no
such thing as a quick fix. I'm still working on all of this.
It's something I deal with every day. It doesn't go away
simply because society wants it to.

Michael's observation and concern that adoptees may
be more susceptible to abuse is an important point to consider. With self-esteem issues paramount for many adoptees,
adoptive parents may need to be even more vigilant for potential situations of abuse.

Sometimes when a man locates his birthmother, he may
feel attracted to her. On rare occasions this attraction can be
so intense it is almost sexual. But more often it is just a
strong emotion of mother-son love. This is what Steve felt
when he first located his birthmother.

In the beginning, when I first found her, the honeymoon period, things couldn't have been better. We
were both so happy, thrilled, in love. I could do no

wrong in her eyes, and I felt the same way about her. It was only natural.

I was amazed at the similarities of our bodies, our eyes, mouth (pretty amazing!), and she was so soft spoken and gentle, warm and loving. That first meeting, *God!* I'll never forget that beautiful day, including the telephone call when I first spoke with her only hours before actually meeting her. I remember it word for word!

That's the honeymoon. At first, I could see no faults with my birthmother, nothing bad. I saw her problems clearly, the burdens of her life, her worries, etc. I immediately wanted them to all become *my* problems and concerns and worries, etc., etc.

I had had some anger toward my adoptive mom as I was growing up. Nothing major, but it was there. For a while after our reunion, I began to accept my birthmom as my mom, period. But then, as time passed, reality replaced this fairy tale. Once I had a chance to really get to know her, the whole person, the good and the bad, I've learned a lot about myself.

I had told her from the beginning that, instead of mourning the fact that we have lost time together growing up over the years, we should be enjoying the fact that we are finally together. We should live in the present, not in the past. Life is full of disappointments. She tends to dwell on them. She's had so much of it in her life, I guess.

Possibly one of the best outcomes of the reunion is that my relationship with my adopted mom has grown stronger and closer and clearer. There's no doubt in my mind anymore, no more anger or resentment toward her. Recently, I wrote her a letter which said in part:

"I denied [my anger] at you for a long time. When I examined it I found that I was most mad at you because you weren't my real mother.

"Then I found my birthmother. That was great, but after the initial excitement wore off, I began to look at my life. I feel like a whole person now because I've found all the pieces to the puzzle. Now that I have the whole puzzle, I realize how wrong I was. *You* are my real mother. You made me what I am today. You and Dad.

". . . Funny, all this time, I was thinking the main piece was missing, the foundation for the entire puzzle called me. Actually, it was only a very small, yet still important piece. What I never knew was that I always had the main piece, the foundation. And that's *you* and *Dad*."

When I set out to find my birthmother, I had one wish: that by finding her I would make her life and my life, and the lives of those around us, better because of it. I was prepared for the worst, but I prayed for the best. I got lucky.

One's perspective can change dramatically throughout a reunion. If Steve had written during the early months following his initial reunion about how meeting his birthmother had affected his relationship with his adopted mom, he might have told a completely different story. Steve's experience is a beautiful example of how, given time and patience, the reunion can be one of the most bonding adventures that an adoptive parent can have with their child.

But many adoptees wait to search until both of their adoptive parents have died. Fearing they may hurt the parents who raised them, their reunions occur much later in life.

Paul spent the first six years of his life in an orphanage. Then a couple in their mid-fifties, who had never had children of their own, took Paul just for the summer. By August, he had endeared himself so much to them that they adopted him. He always felt that they were his parents, but he was curious about his heritage.

The subject of searching had come up in our house and my adoptive parents agreed to help me if I was interested. But I could see the hurt in their faces. I didn't feel right pursuing it.

Both my parents passed away before I turned thirty. Five years later, I began to search. I felt a need to know the "whys" and "wheres" of my birthmother. After fifteen years of searching, all I had been able to learn was that my birthmother was eighteen years old when I was born.

Then one day my wife, Ginny, saw a television program that was highlighting an organization called The Adoption Connection, which I joined. This organization was great, not only for their assistance in my search, but also because of their support. A few months later, I got a phone call at my office: for the first time in my life, I knew my birthmother's name. I was fifty years old.

Four weeks went by. Then, a second call. This time I put Ginny on a conference call so that she could share in the joy that I was experiencing as the agency gave me my birthmother's full name, address, and telephone number.

That night, I wrote a letter to my mother. I mailed it the next morning. Now, the most difficult part of the search began: waiting. Those five days seemed like an eternity. I thought I had prepared myself for the worst situation that could happen. But as time went on and days went by, my anxiety and my fears grew and grew. The question "what if" started to play a mind game with me.

Then on Thursday night I picked up the phone and a voice said, "Paul, this is your mother." That was the first time I had heard her voice in half a century. We talked for three hours. I learned that I have a brother and six sisters. I also learned that my mother had for years been searching for me, but she ran into the same roadblocks that I had. She was sure she would never see me again. We agreed to meet in two days, on Saturday, at one of her daughter's home.

After our phone conversation ended, my oldest son came home, and Ginny and I told him that we just got through talking to his grandmother. In an emotional moment, my son and I stood in the middle of the kitchen floor, hugging each other.

I talked with my sisters and my brother by phone. We were all excited. My sister Mary who lives over a thousand miles away told me she was sorry she wouldn't be able to make it to the reunion.

On Saturday, I asked my son to drive. My mind would not be focused on the road. We finally arrived and drove up the driveway, where everybody was waiting for us. . . .

My mother came out to see me as I got out of the car. Our eyes met. Seeing her was like a shock—she was real. Then I turned and one of her daughters came up to me and introduced herself as "Mary, your sister." Mary had driven with her two boys for seventeen hours to be there that day. It was at this moment that I became very emotional. . . . I lost it. The tears came. As each one of my sisters came forward to meet their brother for the first time, it became a reality that I had indeed found my family. Two weeks later I would have a chance to meet my brother when he made a surprise visit to where I was vacationing.

There are few words to express a reunion like this. Your inner feelings take over—it is indescribable. I feel that I found my family. Each one of my sisters has her own way of bonding with me. I enjoy being with every one of them. There is a family joke that I like my brother more. There is a special bond when I get to see my brother. We have similar interests like golf, and I find it a tremendous thrill to play with him (even though he beats me every time). Not having a brother for all of these years, I find it difficult to try and make up for lost time. I know that you can never bring back what you have lost, but I sometimes wonder what it would have been like.

I feel now that my life is complete. I loved my parents. And I love the mother and family that I have found. I have to say that over the last fifteen months since we all first met, this has been the experience of a lifetime. If you were to put this whole search and reunion on a scale of 1 to 10, I would classify it an 11.

Paul's reunion with his family is "the fairy tale." Perhaps a reunion is easier, less traumatic, when all the individuals are older, more mature. The downside of this, though, is that so many years have been missed.

But not every adoptee wants to search, or desires a reunion. What about adoptees sought out by birthparents they have no desire to meet?

Ice skater Scott Hamilton, because of his celebrity status and the media focus upon the fact that he is an adoptee, is more susceptible than most to being approached by an outsider believing him to be a birth relative. This occurred several years ago when he was approached by a woman claiming to be his birthmother.

A woman came up to me one day. She was sure she was my birthmother. I didn't think that she was. She didn't have most of the facts right as far as I was concerned. But even if she *was* my birthmother, it wouldn't matter to me. I just wasn't interested in making this connection.

The problem was, this woman began to push. She was always around, always showing up unannounced. I live a very public life that puts me in a vulnerable position. I finally said, "No more."

I can only imagine what a birthmother is going through. But this woman, whether she was my birthmother or not, never seemed to *hear* me. I didn't want a relationship. She was a nice lady, she seemed very pleasant and all, but she began putting herself in a no-win situation. She was pushing so hard that I told her she had overstepped her bounds. She had become counterproductive.

She finally left me alone. But this whole episode made me frustrated and angry. I don't believe this woman was my birthmother—but even if she had been—I have no desire to have my birthfamily in my life.

Over and over again, it seems the stories where discomfort occurs are the ones where the searcher expects something, and attempts to force a relationship. What is especially troubling about Scott's story is that he didn't even know if he believed the woman who claimed to be his birthmother. Ultimately, this woman was stalking him, interfering in his personal life.

The flip side of this is that not all adoptees are welcomed into their birthmothers' lives. This can be difficult to accept when an adoptee has spent years and considerable emotional energy searching.

When Grant found his birthmother, he wrote her a letter, careful to make it so vague only his birthmother would understand who it was from. Grant was concerned about protecting her. But his birthmother, in fact, wanted nothing to do with him. At first he was angry and dumbfounded that she didn't want to meet him. Her response after his two-year search was worse than anticlimatic. It was a rejection.

After he overcame his shock, he wrote her once more, this time for himself alone.

Over the past years, I've seen more and more attention being paid to reunions of children and their birthmothers on television. With each show, the outcome was always an immediately positive one, filled with joy. This is something I did not experience. Television depicted these reunions as a wonderful thing, and with good reason. I couldn't believe it could be any other way. How could it be that a mother would reject contact from her own child and live with herself? That child is an innocent by any standard. . . .

I recall growing up, I would be attending a barbecue or family function with all of my family and cousins in attendance and I would scan the room. I would first notice, and still do, my brother, who would be standing next to my father. The resemblance between them was and is remarkable. Continuing to survey the rest of my family, cousins, etc., the conclusion was always the same. "I look like no one in this room."

I would ask you to imagine what it would be like if you never had a chance to meet your own flesh and blood. I want you to look at your children the next time they walk through the front door and ask yourself how you think your children would feel if you turned your back on them. Their knowledge of you could never be erased, regardless of the fact that another family grew to love them as their own.

They would wonder, the same way I do, how any warm-blooded human, a mother, could turn her back on her own offspring.

I want you to know and understand that it's not that I was given up for adoption that bothers me. I'm certain you did what you thought was best and most prudent. I respected you because it must have been a difficult decision to relinquish your own baby. However, what you need to know is the letter you sent was the most callous, cold, cruel, and terse letter I've ever read. What did I do to deserve this?

I am not a random stray cat but a human being. . . .

In your letter you wrote that what happened a quarter century ago was from another time, another life. I will respond by (partially) agreeing with you. It was another time. However, your particular statement about another life was quite wrong. As humans, we live only once. You are having serious delusions if you think that you're living a second life. Life is not like that. It cannot be denied.

I will not go away. But I will respect your privacy and confidence. I'm not looking for anything from you . . . merely your respect.

Unlike the birthmother who contacted Scott Hamilton, Grant was not pressing for a relationship, but a *validation*. There is a difference.

Adoptees face rejection, not just from birthparents, but from outsiders, strangers. As incredible as it seems, some adoptees who have critical health problems are turned down when they request information on their birthfamilies. Stephen survived an unbelievable ordeal growing up. That a state adoption unit refused to help him in his search efforts seems to me almost criminal.

The desire to know my beginning was always deep inside of me. But I also searched for medical reasons. I was born with a physical disorder. I always thought I was put up for adoption because I had to have extensive surgery. I was eleven years old when I was finally adopted. I didn't take my first step until I was seventeen years old. I've had thirty-one operations. I made medical history as the first person to have a muscle transplant.

It was really the birth of my own child that made me decide to search. My wife and I were blessed with a child who was physically "normal," and I wanted to let her know what the future may hold. Meeting members of my birthfamily would help fill in the blanks of my medical and genetic background. I'm very close to my adoptive family—my adoptive mom is also an adoptee. She's never had any ambition to search, but she understood and supported my desire to look.

So I began to search. The court denied me full

access to my adoption records. I could only get non-identifying information even when I had letters from doctors stating I needed full disclosure of this information for my medical history. When I hit roadblocks like this, my wife was my sounding board. She supported my decision all the way, and did the legwork for me at the times I couldn't.

I finally used an adoption support group to help me locate my birthmother. Three months later, I had my birthmother's phone number. I called her and told her who I was, and asked if I could meet her. She agreed. She was single, so my "arrival" was not too disruptive.

She lived only twenty minutes from my home, but it took me five hours to get there. I would drive, then stop. I was so nervous. Drive a little further, then stop again.

Meeting her was wonderful. First off, seeing how tall she was (four feet eleven) and realizing that I looked like her (I'm five feet tall) made me feel that I had a definite beginning—I was born. She's a nice lady, hard-working. She held the same job for twenty-five years.

She didn't even know I was handicapped until we met. I always thought that was why she gave me up—that I was too much to care for. This bothered me a bit, to be honest. Before we met I'd had a rationalization for why I'd been relinquished. Then I had to adjust to the fact that she'd given *me* up.

We've become friends, and we talk on the phone about once a month. Finding her has made me a little more at peace with myself. It's given me a beginning.

The hard part is that I haven't found my birthfather yet. All my birthmother can remember about him is his first name. She thought he walked with a limp. She's obviously blocked what happened out of her mind, and I don't want to make her dwell on it. But I'd like to know what he was like and to see if we have any similarities. And I'd still like to complete my medical background for my daughter.

Some adoptees grow up without ever knowing that they were adopted. When they learn the truth about their origins, they can be drawn immediately to a search, as they try to assimilate this critical information into their adult life. Travis didn't learn that he was adopted until he was in his forties. He quickly embarked on a search.

My mother died three years ago after a long, painful struggle against cancer. Shortly after her death, I turned forty, and my father invited me to lunch to celebrate the occasion. After eating and sharing our continued feelings of loss, my father told me that the woman for whom I grieved was my mother in every way but one: she was not my natural mother. I was adopted.

I was stunned. I asked my father why I had not known this earlier in life. His only explanation was that my mother had insisted that my sister (also adopted) and I be "protected" from this knowledge and its potential emotional effects. That this secret had been kept within the family and among neighbors who were all very well aware of the situation still amazes me.

My initial reaction was anger . . . this is my life, my background, my "birthright" that had been denied to me. Upon reflection, my attitude changed more to one of profound sorrow: sorrow that my mother could not trust herself or me with the truth, and sorrow that I would never be able to share with her the memories of her experiences about my adoption. My third level of reaction was intense curiosity. I had to know what my "biological" background really was.

I went to the County Probate Court to petition to have the records of my adoption opened. I met there with a probate officer who agreed to escort me before a judge to acquire permission to access my sealed records. The formality of permission granting accomplished, we returned to the probate office, and I was allowed a few minutes alone with my past.

I can still vividly remember this first introduction to "Angie," my birthmother. I wrote down as much as I could (copies of documents were forbidden). There were only a few details about Angie: her date of birth, residence, educational background—enough to further stimulate my need to know more. I left the court with an admonition from the probate officer not to call all the people in the local phone book with Angie's surname. I drove from the courthouse to the town where Angie had lived prior to my birth, and spent time at the town hall researching old residence records. The trail, however, was cold. Angie left in the early fifties, and there were no other obvious relatives.

My adoptive sister, who had already searched for and located her own birthmother, provided the next step—a search and support group. I forwarded them all the information I had and waited. And while waiting, I imagined and worried about the potential reunion scenarios. Was Angie still alive? Did I already know her? Was she someone who hovered around the edges of my world, watching my life but afraid to be known? Would she want to acknowledge me? How had the experience of giving me up affected her? Was she a lonely spinster? Had she married and put the experience behind her? Did her husband or family know about me? Was I a "love" child or the product of some more sinister activity?

Late in summer, I received a phone call: "We've found her . . . she lives out West." Okay. Now what do I do? "You must write a letter . . ."

I wrote the letter: "We last saw each other in 1949 . . ." I waited again. I wondered how the letter would be received. When I didn't get an immediate reply, my apprehensions grew. Finally, three weeks after I mailed the letter, I received a phone call from Angie's brother. "Angie got your letter, and she's very upset. . . ."

This initial contact from my "birth uncle" was both exciting and a little disappointing. I did not want to be dealing through an intermediary in this process. I assured him that I was not trying to cause trouble and that I had no obvious maniacal tendencies—I'd provide references if necessary—and that I just wanted information. I must have been convincing, because twenty minutes later the phone rang again. It was Angie.

This first conversation with the woman who had given me life was one of the most moving experiences of my life. Her pent-up love came pouring out through all the years and miles. She tearfully opened her heart to me, telling of the painful loneliness of being rejected by her family and my natural father during her pregnancy, of the years of grieving she had experienced after giving me up for adoption, of the prayers she had offered through the years for my well-being, of her tears she shed thinking of me, of searching faces on the street or on television and wondering who and where I was, and of her love for me that had never stopped. My own emotional response was one of relief, of course, but also included an almost tangible feeling of comfort and peace . . . as if I had finally bonded after all these years. These same feelings continue today as I think of Angie, or read her letters or speak to her on the phone.

By coincidence, she and her husband had planned a trip to my state about a month after our first contact, so we were able to meet face to face. Experiencing first-hand the love she had carried for over forty years was an incredible experience.

We correspond regularly, and speak occasionally on the telephone. We are proceeding to get to know one another, and to build a rational relationship on the foundations of the emotional one that seems to already exist. Our families have been tremendously supportive.

I continue to think about my adoptive mother and wonder what her feelings would be about all of this. During my first telephone conversation with Angie she said, "I wanted you to know that your mother is a very nice lady." She was referring to herself, but I misunderstood. I said something to the effect that my mother was indeed a nice lady, but that she had recently died, and I went on to ask when she had met my mother and what dealings they had had. Of course, they had never met, and after some discomfort, we were able to get the conversation back on track.

I call her "Angie" and I refer to her as my "birth-mother." I cringe a little when friends, etc., refer to her as my "mother." Angie is a special person, and I am not afraid to say that I love her, but she is not, and never will be, "mother" to me.

Dirck's perspective is from the point of view of a sixty-year-old. He was adopted as an infant of two months. His adoptive parents literally walked down rows of newborn white infants in a large maternity home called The Willows. They picked him out from the hundred or so babies available for adoption that day. He was always told they liked his smile.

I grew up knowing I was adopted but I don't remember asking any questions. On my first date in 1947 with Molly, who would later become my wife, I asked if she knew I was adopted and she said yes. We never mentioned the word "adoption" or spoke about it again for twenty-two years, until I became interested in finding out about my origins.

I was studying for my Ph.D. in psychology and was going through psychoanalysis as a part of that program. I was in analysis for about a year before I finally had the courage to confide to the analyst that I was adopted. We began to explore my feelings about being adopted. He asked me what I would like to do if I met my birthmother. I told him I would like to hold her and be held by her. "Any other feelings?" he queried. I said I didn't think so. My analyst commented, "I think you'd like to strangle her!" Although it was difficult for me to admit it, he had put his finger on another set of feelings I had about my birthmother: feelings of intense anger and frustration.

Not long after that, for the first time I asked my adoptive father for information about my adoption. He sent a large folder of material special delivery airmail—material that he had carefully collected and saved for me all through the years. Asking my father for those documents and having him send them so promptly was a very significant early step in my journey.

I learned from that packet of materials that my birthmother had tried to get me back after she gave me up. Somehow, she had obtained my name and whereabouts. She came to my father's office about a year after she had relinquished me, demanding my return and threatening legal action. Years later my adoptive mother confided that she was afraid to take me out for walks for fear I would be kidnapped. The packet also contained a carefully preserved letter from my birthmother, to my adoptive mother, which relayed how despondent she had been since my adoption.

When my search began, almost no week passed that we didn't search for some piece of information, make a trip somewhere, or spend hours on the phone. My search ended almost three years later. I had located my birthmother and called her at home. Her husband answered the phone. When I introduced myself as Dirck he said, "Oh my God, just a minute, I'll get her." It seemed like a long wait. Finally my birthmother came on the phone and said, "This is your mother. I have been expecting this call for a long, long time."

I met my birthmother three days after that phone call. It was an experience I will never forget. On a subsequent visit, she told me the story of how she and her mother had traveled hundreds of miles from their home to the small town where I lived when I was six years old. They came to my school and asked the teacher if they could take me outside just for a few minutes. The teacher agreed and we went outside in front of the school. They wanted to take my picture.

Word got out—it was a small town, where my father was a college president—that I was being kid-napped by two strange women. My father rushed to the school. He realized that all my birthmother wanted was to give me a hug and a kiss. They were there to say "goodbye" to me. I did not see her again for forty-two years, but I learned later that my birthmother kept that picture on her table by her bed for all those years. She gave me a copy of that picture on my forty-eighth birthday.

After I completed my search, I visited my adoptive father. As I talked with him and told him about my reunion, his face filled with an expression of joy and peacefulness. He felt the same sense of peace and re-solve that I felt in completing this long journey of self-discovery.

My adoptive mother had a more difficult time knowing of my reunion. But in her remaining years she came to understand that I dearly loved her and cared for her as my nurturing mother.

The realization that I needed to search, and the decision to take the first step, were significant events in my life. Looking back, they were necessary steps if I was going to come to terms with the anger I felt and over-come feelings of loss and pain, which are central to the adoption experience. Before I searched, I felt much like a bystander and often like an imposter, masquerading as someone else.

I believe that the majority of adoptees will ulti-mately want to and need to search and be reunited at some point in their life. Fear and anxiety about search and reunion tend to be based on a short-term view. That fear, it seems to me, is often a fear of the unknown and a mistaken concern that the searching adoptee will somehow reject his adoptive parents in the process. Most adoptees I have worked with have found that the search and reunion bring them into an even closer relationship with their adoptive parents. That certainly was true in my experience.

Many adoptees want to search, but hold off, sometimes for several years, before beginning. It's important to pay attention to your own instincts, to know when you're truly ready to begin. But waiting can carry consequences. Spencer will always have some regrets that he didn't begin his search just a little sooner.

It took me ten years to say, "I want to find my birthmother." Then it took me another year to finally contact a search and support group. I wish I had done the search earlier. I feel I have missed a lot. My birthfather passed away just months before I located my birthmother. And my birthmother is dying—she has cancer. If I learned anything it's that, when you have the urge to search—DO IT! Don't wait.

The last story in this chapter is one that is very special to me. Fred is not an adoptee. But, because of divorce, he had not seen his father since he was two years old, and had no conscious memory of him. Shortly after the story of my reunion with Lee appeared in *People* magazine, Fred and I talked briefly about how to search. I did not anticipate that he was going to immediately go out and locate his father. But it turned out that our chance discussion about searching would spark an incredible event.

My parents divorced in 1962 when I was just two years old. My brother was one, and my mother was pregnant with my sister. After the divorce, my father moved to California and my mother had no further contact with him. By 1988, I had not seen or heard from my father in twenty-seven years.

In 1988, my wife, Kirsten, stumbled across the reunion story about Jean Strauss, wife of the president of my alma mater, in a copy of *People* magazine at the grocery-store checkout. Kirsten bought the magazine, and I read the article with interest. Kirsten and I had talked about possibly searching for my father someday. Soon after, I spoke with Jean at a college function, and asked for her recommendations regarding a search. I was not, at that point, committed to the idea, but I thought I would at least gather some information should I ever decide to look.

The following Monday, I decided to call my mother to gather some preliminary information. She offered two names I had not recalled of a couple who had been foster parents to my father during his teenage years in a small town. On impulse I called directory assistance for the town and was astonished to obtain their number.

Kirsten joined me on the call. An elderly woman answered the telephone and I asked to speak to this couple. She responded that her husband had been dead for ten years but that she was the woman I was seeking. I then said, "My name is Fred. Do you know anyone by that name?" She responded, "Yes I do! He's my son." I then said, "Well, I'm *his* son." In the next moment I went from euphoria to dread as she continued, "He's on his deathbed in a hospital."

I don't remember the exact words of the rest of the

conversation, but I was able to gather from her the name of the hospital where my father was dying of cancer, the name of his wife, whom he had married twenty-six years earlier, and the names of my two half-brothers. When our call ended, Kirsten and I sat in silence. We were stunned.

That evening I called the hospital and my father's wife, Jan, answered the phone in his room. I clearly shocked her, but she was excited and asked if she could call me back. She called a few minutes later and explained that due to my father's delicate condition she preferred talking with me outside of his room. She said that she knew of us children and she was happy to hear from us. At the onset of my father's illness (brain cancer, which had spread throughout his body) they had discussed trying to contact all of us but had agreed that it would be inappropriate, given the lack of contact over the previous twenty-seven years.

Predictions had been that my father would not live through the previous spring, but he continued to hang on. Jan told us that it was expected he would not live through the next few days. I raised the issue of traveling out there with my brother and sister so that we could see our father for what would feel like the first time. Neither my brother nor I remembered him and my sister had never seen him. Jan said she would discuss it with the hospital staff and with my father, who, in spite of his deteriorated condition, was still lucid and able to talk.

I then called my brother and sister to share the astonishing events of the day. Both, especially my sister, were interested in going to see him. In the meantime, Kirsten and I express-mailed a package of pictures of all of us and our families so that our father could at least see what we looked like.

The next day, Jan called to tell me that the hospital staff recommended that we *not* come because of the potential impact upon our father. I accepted this feedback but my sister was not at ease with this decision. She felt an intense need to see our father.

On Wednesday our pictures arrived at the hospital. Jan and my father talked more about a visit. It was finally decided that we could all go out to see him, but under the condition that we not press him about specifics regarding his separation from my mother and us.

On Friday, all of us, including Kirsten, were on a 7 A.M. flight to see a father that we had not known, nor had anticipated knowing five days earlier. At the airport, we were met by our new half-brothers. We exchanged hugs and small talk, then we headed to the hospital. En route, we all shared bits and pieces of our pasts, and everyone was highstrung in anticipation of the coming meeting. Our brothers told us about relatives we had never known. They told us about growing up with our dad and what the last months had been like. Jan met us at the hospital. She had been very warm and welcoming on the phone, and was even more so in person.

The next minutes were euphoric as we walked into the room and laid eyes on the man that we knew of, but never knew. I was surprised to see an essentially normal-looking person, not one that looked like he had been living beyond all predictions for the last six months. He smiled with pleasure as he made eye contact with me. I introduced myself (what a funny thing to do to your own father!) and started to introduce my brother and sister, when he looked at my sister and asked, "Who's she?" This was a fairly awkward moment, but I quickly explained that she was my sister and his daughter. We later learned that he did not know of our mother's pregnancy when they separated.

We let the moment pass, as we were cautious about our commitment to not delve into that part of our past. We quickly moved into a series of conversations on what each of us children were doing. About ten minutes into this casual give-and-take (no talk about what an incredible thing we were all experiencing) he started to cough and we had to leave for a couple of hours.

During the weekend, we visited three times each day with our father. We developed relationships with our brothers, and we continued to be a little stunned just by the fact that we were there. Our father remained very lucid during our entire visit, and while the focus of the dialogue was on us, we learned some things about our father's interests and life. In many respects, despite not having grown up with him, we had many outside interests in common.

Late Sunday morning, we had an emotional good-bye with our father. We talked about seeing him soon. It was kind of odd, like this was a casual visit with a friend that we had known for years and he was perfectly well. We knew that this first set of visits was our last. Kirsten was visibly more emotional than the rest of us. At first she found this confusing. Then we realized that she was relating our farewell to this man to what a similar farewell to her own father would be like. And they were not the same.

It was expected that our father would pass on immediately, but everyone remarked that after our visit he seemed a bit stronger for a while. He died at age fifty-two, exactly one month after our departure. Kirsten and I flew out for the wake and funeral. We met lots of other members of the family and toured the towns and farms where my father grew up.

Looking back on this experience, I can say that I never really got the total fulfillment that I had hoped for. While I felt good about finding this man who was responsible for my coming into this life, I did not get the sense of closure I sought because I never heard his explanation of the events that led to his decision to not be a part of our lives. The prospect of never being able to learn everything is disconcerting to me. In many respects, I think I have emotionally detached myself from this experience, as if it were more of a staged event that I simply witnessed. The circumstances and speed at which the experience unfolded were so incredible that I felt then and now that I was given grace from God in meeting my natural father before it was impossible to do so. I said farewell to this man that I never knew, but I did not truly mourn his passing.

Children separated by divorce can share striking similarities with adoptees. The notable difference is that society "gives permission" for children separated by divorce to reconnect. This permission does not yet exist for adoptees. Certainly any child cut off in his or her relationship with a parent will be permanently affected by the severance.

~ 11 ~

ADOPTED WOMEN

THE STORIES OF REUNIONS BETWEEN WOMEN and their birthmothers differ in subtle but significant ways from the reunions of men with theirs. Many women begin their search only after they have given birth, as if the very act of bearing children gives them permission to seek out their own origins. Some feel an awakening, a realization of a loss that has affected their entire lives. Many, like Karen, have inexplicable fears of losing their babies. Interestingly, in Karen's case, this did not occur until she gave birth to a daughter.

My need to search for my birthparents began when, after having had three sons, I gave birth to a daughter. It was as if I were seeing myself as a baby.

The feelings started right away. I thought she would die, be taken away. In some manner, I was sure

I would lose her. I wondered where I had been at her age, two hours, two days, two weeks. Who held me and loved me as I loved her so dearly in those very early moments? She was strong-willed from the very beginning, a lot like me. But why was I so strong-willed? Questions about myself suddenly needed to be answered.

I enlisted the help of a search agency, and five months later I had my birthmother's name and other information regarding her whereabouts. I remember my mixed feelings upon learning the name she had given me. It was a beautiful name. I wrote in my journal:

> There is something more to me than before. Part of the incompleteness has been returned. There is also a sadness. This name is a stranger to me, but it is also me. I feel sad that the connection was broken and this person never got a chance to be. She is a hollow shell.

As I suspected, the middle name I had received at birth proved to be my birthfather's surname, and I found him on my own in three days. My brother made the initial phone call to confirm that we had the right person, to see how he felt about speaking with me, and to allow him a bit of time to absorb the situation.

I called him immediately afterward. Yes, yes, I'd found the right person. He felt ashamed of the past, but was very excited that I had found him—it was his sixtieth birthday that day. He spoke slowly, but assuredly, and with great emotion. How would he tell his children? We shared all sorts of information about ourselves and our families. Learning my birthfather was six feet seven was a significant detail to me since I am six feet one, and my height has always been a critical part of my identity.

We rendezvoused shortly thereafter for dinner, choosing a location between our two homes, and then I visited my birthfather's home a few weeks later. It was lovely, though a bit awkward. Being related and being a stranger at the same time was cause for considerable confusion. Since we were unfamiliar with each other in traditional family roles, we tried to communicate our thoughts and feelings openly to each other in an attempt to establish our new relationship. I refrained from judging his past actions. Today, I feel a strong pride in my birthfather. He is where I came from.

I wrote my birthmother a discreet letter, designed to break the ice yet protect her secret. Two weeks later my phone rang. It was a lawyer, a gentle-sounding woman hired as a voice for my birthmother. The attorney told me that my mother was "A very lovely lady, a very private lady. She does not want to be hurtful, but she cannot contact you. She is frightened, and asks that you not be in contact with her. She wants closure."

Closure. Now that was something to think about. What did she think I was doing? I also wanted a little closure. I explained my intentions to the lawyer, and firmly stated that, though I could promise respect, I would not "evaporate." In the real world, people do not disappear. The lawyer agreed to receive letters to my birthmother, and guaranteed my birthmother would read them.

Since I'm a mother myself, my birthmother's response stunned me. She chooses to live in a confining state of denial. I pity this denial. It is a loss that she cannot enjoy a life rich with emotion, risk, and commitment. In closing herself off, she shuts out the pain, but she also shuts out the joy and the ecstasy.

I was frustrated. Her response did not meet my craving for information regarding my background. I had a million questions I wanted to ask. I decided that I would have to find the answers on my own. Using a combination of old census information, city directories, obituaries, town records, the Chamber of Commerce, and a healthy dose of intuition, I answered almost all my questions. I even located a recent photograph of my birthmother. I felt euphoric.

Yet it would have been far more satisfying to have direct contact with my birthmother and be able to learn details from her. Maybe someday that will happen. But whether it does or not, I *do* feel empowered by what I've been able to learn on my own. I feel happier, more complete, and more comfortable with the person that I am.

At my birth, the mother-infant bond was severed. I believe I have mourned the breaking of this first bond. A split occurred, and I left part of myself "back there." The search and reunion process provided a vehicle by which I can mend this split. It's given me a foundation of reality in which to grow and thrive. It enabled me to see that, although I am connected to all of the people who contributed to making me who I am, they are not really "me," the same way my daughter is not another version of myself. I am myself, alone and unique in this world.

Karen has kept her promise to respect her birthmother's privacy. Although she sends an occasional letter, she has backed away, giving her birthmother time to adjust. The reality is Karen had a long time to prepare for a reunion; her birthmother did not. She may need just as long, or longer.

One risk that all searchers faces is receiving information about themselves that they had not anticipated. The truth about one's origins may change certain realities in the searcher's life. Elizabeth discovered something about her birthfamily that would change her perception of her own self forever.

When I was ten years old, I was told I was adopted. My parents told me my birthparents had died, and that was the reason that I had been placed for adoption. This news both shocked and saddened me.

At age forty-four, I went to my first adoptee support-group meeting, and was thrilled to hear that many adoptees are told their parents are dead. For the first time, I thought mine were probably alive. But a few months later I learned that my mother had, indeed, died of toxemia when she was seven months pregnant with me. A year and a half later, my birthfather had died at the age of thirty-nine. I felt depressed. It was like losing them twice.

But . . . the biggest shock that I had to deal with is that I am not Jewish. My adoptive parents told me they asked for a Jewish baby girl. I always believed I was Jewish. This is my identity. I was not raised as an Orthodox Jew, but I grew up celebrating all the Jewish traditions, and I brought up my children with religious training.

From the time I was told I was adopted, it was the only thing I knew about my birthfamily. But it was all a lie. No one in my birth family is Jewish. My identity as a Jew was shaken to the core in learning this. I have been told by conservative and Orthodox rabbis that I'm not considered Jewish because my birthmother wasn't Jewish. Even though I've been brought up believing myself to be a Jew, and raising my children according to all the Jewish traditions, this is not given an ounce of consideration. My children and I may have to undergo conversion to be viewed as Jewish.

I now look at myself as coming from two different cultural heritages. I refuse to make less of one than the other. I was born Christian, and I'm proud to be a part of my birthfamily. This is now part of my heritage. However, I have been raised as a Jew, and this is the religion I know, and wish to follow with my family.

I have had pain and confusion in dealing with this. But, even though I've had to deal with the difference in religion, and the loss of never meeting my birthparents, I'm still happy that I know the truth. "The truth shall set us free."

By odd coincidence, not by design, several of the women in this chapter did not learn until later in life that they were adopted. It's intriguing how varied their responses were.

A friend of mine found out that she was adopted when she was in her late forties. Both of her adoptive parents had passed away by the time she learned this, so she was unable to discuss it with them, but she wasn't at all angry that she'd never been told. She viewed it as a generational thing: it was normal to keep adoption a secret in the thirties and forties. Her way of looking at it was that her parents had kept this information from her thinking it would protect her, not hurt her. Thus, she did not feel in any way deceived or betrayed.

The information didn't faze her at all. In fact, it seemed to give her an inner peace. Discovering she was adopted ex-

plained for her some of the feelings she'd had growing up
—feelings of being different from the rest of her family.

She was given enough information about her birthparents so that a search for them would have been relatively
easy. But she had no desire to seek out any members of her
biological family. She was glad to know the truth, and simply
got on with her life.

Patrice also learned as an adult that she had been
adopted. Initially, the news drove her away from her adoptive parents. She felt hurt and betrayed. It took a search and
a reunion to give her some perspective.

> I was born in June, under the zodiac sign Gemini,
> the Twins. I always felt that I had a split personality, or
> another side to me. Little did I know . . .
>
> Just before my thirty-third birthday, I learned that
> I was adopted. I had always wondered. My parents
> never spoke of pregnancy or childbirth, and I didn't
> look like anyone in my family. I never felt "connected"
> to anyone or anything around me. But every time I
> asked my mother if I had been adopted she would re-
> spond, "Don't be ridiculous."
>
> Then one evening I was talking with my father on
> the phone, and the subject of adoption came up. He
> started talking so positively about adoption that I asked
> him if I was adopted. He paused for a fraction of a
> second, then kept speaking. When he finished, I asked
> him again. "I'm not going to answer that," he said. He
> didn't have to—he just had. "I'll be right over," I said,
> and hung up.
>
> The news was staggering to me. I suddenly had no
> idea who I was. The family I had known all my life
> suddenly seemed like strangers to me. The parents I

loved so much had betrayed me. I couldn't believe it. I didn't want to believe it.

That night when I visited my parents, they had very sketchy information and clearly didn't want to discuss it at all. I did. I needed answers. I was devastated. I couldn't call my brother and talk to him because my parents begged me not to tell him. He was also adopted and didn't know about it. They said they would tell him soon.

The next day at work I was a wreck. My coworkers were very comforting and helpful. One person recommended that I search for my birthfamily, and gave me the name of a search and support organization. I gave it some thought for a few days, and then made the scariest phone call of my life to The Adoption Connection.

That phone call changed my life. The people at TAC were absolutely wonderful. They reassured me that I was not the only person in the world who had been adopted; that I was not alone; that I was not a reject. I remember standing in front of my mirror repeating out loud, "I'm adopted . . . I'm adopted . . . I'm adopted . . ." until I finally started to accept it.

The search for my birthmother made several twists and turns before we finally found her after ten months. I was filled with excitement and anxiety the entire time. Each phone call I received from TAC could have been *the* call I was waiting for. And then one day, it was.

Now came the truly scary part—contacting my birthmother. TAC suggested that I write a letter, so I wrote to her, mailed the letter, and waited. And waited. And waited.

Three weeks later, I received a phone call from a man who said he was my brother. He was so excited to hear from me he wanted to get together right away to meet me. It was everything I hoped for. He told me that I had two half-sisters, and one half-brother, and that he was my full brother. He said that my mother was not very healthy and, at this time, she didn't want to see me. He said she needed some time to get used to the idea. I agreed and said I'd be patient. The phone call ended quite positively with a promise to be in touch very soon.

A few days later, however, my sister called to say that my mother would not be contacting me. I later found out that the letter to my mother had been intercepted by this sister, and that my mother had not been told about me.

Eventually, I met my sisters and brothers, but I never had a chance to meet my mother. Three months after I found her, she passed away. I went to her wake just so I could see her face and touch her. I wish I could have heard her voice, just once.

When Sally was fifty-three years old, her mother died. Shortly after her death, one of her mother's closest friends called Sally. It was ten-thirty at night. They chatted, and were just about to hang up when the woman said, "Before you go, tell me how you reacted to your mother's letter."

"What letter?" Sally had no idea what she was talking about.

"The letter that explains how you were adopted," the woman continued.

"Adopted?"

Her mother's friend's voice suddenly got very shaky, as she realized that Sally never knew. For Sally, a new adventure began that night.

My mother had told her friend that she was going to tell me I was adopted in a letter, to be read after her death. I never got it. That night after that phone call, I didn't sleep. I brought out all these old scrapbooks and looked at the baby-announcement cards that my parents had received when I arrived in their lives. Not one of them said anything about a birth. I started going through old newspapers to find my birth announcement in 1932. There wasn't one.

Ultimately, I learned that I wasn't the first baby that my parents had tried to adopt. They had had to return another little girl, whom they had had for several months. They gave me the same name they had given her.

Since both of my parents were dead, I couldn't talk to them about any of this. But after I got over the initial shock, I was really glad to know. I had always wanted to be French—I'd studied French and liked French music. When I met my birthmother I found out that I'm French Canadian. And Jewish.

To be honest, I've had fun learning this. I still have terrific respect for my adoptive parents. My mom and I were best friends, and learning that I was adopted hasn't changed any of my feelings. If anything, I admire them more. They had adopted me at the height of the Depression. My dad was a fireman, and civil service jobs back then paid nothing. But they took me in, made a home for me. They were gods in my eyes. To me, it showed even more how much they loved me.

I met my birthmother on the day that she found out she had terminal cancer. The doctors gave her three months to live. She made it for nine. So we shared nine months together, twice in our lives. . . .

Learning I was adopted has opened up a whole new horizon for me. My search and reunion gave me a new, expanded identity. I had roots from my adopted parents. Now I have roots from my birthmother and her family. I've looked upon this as an episode that has given me something special—not taken anything away from who I am.

While some adoptive parents never informed their children that they were adopted, others told their children half-truths or outright lies, feeling this was in their child's best interests (or their own).

Emily never forgot what her parents told her had happened to her birthmother. It was a story that would haunt her in her youth, and then cause her enormous problems later on.

When I was six or seven, my parents had told me that my birthmother had died. My mom said that she'd gone to heaven and was with God. I felt I'd killed my birthmother when I was born, and that my birthfather had given me away because he hated me. That's what I believed.

Then, when I was twenty-seven, I learned that my birthmother had not died. I was shocked and depressed. Rather than being overjoyed at knowing she might be alive, I felt this meant my birthmother, like my birthfather, had rejected me. Finding this out confused me so much that I knew I had to "untangle the web."

I was afraid I might lose my adoptive family if I searched, but my adoptive mother was very helpful. She gave me my birthmother's name—it had been written on some papers the social worker was showing her when I was adopted, and my mom always remembered it.

My search took ten years. When I found my birthmother, that first night on the phone was a little difficult because she had never told her husband. After I explained who I was, she asked me if she could call me back, and then she didn't call until the next day. It was torture.

Initially, she wasn't resistant to my contact. Her own mother was out-of-state at the time, and her daughter lived across the country. While they were away, everything was fine. But when her mother found out about me, she was furious, and her daughter, my sister, didn't want to hear anything about me. So my birthmother felt unable to integrate me into her family. I felt like a mistress, a skeleton in the closet.

Early on, I had asked about my birthfather, but she didn't want to talk about him, and refused to share any information. She refused to give me his name and threatened to end our relationship if I searched. I didn't settle for this. I learned what I wanted and needed, and decided that I had to take the bull by the horns.

Ultimately I was able to meet my birthfather. We have a warm and caring relationship. He lives far away, but visits my area a couple of times a year. The fact that he's been so welcoming and accepting has made all of this much easier.

Sometimes, adoptees have wanted to search for most of their lives, but for one reason or another held off for years, or even decades. Shannon waited until she was forty-nine years old. For her, the wait would carry a heavy cost.

Searching was something I had wanted to do since I was nine years old. A piece of the puzzle of my life was missing and it wasn't my fault it was lost. But it wasn't until forty years later that I decided to search.

I hired the Musser Foundation to help me search. Within four hours they called me back with the devastating news that my birthmother had been "located" but that she was no longer alive. Upon hearing of my birthmother's death, I fell apart. This puzzled me, that the loss of someone I didn't know would have such a profound effect upon me. The Musser Foundation had two women call me who had also learned their birthmothers were dead at the end of their search. The sharing of their own experiences was a tremendous help to me.

I sent a letter to my birthmother's sister, to at least have some contact with my birthfamily. She was going to throw the letter away, but another member of the family urged her to give the letter to my birthmother's husband, which she ultimately did.

He had known about me, and after some thought he decided to share the secret with his daughters—my two half-sisters. Both of them immediately phoned me. From the very first moments that we talked, I sensed strong feelings of love and acceptance on both their parts. These feelings of closeness have gotten stronger and stronger as time goes on. We decided to meet about a month later, and the long phone calls we had before this meeting allowed us to be very comfortable when we met. I felt as if I was coming home.

During that first visit, my sisters took me to my birthmother's grave. It was there that I "talked" with her, and thanked her for the gift of life, and told her that I understood the circumstances that necessitated our separation. Then each of us placed a single pink rose—her favorite flower—on her grave, to show her that her three girls were reunited at last.

Abby was luckier than Shannon. She was able to meet her birthmother and have some sense of closure before her birthmother died.

I became more and more curious about my roots as I watched my own children grow. Then I read an article in a local paper about a support group, attended a meeting, and joined. That was fourteen years ago.

My adoptive mother made me feel I had a birthright to the information about my original family. In fact, she told me that I would have to be numb not to wonder. She gave me her love and support, as well as all the information that she knew.

My search took two years. When I finally located my birthmother, I wrote her a letter. She called me by phone on Holy Thursday.

It was very exciting. I had so many questions. We decided we would write to each other for a while, to get to know each other before we met. This arrangement didn't last too long, since we were curious to see one another. We met at a restaurant, just the two of us. As soon as I saw her and we had eye contact, I knew it was her. I felt I had seen my roots and had a sense of having had "a beginning." I now knew where I came from. . . .

We talked very openly and easily with each other. The title of "Mom" was difficult for me to use, so I called her by her first name. I grew to love her more and more, and wished we had been able to be a part of each other's lives sooner.

I did experience some difficult feelings toward my birthmother. As much as I felt love and gratitude for her for having always thought of and loved me, I felt I could not be the child that she would have liked me to be, and to have the mother/daughter relationship she wished existed. This was difficult for her, and I know it was a disappointment.

Three years after our reunion, my birthmother died on Holy Thursday. I'm so happy and grateful for the close love and friendship we shared for those brief three years. I feel my finding her and being reunited gave my birthmother peace of mind in knowing that I was well and happy in my life, which she gave to me.

Diana has found her reunion with her birthmother and family to be a deeply satisfying and enriching experience. Interestingly, her desire to locate her birthfamily was not shared by her twin sister.

I'm a twin. My sister and I were adopted as infants, and are alike in many ways, but different in others. As I got older, I became more and more interested in searching for our birthmother. Finally, when I was thirty-three, I decided to search. But my twin has no desire to meet our birthmother. Even after I completed the search, and found our birthmother, she has expressed only anger and anxiety at the idea of reconnecting.

I remember thinking the phone call to my birthmom would be the phone call of my life. I was nervous and excited. I was also apprehensive that she might not acknowledge me, but I felt I'd prepared for that. My one and only goal was to speak to her directly and tell her thank you for giving me a gift that no one else in my life could give me: the gift of life.

When she answered the phone, I identified myself by the name she had given me at birth. She denied knowing who I was. I then gave her my birthdate and my twin sister's birth name and asked her once again if she knew who I was. Her reply was, "Yes, I do, but I don't want to."

At that moment I felt disheartened, but I was determined to have her hear what I wanted to tell her. I told her all the things I had always felt deep inside. I told her that my sister and I were both happy, that we'd been raised by two of the best parents in the world, that we had both gone to college and become nurses, and that we were married. I told her I loved her.

There was now dead silence on the other end of the phone. When she finally began to speak, the tone of her voice was different. She began to tell me things, about the guilt she felt at having twin girls out of wedlock, about the family's medical history, and about the sister and two brothers I never knew I had. We talked for over an hour, and during that time, she consented to meet with me later that week for lunch.

Five days after our initial phone call, we met. I was so happy and excited I cried during the entire hour and a half drive to meet her. When I arrived at the restaurant, I saw her standing there, all dressed up. I couldn't get out of my car fast enough.

I ran to her, crying, and hugged her. She told me she was not the emotional type, and I told her that that was okay—I could do enough crying for both of us. One of the first things I remember thinking when I saw her face close up was that my mother has *my* eyes. Her daughter, my new sister, soon joined us. I was pleased that she was as excited to meet me as I was to meet her. She reminded me of my twin. Once seated, we all took turns showing pictures, trying to catch up on the last thirty-three years. They showed me a photograph of my grandparents. I couldn't believe how closely they looked like my twin sister and me. It was chilling. For thirty-three years I had looked at my relatives' pictures and never associated them with me. To see people with similar characteristics was simply amazing.

That was one year ago. In the twelve months since our first reunion, my birthmother and I have developed a fabulous relationship. Knowing my roots, knowing where my genes are from, I feel complete.

But . . . that's me. My twin sister still has no desire to meet our birthmother. She feels we were abandoned by her. I respect my twin's feelings, but I look at all this differently. I've never felt like I lost. I feel like I won.

Not every birthparent wants to be found. Many are afraid. They've kept the birth of children secret for their entire adult lives.

An adoptee who meets with staunch resistance must come to his or her own decision about what to do. Eleven years ago, Ruthanne sought her birthmother and was informed that this woman wanted no contact. Ruthanne became frustrated that her birthmother would deny her even a single meeting. After a great deal of time and thought, she decided to force the issue.

As an adolescent, I was sure that I must look just like my birthmother—and that if I was lucky enough to meet her, it would be like looking in a mirror.

At the age of thirty-two, after both my adoptive

parents died, I searched and found my birthmother, who had been thirty-two at the time of my birth. She would not agree to meet me, although she did not deny who she was. After many letters and much frustration and heartache, I decided I would meet this woman, if only briefly, uninvited and unannounced.

I knew my birthmother lived alone. I also knew the location—a high-rise senior-citizen building, which had a locked front entry. I was sure that she would look out the peephole of her door, see the image of herself standing there, and not open the door. So I felt I needed some disguise. I bought a large straw hat, dark sunglasses, a big plant, and a box of pastry.

I drove the two hours to her home. I had not figured out how I was going to get into the building, but put on my hat and sunglasses and gathered up my plant and pastry, and walked the block to her building. As I was walking along, my heart was pounding, my mind was racing, and I was sure everyone I passed on the street knew I was up to something devious. As I approached the front door of the building, a UPS delivery man was leaving, and held the door open for me. I was sure this was a sign from God that I must be doing the right thing.

As I looked for her name on the directory in the lobby, my hands were shaking, my mouth was dry, and I felt sure my heart was beating so hard someone would see it pounding through my dress. Once on the elevator, it was as though I were having an out-of-body experience—as if I were watching myself in the elevator from three feet above. I walked to her door and knocked. When my birthmother opened the door I was shocked.

My mirror image was not standing there at all. She

was, in fact, a petite woman with blue eyes, not the tall, slim woman with dark brown eyes I'd imagined all those years. I was convinced I must have the wrong apartment, and asked her if she was "Harriet." When she replied yes, I was momentarily stunned, but I put one foot inside her door and said I was her birthdaughter.

She started shaking all over, put her head down, and demanded that I leave. I assured her that I was not there to harm her in any way, that I just wanted to meet her and get a little bit of information. I told her that I had brought some pastry, and if she would just make some tea, we could talk. Much to my surprise, she agreed and showed me into her kitchen.

As she made tea, she gradually opened up. She told me that no one in her family knew of my existence, that she had never married. Yes, she had thought of me often, and wondered what had happened to me. She was glad to meet me after all—it was just something that she couldn't *agree* to do.

I stayed about an hour, and asked all the questions I could think of without trying to pry too much. She gave me a kiss on the cheek when I left, but made it clear that she was not interested in having any sort of a relationship. She did not even want to have lunch for fear a relative might see us together.

I am her deepest, darkest secret and she intends to take that secret to her grave with her. I respect her wishes and have not tried to make contact since. I feel I had a very successful reunion in a rather unorthodox way. Meeting her face to face was a dream come true. The most healing thing was to know that she was just glad to meet me.

Having a closure to my search was a milestone. It

enabled me to get on with my life. It's hard to know where you're going if you don't know where you came from.

That need for closure is heard over and over again. Holly's story is an excellent illustration of how even a little information can help a lot. Her sister assisted her in getting started by getting Holly to request a reunion through a state mediator. But for Holly, using a mediator as a first resort was a mistake with lasting results.

I didn't prepare for my search. If I had, maybe things would have turned out differently. I had very little information to go on: my birthmother had been twenty-two years old, paid sixty dollars for my one-month foster care, and took three weeks to sign the termination papers. I was told she named me.

In the beginning, I told myself I was searching only for medical information. I was twenty-three and pregnant. But as time passed, I realized I couldn't suppress my real feelings anymore. I had so many questions. Why was I placed for adoption? What was my birthfamily's history? Did I look like anyone in the family? For a long time I didn't think I was worthy of that information.

My search was conducted by my state's intermediary system. My searcher was a very nice person who, I'm sure, thought she was doing the best she could. The problem was, my birthmother never heard from me. She only heard what someone else chose to tell her. It might have been easier for her to tell them, "No, I don't want any contact," than it would have been to tell me, her birthdaughter. When she was contacted, she was shocked and angry, asking, "How did you find me? This has got to be illegal!" Soon after that, she hung up.

I very much respect my birthmother's feelings and privacy. I assumed that the searcher would wait one year to make a follow-up call to see if she had changed her mind. If that wasn't possible, then I assumed they would at least attempt to get some updated medical history for me. But that didn't happen. Instead, I was told by the searcher that five months earlier she had sent a form for my birthmother to sign to confirm her decision.

I had filled out a state form from the Department of Human Resources—I was allowed to write ten questions and a brief letter that were to be given to my birthmother to answer. These were never given to her. My searcher never told my birthmother how I felt, or why I needed to contact her. My birthmother never read the letter I wrote telling her my feelings and intentions. My searcher never even asked about her medical history. Now that my birthmother has signed this form, my searcher can *never* contact my birthmother again without being sued for harassment. I wouldn't have taken the time and extreme emotions it took to fill out those papers if I had known they would never be passed along.

The most difficult thing about my search was that I had *no* control over what was done or even what was said to my birthmother when she was contacted. The social worker made all the decisions. I saw no proof. I had to take her word for everything—how she searched, what she said during the phone conversation with my birthmother, and most importantly, that my birthmother had signed the form. I wasn't allowed to see her signature, because then I would know her name! As far as I know, my medical and family history will die with her.

Several months later a different file was found on Holly's adoption. A reunion with her birthmother still wasn't possible, but new information from the file would at least give Holly more knowledge about her origins. The resulting impact of this information on Holly should not be minimized.

One year after my birthmother was contacted, the agency located a different file on my adoption. This contained a great deal of new, nonidentifying information on my birthmother and her family and a small amount on my birthfather. They had both been working on their master's degrees. She had a highly educated family who were well known in their community. There was musical talent on both sides of the family. I read that being pregnant out of wedlock went against all of her morals. She waited until the last minute to go to the agency—even to tell her mother. The file said that she was very emotional about the whole situation, but she decided not to see me after I was born. She sent a social worker to check up on me, and I believe that she helped her name me.

It makes me feel much better about myself to have this information. I feel like I should go back to school now. It's given me this big push. I tell myself, "You can do it, Holly—you come from this educated family." This small bit of information has given me a new sense of self-worth. I noticed it just today. I was looking people in the eye, and smiling. I'm somebody now. I'm real. I now feel like I was born. Before, I just felt like I was brought here by the stork.

I hope and pray that my birthmother will someday change her mind. Every year around my birthday, I think of her. What a great gift it would be to hear from her.

Paige says that there is no way she would ever discourage adoptees from searching for their birthparents. But she would caution them not to expect to resolve all of their problems by completing the search. Life is just not that easy. And for Paige, the way some of her birthfamily reacted to her compounded the feelings she already had of low self-esteem.

I was raised by two very loving parents and always knew I was adopted. I was always made to feel that I was special because they wanted me so much. I lived in a small town and never had an opportunity to talk with anyone in similar circumstances. In fact, I don't even know anyone near my age who is adopted.

I never asked my mother much about my adoption nor related that I desperately wanted to find my natural parents. I was afraid I would hurt my adoptive parents. Finally, as my adoptive mother was aging, I knew it was then or never. I realized that if she died, what little she knew would go with her. I was in my forties when I finally told her I wanted to search for my birthmother. She was in complete agreement with me and very supportive. She told me what little she knew, which really did not help me at all.

I undertook a search for my birthmother, and was able to locate her using the court system and a systematic search through phone directories. With shaking hands, I dialed her phone number and for the first time in forty years heard my mother's voice. Only someone who has experienced it will know the emotion of such a conversation. The moment I opened a letter and saw photos of my mother, her mother, and other relatives was one of the high points of my life. All the years of wondering what my relatives looked like were finally ended.

Two months later, I took the most nerve-racking flight of my life to meet my mother. We ultimately formed a good relationship. Her husband is a jewel, and considers me his daughter—they had no children. My birthmother and my adoptive mother became very close before my adoptive mother died in 1985. I think it was a good experience for both of them.

But the jubilant feelings in the first year after meeting my birthmother gave way to many mixed emotions. I can't summon up the same feelings for her that she feels for me. I care for her deeply, but naturally the feelings do not come close to those I felt for my adoptive mother. My birthmother seems more like a close friend.

My feelings for my birthfather were different. My birthmother had told me that I was the result of a teenage romance. When she became pregnant, which was quite a scandal in 1937, my birthmother was sent off on a bus to a different state to have me. My father denied he was the father. She never heard from him again. Naturally, she was quite bitter.

A year after meeting her, my husband and I were driving through the town where my mother met my father. Just on a lark, I stopped and looked in the phone book. You can guess my feelings when I discovered my father's name there. I asked someone about him, and they told me where he worked. I inquired about him at his place of business and was told that he was on a business trip in my state!

We drove home and I just could not let it go. I called his company and asked them to have him call me. He returned my call and I told him that I wanted to talk to him about some relatives of mine I thought he knew. I asked where he was staying and was told that he was only thirty-eight miles from my home.

I made arrangements to meet him at the hotel. My husband and I walked into the lobby and there sat the man who was my father. We talked for a long time. Of course, it was quite a shock to him. He would not commit himself to the fact that he was my father. But he came to our home the next day and we met once more before he returned home.

We became very close. We had so much in common. His outgoing personality was a match for my own. He was a joy to be around. That made it all the more painful that his wife and children totally rejected me. They refused to ever talk with or meet me. Their almost venomous dislike of me, a person that they didn't even know, didn't help my self-esteem. I always sought the approval of other people, way beyond that of a normal person, as if I had to achieve all that I could to prove I was a person of some worth. I have struggled with their rejection through all these years.

Despite how his family felt, my father came to visit us once a year, and called me every week. I never wrote or called him, as it upset his wife. When he died two years ago, his family told me they didn't want me at the funeral. That was very hard for me. My father and I had become so close over the years. Later that year my husband and I made a trip to his grave so that I could place some flowers there.

Hell or high water probably would not have stopped me from searching until I found the answers I needed. Even though I found the answers, I do not feel everything is okay. Somehow, I still feel I do not really belong to anyone. I just sort of feel as if I "just happened." As I get older, it doesn't seem to matter as much, but these feelings are always there, still hidden below the surface.

If the search and reunion process is really the first step in coming to terms with the early sense of loss and abandonment, then pain would seem a necessary and acceptable part of reunion. There have been levels of pain in all these stories, but that shouldn't be viewed as a negative. Loss and pain are a part of adoption. They are inescapable.

Certainly how one is responded to by birthfamily members can affect, to a great degree, how much pain is suffered by the adoptee. Rejection can compound the sense of pain, but there are different kinds of rejection. There is the rejection by a birthparent who says, "I can't meet you. My family doesn't know about you. Please understand." But, at the extreme is the response that purposefully causes pain. That, to me, is the hardest to ever understand.

Sarah searched to learn about her roots. But she received a "double shotgun blast" that she was totally unprepared for from her birthmother. Her metaphor is not inappropriate—words can inflict physical pain.

The woman you are looking for does not exist—and even if she did, she wouldn't care about you.

These were the first words that Sarah ever received from her birthmother. After a search for her birthfamily, Sarah had written a gentle letter of introduction to the woman who had given birth to her. She was not prepared for this hurtful reply. It made her feel unworthy and useless, confirming all the negative feelings she had felt about herself her whole life.

Sarah would wait three more years before gaining the courage to write once again. With her second letter, she sent along a copy of *Birth Bond*, a book that contains several interviews with birthmothers, in hopes it would give her birthmother a sense of connection with others. In her letter, Sarah was discreet and understanding. Her birthmother's reply was devastating, calling Sarah an evil, sorry bitch, and demanding that she leave her alone. She ended by saying all she felt for Sarah was hatred.

The first time I met Sarah was when I heard her birthmother's letter being read aloud at a conference. I'd met adoptees before who had had to deal with rejection, but nothing as cruel as this. I was inspired by her courage in sharing her experience, and her ability to move forward despite such a cold-blooded response. This is Sarah's story.

I initially searched because all of my life I have felt disconnected from the world. I lacked a sense of connection with my adoptive family and always felt in my gut that I would feel connected to my birthfamily if I could just find them. I wanted to know my heritage. To ultimately learn that my first ancestors set foot in the Colonies back in the 1600s has made me feel proud. It's given me a sense of belonging I'd never had before.

When I began to search, I felt at times that I was falling into this dark hole. I worried that I might die during the search process. I remember feeling so relieved upon reading one of Betty Jean Lifton's books to learn that the feelings that I was experiencing were quite normal for someone getting close to moving through that "veil of secrecy." Prior to reading her book, I really was becoming convinced that perhaps I was going crazy.

Contrary to what a lot of people experience in a search, I never had anyone turn down a request for information—except my birthmother. The person who helped me search gave me a piece of advice that was extremely helpful. She told me to "Take this search and reunion process at *your* pace. Don't let anyone else push you into something you're not ready for."

It surprises people, but when I read my birthmother's first letter to me, I felt nothing. I put it down and turned on the news. I had just lost my life partner and my life was in such an upheaval the letter seemed almost inconsequential. It was just one more loss. It didn't impact me at all at the time.

I seriously doubt that I could have pulled off the next phase of my reunion very well during this time. I was too vulnerable. By the time I did meet my aunt, grandmother, and brother, I was feeling fairly strong again.

Excluding my birthmother, I've been able to become quite close with members of my birthfamily. The first meetings with my aunt and cousins were incredible adrenaline highs, which were always followed by a time of quiet depression and anger. It took me a long time to figure out why, but I believe it stems from being kept away from my birthfamily and my heritage for so long. I go through times when I feel very cheated, very resentful of the system, then it evens out and a comfort level happens. I call my reunion experience an "E-ticket ride."[1] The roller coaster of emotion is unbelievable. I doubt that any person, any book, any support group can really prepare another human being to go through this experience.

Today, I am a part of my birthfamily, except, of course, for my birthmother. I *am* very different than anyone else—different politics, different lifestyle, etc.— but I feel very accepted. Maybe that is my need, more than their reality. I don't know. But my perception of our relationships is very positive. I feel incredibly lucky to be a part of this family. I've met a wonderfully amazing array of people, from my eighty-six-year-old grandmother, who "always wondered" where I was, to my new third cousin born this week.

When I received my birthmother's second letter, I cried, really cried. I didn't go much beyond the first line for a while. It was pretty devastating. I knew from that letter that I would never meet her. I had to give up any hope of that.

While it has admittedly been disappointing to find a mother so full of rage that she cannot bring herself to allow me in her life, meeting my aunt has made the closure of the circle possible for me. We have a special, unique relationship, and she has filled much of the void I used to feel.

When I began my search, I had only questions. Now I find that most of my questions have been answered. I feel connected for the first time in my life. On the good days, I wouldn't trade this experience for anything in the world. But there are also days when I feel the losses of this journey more than the gains, and down times when I am not certain I would do it again if I had the chance. The roller-coaster ride never ends.

Sarah's story is one of survival. She is working hard to incorporate the positive aspects of her reunion into her life. Rejection is one thing. But the cruel missives she received from her birthmother are difficult to surmount.

When people hear of reunion stories that involve difficult situations, a frequent response is "Well, maybe people are better off not searching. Why put yourself through all that pain?"

Perhaps it's impossible for someone outside of adoption to understand how it feels to be an adoptee. Searchers don't seek pain, they seek answers. They seek knowledge and a sense of completeness. Almost intuitively, instinctively, they are drawn to the search.

Pain is frequently a part of the quest. Do not misinterpret the pain in reunion stories as an indicator that reunions are not good for people. They *are*. But reunions are not black-and-white events. They are rarely all good and rarely all bad. They just "are." They occur because they are necessary. And somewhere, on the other side of the ocean of pain, is self-awareness and empowerment.

~ 12 ~

BIRTHMOTHERS

THE NATURAL RESPONSE TO A TRAUMATIC loss is grief. To not grieve, to stifle one's pain, would be unhealthy. Today we call it "denial."

When a relationship is terminated or a climactic loss is suffered, the bereaved is supported, consoled. People extend empathy and sympathy. No one would callously say, "Forget about it. Just get on with your life." Yet that's just what birthmothers were told to do.

Just because they were not able to care for a child or did not assume that parenting responsibility did not mean that birthmothers didn't love their children. Most were counseled to sign away the rights to their child before the baby was even born, never anticipating the physiological changes and emotional attachment they would experience after giving birth.

Hundreds of thousands of birthmothers were sent home from the hospital with the admonition to put this event behind them. Furthermore, they were never to mention to anyone what happened. They were supposed to simply pretend the pregnancy, the birth, and the baby never happened. Grieving was not allowed or encouraged. The inner anguish they felt upon relinquishment was to be hidden and ignored. This game of denial and pretending was required of birthmothers if they were to be accepted "back into society." So for decades they kept their feelings about the loss of their children secret, locked inside them. Is it any wonder that they then face enormous upheavals during reunions?

My own birthmother went through an emotional tailspin after I first called her. She relived an event she had never really given herself permission to think about, much less resolve. I wish I had known ahead of our reunion what she would go through. I hope that that knowledge would have made me more empathetic.

I have taken up a great deal of space with my version of our reunion process. It seems only fitting that Lee share her own perspective. This is her story.

I am an adoptee. I was born Lenora Cecelia Brown. My birthmother is somewhere out there. I want to find her because I know how she feels. I am also a birthmother.

I didn't find out I was pregnant until I was over four months along. I was initially sent to a home for the aged in Seattle. Above the doorway was a sign which said ENTER YE INTO THE TWILIGHT OF YOUR LIFE. I thought it probably was my twilight. I was terrified. I slept in a ward with the old people and one of them died that first night. I was so scared I just ran. I ended up in northern California where friends of my parents took me in. There I stayed, pregnant, unmarried, and scared, rejected by my family. Everybody.

My first child was born in April of 1955. I named her Cecelia Anne. I cried to the depths of my soul when she was taken from my arms. I thought I would never see her again. I remember watching the taillights of the social worker's car until it disappeared from sight.

When I returned home two weeks after giving birth, my mother introduced me to Lou. We married five weeks later. Throughout our marriage, he was constantly dealing with someone who felt worthless. For years I would say to myself, "Remember who you are and where you came from. You're not worthy to tie his shoelaces." I wasn't happy.

We had seven wonderful children together. But I had never dealt with the trauma of losing Cecelia. My self-esteem was nonexistent. It ultimately caused problems in our marriage. I blamed my unhappiness on Lou. What I really needed to do was grieve the child I had lost. But no one knew anything about the impact of adoption on birthmothers back then. So I transferred the burden of my unhappiness onto Lou.

We divorced. I moved to a different state. Lou died of cancer several years later. Then in July of 1988, I thought something terrible had happened to one of my seven grown children when the local priest called. He had to repeat his question: Would I be willing to talk to my daughter? I caught my breath. My heart was pounding, and I felt faint. "You mean Cecelia?" It was too good to be true. She had found me! I never expected this.

She called me right away. I was thrilled but scared. How do you tell someone you had to leave them? I pictured this sweet little baby. Her voice didn't match my fantasy. It was a stranger's voice, stronger than I expected. She told me she had a great life, and that I had done the right thing by giving her up. Feelings and words ended thirty-three years of suppressing the reality of Cecelia.

She was called Jean. I felt disappointed. Her name was the only thing I'd been able to give her. The agency told me I could do that. Why didn't her parents like the name? It was such a little thing to be able to do. . . .

Jean's voice was friendly, but she asked such probing questions—questions about things I hadn't dared to think about for years, trying to dull the ache. Now I had to answer. Could I remember all the details correctly—particularly about her father? Did I have to remember him?

To cope over the years I had literally blocked things out. It was not easy to gloss things over. I don't think Jean knew how difficult it was for me to answer those questions, and suddenly have to confront that past. I didn't tell Jean how I really felt about her birthfather. To me he was a stranger in my life, an intruder. During the weeks before our reunion on my birthday, I found my memory whipping me back again and again to the mid-fifties. It made me physically ill.

But I was also elated. Eight! Yes, world, I have eight children. Count 'em. No longer would I mentally subtract one when people asked how many children I had. And the whole world was going to know my secret. *People* magazine was covering the reunion. What would my parents have thought if they were still alive? Was I trying to get back at them? I felt swept along. I had no time to work anything through. I cried a lot.

I sensed a tension in Jean's voice shortly before I

left for the reunion in Minneapolis. Things were changing between us, getting uncomfortable. At the airport, the day of the reunion, my kids organized everything. It was as if I was "just there." After a mixup at the gates, we finally connected over a white courtesy telephone. Then everyone ran to meet her at baggage claim. I ran too, thinking STOP! Let me find her! They all crowded around her, laughing and crying. I held back. I felt like a goddamned afterthought. What about this mother and baby—forever lost? Finally, my kids stepped back and there she was looking like . . . a stranger?!

Jean hugged me and I hugged her back. It was a miracle. But a strange feeling came over me. Rather, a loss of feeling—or maybe not enough. Maybe the moment was more than we could manage. Why couldn't we walk away together and just talk?

I felt put off and strangely out of place. I was trying too hard. My kids were videotaping the day, and with a national magazine there, I felt I better act deliriously happy. It was my fifty-fourth birthday after all, and *she came.*

Later, Jean and Sue were in the kitchen when I heard Jean say "Mom." I started toward her saying, "Oh Jean!" when she said pointedly to Sue, "Your mom." I felt mortified, my heart pounding, I went off by myself. I blew it . . . I blew it. Why was this so hard? Inside I knew I lost Cecelia a long time ago.

I needed time alone with Jean. I understood how she felt more than she knew. We did get together but at arm's length. I couldn't clasp her to my breast but I didn't want to lose her again. Why did she find me? This wasn't fair, I thought. I was really hurting over this stranger who was really not a stranger.

By the third day of our reunion, I wished I could just disappear. Jean just didn't seem to like me. But she sure seemed to like her new siblings. I sat away, withdrawn, hoping Jean would notice and give me some sign that she thought I was okay, or that we'd be okay—someday.

Jean had kept a log of her search, pages and pages. It hurt to read it. I acted interested. I must have been a real disappointment after all that work. I felt sorry for myself.

The last day of our reunion our laughter was forced. We said goodbye, agreeing to keep in touch. We communicated infrequently in the months that followed. Where was the "bible" to tell a person how to feel or how to act? She was busy. I was afraid to call.

On my next birthday, Jean sent flowers. I was touched she remembered. Yet when Jean visited that Christmas, she was barely cordial to me. I suggested that I might have a chance to visit her. She told me she and her husband appreciated the fact I hadn't interrupted their lives. My sons had visited her. I felt embarrassed I'd mentioned it.

A few days later I wrote a long letter to Jean stating all the hurts I felt, mistakes I'd made, misunderstandings we'd had. I said I wanted to remember Cecelia the way she was—and that I felt I couldn't and didn't want to see Jean again. It was too hard. It hurt too much. I wished her well.

The letter sat on my desk. A week later I tore it up.

In April I spent an hour looking at birthday cards for her, trying to find one not too possessive, not too personal. Was there a right one?

The following summer, the family organized a two-year reunion with Jean. I thought, "Oh, good grief. What for? You think it will help?" To top it off, all of us, my kids, myself, and Jean were to meet with a pair of family counselors to discuss the "trauma" that followed the reunion.

At the airport, Jean looked good. We were pleasant toward each other. I was wary how to act, but glad to see her. Why couldn't I just be me?

With the counselor, Jean talked about how it must have been for me—the difficulties I had faced as an adoptee and birthmother. I was touched. I sensed for a moment a kind hand on my shoulder mentally—Jean's.

After the meeting, we went to lunch, just the two of us. My kids were surprised we would do that. But it felt great. We started to talk of our mothers and many things.

The time since our first meeting had not been easy. I had felt anger and loss. I wondered frequently, "What in the world does Jean want? Why did she search for me?" She must have been afraid of me, of meeting me, thinking that I wanted to mother her. How could that be? One little incident in the kitchen? But it wasn't little, and I knew in my heart of hearts that maybe I did want that—the whole nine yards. Still, I can't feel the same way about Jean as I do about the family I raised.

Two years after "Cecelia" first found me, I sat and watched a video Jean made for us of herself and her family. I suddenly felt good about Jean's life. Betty, Jean's mother, and her father, Lou, seemed so happy together. Jean looked like such a happy child. I said to myself, "I did the right thing." When I first met Jean, I could not honestly say that. It hurt too much. But the past was beginning to heal.

An ending or a beginning? I still would want to have met Jean. Yes, I feel lucky. She's added a new dimension to my life—helped me to begin anew with the closure of reunion, and to find new inner strength. And we are becoming friends. Who could really ask for more?

More than ever, I need to find my own identity, my own roots. Somewhere. While there's still time.

The anger and disappointment that Lee felt after our reunion was not unique. It's easy to see how birthparents and adoptees will be seeking different things when they reunite.

Lee needed to rescue "Cecelia"—to find that three-day-old-baby. But I was grown, with a voice stronger than she expected, or, perhaps, wanted. I didn't need her the way baby Cecelia had. That unretrievable past had to be reconciled before we could live in the present.

Some birthmothers can clearly see their fantasies aren't matching reality early on. But others hold out, hoping that sometime the adoptee will fulfill their deepest hopes.

When I first began a dialogue with Penny, a birthmother who had sought out her birthson, she painted a fairly rosy picture of her postreunion situation. But over a period of a few months, Penny's feelings toward her birthson drastically changed. As she began analyzing the difficulties in her relationship with her birthson, something inside of her psyche said, "Let's get on with it."

I think there's something in our human nature that needs to believe in fairy tales. Many a birthmother's heart holds fast to a nonexistent "happily ever after" and mine was no exception.

Reality usually hits us in small doses. We rarely hit that brick wall all at once. This was true for me throughout my years of postreunion with my birthson. The reality of "here and now" was simply not making the adjustment with my heart that was still clinging to "happily ever after."

When we find our birthchild and make a connection, we're not always a welcome intrusion. This is understandable, but when a birthchild accepts a birthparent into his life (as mine did) and then sets restrictive conditions, I don't think there is much chance of building a relationship for the future that's going to stand the test of time. My own birthson, perhaps without realizing it, has caused me to feel ashamed in front of others and often leaves no room for growth with the power he exerts over our situation. For instance, my presence in his life, along with my husband and five children, has been kept a secret from his adoptive parents. Our first reunion was almost four years ago! This continued secrecy affords no opportunity to break the original compact of lies upon which the adoption was built back in 1960.

I've had to sort the facts from fiction and have only recently come to the realization that what the past has taken away is gone forever. My place as my birthson's mother has been permanently filled by someone else. All my hopes and dreams of finding a special place of belonging in his heart must die. With pain, I must accept the fact that the adoptive mother takes my place, in its entirety, as my son's only mother and grandmother to his two little girls.

I could have done without the pain the reunion has brought. I know a small part of me will never be the same again. There are people who are timid about opening that door to the past. I used to encourage them, but now I think they might be the smart ones. They weigh the risk before they take it and don't let their hearts rule their heads. I've got to learn to do that. It's never too late.

It's painful to let go and move on, but my heart is finally at peace where it used to be so painfully torn. The time for closure has come. Looking back, I have learned first and foremost that blood is not thicker than water. And you can't make somebody love you. No matter how much you give to the other person, love cannot be forced. That's the one honesty all love possesses. You know when it's there and when it's not. It takes both parties, working together, to make a successful relationship.

The best part of closure is the peace you find on the other side of the pain. "Happily ever after" may exist after all, but it's up to each and every one of us to make our own . . .

There's a lot of anguish in Penny's words, but also a sense of growth and resolution. She no longer expects her birthson to make her okay. She senses she must do that on her own. She is taking control of how she feels about herself. After all these years, Penny is moving forward, alone, and in many ways finding peace.

This does not mean, however, that a birthmother should just metaphorically walk away and close the door. Penny is dealing with her own issues, but she is not turning her back on her birthson. As psychotherapist Nancy Verrier writes in *The Primal Wound*, "Sometimes a reunion, which started off gloriously, begins to deteriorate to the point of an almost nonexistent relationship. Many birthmothers, themselves hurt and feeling rejected, don't know what to do at this point. Because of their own feelings of rejection, there is a tendency to want to just forget it, to try to get on with life. She should not forget that she tried this once before."[1]

Some birthmothers are unable to let go. The wound is too deep, the need to connect is too strong. This is especially true when the birthmother and birthfather ultimately marry. Even if they go on to have more children, the missing child leaves an unfillable place in the family.

Maria began to daydream about reuniting with her daughter Crystal even before the baby was born. The knowledge of their impending separation was incredibly painful. Maria knew she could not live her life without knowing about Crystal's well-being, and ultimately knowing her as a person.

My husband and I are an interracial couple and I became pregnant before we were married. Out of fear and in isolation, we allowed our child to get away.

At my insistence, I met the adoptive parents anonymously, and my love and concern for my unborn child was shared. They were informed, as best as I could, that one day . . . I wanted my daughter to know the truth about her background and how she was wanted and loved. The adoptive father commented, "We will do what is best for her." I remember being terrified at that moment that the adoptive parents—who were black—would never tell her that her mother was white and had wanted to keep her. She wasn't yet born and already I felt these two strangers were in control of whether my daughter and I would ever know each other.

When her adoptive mother came to the hospital to pick her up, I quietly, but firmly, refused to sign the release papers unless they allowed me to hold her. I was given only a couple of minutes to say my goodbyes. She was handed to me completely naked. I studied her little body in total wonder and awe. I told her that I loved her and that I would see her one day. "Goodbye for a while," were my exact words. A kiss to her forehead, lips, and her feet, and then, goodbye. The wait for reunion began immediately.

When the social worker came to see me in the hospital to sign release papers, I saw the names of the adoptive parents and their address on the form. I couldn't believe it—their names weren't supposed to be there. I was told to "sign here." I affixed my eyes to the identifying information and memorized it as I scribbled my name at the bottom of the page.

Jerry, Crystal's father, and I ultimately got married. We wanted to write to Crystal's parents and let them know we had managed to salvage our lives. Our minister advised us that we should be happy and content and forget about our daughter. I had mixed emotions of hurt, anger, humiliation, and frustration. I recalled that this minister was a good loving father to his own four children. I wondered which of his children he could forget.

I know people meant well when they said to "forget." I don't think they really realized what they were asking us to do. It was as if we had entered into another realm of beings. We were to deny our feelings and needs, to become instead invisible, content, and grateful and spare everyone else discomfort forever.

Jerry and I ultimately contacted the adoptive parents. Over the years we had periodic communication with the adoptive father. His reserve and guardedness prompted me to worry that they were really not open to Crystal's knowing us when she reached adulthood.

We had unrealistic expectations. Many people who knew of our situation, and thought highly of Jerry and me, were convinced that Crystal would be thrilled to meet us and discover that her birthparents were fine people. This encouragement nearly assured us that Crystal, too, would see us in a positive light.

When we finally met our daughter after she was eighteen, it would take me a long time to realize that her dreams were not my dreams. There is no doubt that I must have presented myself to Crystal as rather desperate. Though I tried to be comforting and cool, I was, in reality, obsessed. The reunion created great hopes in me that the painful separation had ended. So I pushed. My feelings were raw as I was carried back to the original separation. I panicked. The original pain intensified—it seemed that only the reconnection with her could stop the longing and emotional pain. Like an addict I pursued the "fix." I was so high after the face-to-face meeting. I plunged to the depths of a pit when Crystal withdrew.

I realize now that struggling to force things to happen in a certain way was the worst thing I could have done. I wish I had had better insight.

Crystal's well-being is paramount to me. I am working on letting go of the intense need to have Crystal in my life. Letting go does not mean giving up hope on a future relationship. But it is clear I can live without her as an active part of my life. I am living by a "one day at a time" philosophy.

Believe it or not, our reunion has been totally worthwhile for me despite all the disappointment. And, even though it has been a difficult process for Crystal as well, she has told me a number of times that she has benefited.

Recently I received a letter from Crystal in which she requested that I not contact her. She wants to "take control" of the relationship, and she will contact me if she chooses to do so. I view this request as positive. It is a signal, to me, of growth and maturity. All along *she's had no real sense of choice*. Though it's been there, it's been obscured by the relentless messages of our hopes and dreams. Now, she has seized power over her life and has had the courage to express her feelings and exert some control. We will honor that and live with the hope that someday she'll choose to make the contact.

Pain is an unavoidable ingredient for birthmothers in reunions. Beyond the pain of having fantasies left unfulfilled, and of facing a long-buried past, is the pain of facing a different kind of loss. It is every birthmother's nightmare that she might find her birthchild has died. How does a birthmother cope and resolve her initial loss when she finds a gravestone at the end of her search? Amanda had her worst fears confirmed when she searched for her daughter.

In 1960, like most unwed couples, we were convinced, talked into, and counseled that relinquishing our baby was the best thing for our child. Even though this felt entirely unnatural, we were offered no other options. My daughter's future was put in the hands of an adoption agency, who would "do the best thing." I was told I would forget. I would have more children and go on with my life. How little they knew.

This decision affected the rest of my life. There

were a lot of times that I didn't allow myself to think about her. It was too painful, too sad, too empty. I was told I had no right to search for her. I gave up that right.

My daughter was born in April. I named her Stacy. Just to guarantee there would be no way I'd ever "forget," my son was born two months premature on the same date the following April.

Stacy was not forgotten and often talked about. My sons always wanted me to find her, particularly Sean, who shared her birthday. Then my son Bill lost his wife in a terrible car accident. She was the same age as Stacy. This event was a catalyst for me—I had to know if Stacy was alive.

I searched for over two years, then took everything I had been able to find and contacted the Musser Foundation. I remortgaged my house to pay their search fees, but I didn't care. It was time.

Sandy Musser called me personally two days after Stacy's birthday. She said this was the toughest call she'd ever had to make. She wondered if I was home alone.

Stacy was dead. She had committed suicide seven years earlier at age twenty-three. She shot herself in the head in a bar across the street from her adoptive father's business.

It's odd. I had had the feeling she was not alive. I had definitely anticipated it. Still we were all devastated by the news. My sons, all of us. We had all been hoping we would meet her.

I immediately wrote to her adoptive parents, in hopes of learning more about Stacy, whom they had renamed Lynn. Over the next several months, her parents and I wrote back and forth. Their first letter contained a senior picture of Lynn. She was absolutely beautiful. Until you see your child, you aren't able to imagine what she looks like. That picture brought such reality to it—she was a combination of her father and myself—no one could ever deny it.

I flew to Lynn's hometown with a friend from my support group and we drove around the area where Lynn had grown up. I needed to be somewhere she'd been. We went to the cemetery and spent time there.

Her parents invited me to their home. Wild horses couldn't have kept me away. Her mom shared photo albums with me, then took me up and showed me Lynn's room. It meant the world to me to be there. We hugged and cried together. I believe this was therapeutic for all of us.

I had to make that trip to complete the circle. Visiting her grave, meeting her family and friends, helped. Even her dog. He was twelve years old, and was so friendly toward me I felt he knew I was a part of Lynn.

We've all lost something we cannot regain. I lost a dream of meeting her, putting my arms around her, telling her I always loved her, and sharing her history.

When Lynn's adoptive parents were first contacted, they were not going to agree to talk with me. They felt it was better for me to have a dream, rather than reality. But, despite the enormous tragedy that I have found, I have also found peace. I know my daughter's destiny.

Amanda's story is a powerful one. She feels she would have been lost when she learned of Lynn's death if it had not been for the support of her friends and her husband. It is important to acknowledge that this news, though horrible, has, nonetheless, given Amanda a sense of peace and completion to know what happened. There are many who argue against searching, citing the devastating potential of the unknown. Yet, again and again, searchers reiterate that no matter what the outcome, reality is preferable to fantasy.

What are a birthmother's innermost fantasies? Getting the baby back? Changing the past? Reclaiming the child? Does it ever really happen?

Janice is a birthmother who was sixteen when she came home with the news that she was pregnant by her high school sweetheart. Wedding plans were made and canceled. She was sent off in disgrace to a Catholic home for unwed mothers. The name on the building was St. Agnes's Asylum.

I learned too late that St. Agnes's sent home 98 percent of its young mothers without their babies. I still can't believe to this day that I was one of them. I wanted my baby from the moment I learned of his existence. I was told that adoption was in my baby's best interests. He would be raised by wonderful people who could give him everything I couldn't. If I really loved him, I would understand that this was best for him.

He was born in St. Ann's Hospital. I named him John. There were no flowers or congratulatory cards. I fed him and rocked him before I was sent home, five days after his birth, with leaking breasts and empty arms. I cried every day for months. The pain and loss were not spoken of in my family for seventeen years.

I married, had four other children, but in many ways was just going through the motions of living. My soul felt dead. I often stared at little boys on the street. I wondered if the ones that I saw on the evening news that had drowned or been hit by cars were my baby. The inhumanity of traditional closed adoption for birthparents is that we are not allowed to know if our children are dead or alive.

Ultimately I searched. Concerned United Birthparents was my support. John was sixteen when I found him. I waited as long as I could before contacting his family, but found I could not wait until he was eighteen. I sent a well-thought-out letter to his adoptive parents.

They had renamed him "William." After an initial angry phone call from William's mother, my family and I were invited to his seventeenth birthday party. The reunion was exciting and happy, yet disappointing in many ways. I could see that my son did not have the life I had been told he would, with those supposedly wonderful parents who could give him everything that I couldn't.

His adoptive parents tried to portray a picture of an intact and stable family. But I ultimately learned that, due to alcoholism, the parents had divorced when William was two. William was raised by a single mother, who was angry, abusive, and overwhelmed by the responsibility of raising four children.

William expressed a need to get to know me and his siblings through frequent visits. His adoptive parents became increasingly anxious, then angry. Finally, his adoptive mother told him we could have no further contact. William obeyed her wishes for a while, but within a few months, he visited us again. His adoptive mother decided to end her relationship with him. Completely.

We've had many ups and downs. William has withdrawn at times to integrate his new self. Early on, I'm sure I overwhelmed him with all my stored-up love for him. Being reunited is not a simple process. But we have found a wonderful, comfortable place in each other's lives. I am his mother, and he is my son.

William and I plan to legalize our relationship. We will go to Probate Court and I will adopt him. We will right the wrong that was done almost twenty-three years ago. In our case, adoption was not the best thing for all concerned.

One year ago, I walked up the hill toward St. Ann's Hospital, my heart pounding. I hadn't been there since my son's birth. I walked through the double doors into the same labor and delivery room where "John" was born. There, William handed me my new grandson. He looked so much like his father I nearly fainted.

Life does come full circle.

This is an unusual story, one that will probably keep some adoptive parents up all night, and will probably give some birthmothers unrealistic expectations. It's hard for me, having had a close relationship with my adoptive parents, to comprehend that not every adoptee is so lucky. As has been stated before, most reunions strengthen adoptive family relationships. The severing that occurred in this particular story appears to have been totally the adoptive mother's choice.

Janice and her son aside, most birthmothers face, at best, a relationship laced with ambiguities. And some birthmothers face much less. Rejection is a scenario all searchers seem to try to prepare for. Yet preparation and experience are two different things.

Tamara's search for her birthdaughter ended five years ago with a phone call. She has yet to meet her daughter in person.

I remember when I was searching for her that the wait for news was unbearable at times. But in comparison, just locating her was the easy part. When I finally knew who she was and where she was, I wrote to her adoptive parents and included a letter to be given to my birthdaughter. Her parents destroyed my letter to her, but gave her the letter I wrote to them after some time. She held on to the letter and finally made contact with me. I had written in April. She called six months later on her birthday.

We talked on the phone for forty-five minutes. I don't remember the first few minutes of the call, but I do remember our conversation seemed quite natural and full of hope and promises. She said she hadn't told her parents she was going to contact me. She said she'd discuss it with them, and that we'd meet very soon. She asked lots of questions and seemed to really want to become part of my life. That was several years ago. I'm still waiting.

She obviously had second thoughts. She hasn't spoken or written. I'm trying to be patient and just wait until she's ready. Her adoptive parents are much older, and I suspect she's worried about their reaction to the reunion.

Since my first contact with my daughter, I've gone through many emotions. Initially, with her phone call, I was on top of the world. It finally happened! I'd believed ever since giving her up that we would be reunited someday.

As time passed, I've settled into more of a "what happens, happens" attitude. I've been frustrated, angry, disappointed. Why doesn't she want it as badly as I do? I just have love to give. By no means could I hurt her or threaten her well-being in *any* way. I'd like to at least talk with her and help her work it out. I hope she's getting support from her family and friends. I can't help but believe that only wonderful things could come out of a reunion. I pray it will happen one day.

For some birthmothers, the pain of separation grows so strong that the need to find their birthchild becomes an obsession. Julia felt she and her daughter shared a soul. She knew she couldn't grieve her until she found out what had become of her. Foremost, Julia knew her daughter needed her. She always *knew*.

Driven and determined, she began a long, painful search. The day she at last had her birthdaughter's address in her hand, she could not wait one minute to contact her.

I learned she was staying only a twenty-five-minute drive from my house. It was pouring rain, around 8 P.M., and I drove alone to the address her ex-boyfriend had supplied me with. I was on auto-pilot, almost as though I was watching a movie. I found the place with little trouble. The apartment was lit up and loud music was playing. I knocked on the door and waited. My heart, which had up till then been pounding almost painfully, seemed to suspend its action. No response from behind the door. I knocked again, calling out her name several times. Still no response. I couldn't believe how close I had come and still my child was not accessible to me. At last, I went to the caretaker's apartment to inquire as to his knowledge of her whereabouts. My heart sank as he told me that she had flown out of state for the holidays.

I returned home and phoned her ex, who told me that he was certain he would receive a call from her because it was a painful time of the year for her. Six years earlier when she was a teenager, her closest friend had been raped, stabbed repeatedly, and murdered.

Just as he predicted, my daughter called, distraught and needing comfort. He made the decision to tell her I was looking for her and he had spoken to me. He knew she would be pleased for, as long as he'd known her, she'd wanted to find me.

Immediately upon hearing of my contact, she took my name and number from him and phoned me. She was so excited. She kept saying, "Mother, is this really you?!"

While we spent the next four hours on the phone, she had someone use another phone to call the airport and make reservations for her to return on the next flight. I knew she was afraid to hang up, afraid that if we were disconnected by hanging up of the phone, we might again be severed from each other. Finally, it was time for her to catch her flight and we hung up. My husband and I drove in to the airport to meet her plane.

Julia's initial reunion was everything she'd hoped for: intense and intimate. They talked nonstop for days. But then, things changed. A rift began to develop, and with it, distancing in their relationship. The time since their first meeting had been difficult.

I have spent most of the years since our reunion trying to weather my daughter's acting out of her rage over her perceived abandonment. Yet I cannot deal with her issues, only my own.

For me the greatest pain was the reality that I would *never* see my *baby* again. Never hold her or be able to nurture her. Somehow I needed to grieve the loss along with my daughter. I can imagine the experience akin to that of families of persons missing in action. My daughter, to my knowledge, was not dead, yet all contact was severed and she disappeared from my life. I lived suspended in grief, grief I could not process until I met the woman, who was my baby, again and finally come to accept that my baby was forever gone from me.

Sometimes for a birthmother finding her birthchild isn't so much opening a Pandora's Box as it is opening a coffin. The baby she relinquished is gone forever. Julia had to meet her birthdaughter before she could begin to face this reality.

There are common themes of frustration, anger, and pain which run throughout these stories. Dawn's reunion with her birthdaughter incorporated all of these emotions, as well as the insecurity that many birthmothers feel when the adoptee pulls back.

If only one person had told me nineteen years ago how all this would affect my life, I would never have relinquished my daughter. I thought that future children would make it all go away, although I knew I would never forget. Never once did anyone tell me about the ache that would live inside of me until the day I die.

I had to search. I joined Concerned United Birthparents when my daughter was still a young child. I began writing a journal to her when she was thirteen. I wrote to the city hall in the town where my daughter was born to request her birth certificate. They repeatedly replied that there was "no such birth." Having people with the power to give me information pretend that the birth had never occurred was one of my most frustrating moments. I cried, I got angry, and I talked to others who understood what I was going through. My search and support groups were my lifelines. They were always available for help, assistance, and a shoulder to cry on.

The day I finally learned my daughter's name was the end of a long, frustrating nightmare. I wrote a letter to her adoptive parents, with a second letter enclosed to my daughter. This left them the option of giving it to her or not. Her adoptive mother gave my daughter the letter, which made the adoptive father furious. He told her to never contact me, but she wrote back immediately.

Our initial reunion was wonderful, but reserved. I found her somewhat standoffish. I felt that I was the one doing the most talking and expressing feelings. Suddenly, I was afraid she would go away again. Such insecurities. In a way, I felt as if I were eighteen again. My mother said I acted so different around her—like I really was eighteen. I couldn't make the simplest decisions. She overwhelmed my thoughts, my whole life. I wanted to turn back time—if only God would give me another chance. . . .

My daughter has chosen to keep her distance for now. Her father has forbidden her to have anything to do with me and she feels in the middle. I do feel anger at her that she could put me off so easily. It has been eight months and no word from her. I always thought she yearned for me the way I have forever ached for her. She chose not to spend her first reunited birthday with me and no word from her on Mother's Day. This hurt!

I learned you can never expect or plan on anything. I learned you must grieve the loss all over again. And I learned that a birthmother must go slow, approach the reunion cautiously.

My daughter is forever etched upon my life, my heart, and my soul. To me, she is *my* daughter. No matter what she does, she will always be accepted and loved. If I had it to do all over again, I would still never consider an abortion. Her life is sacred and precious. But I would see her as a gift from God—and God doesn't make mistakes.

The strong need for a relationship with the birthchild is an undercurrent in each story. Yet not every birthmother searches to have a close relationship. Some search simply to put their minds at rest. They need to know their birthchildren's fate. In many ways, that was Ruth's quest.

I had a desperate need to know what had happened to my daughter. I joined a search group and read a couple of books and talked with a close friend who is also a birthmother. The support group was very helpful—it was a relief to be with people who had immediate understanding. I felt validated.

At first, I had trouble with my feelings. My daughter needed to hook up with me more than I wanted with her. It was a little more contact than I expected. One of the things that was so confusing to me in my situation was that I was having stronger connections with people other than her. Then I realized that all of my feelings were attached to a baby. I had no picture of her in my mind's eye. This grown-up woman was no one I knew.

It was an emotional moment for me when her mother and I met. I said, "I can't thank you enough." She replied, "Nor I you." I still get teary when I tell that part of the story. Yet it puzzled me that I felt stronger emotion in meeting her than in meeting my daughter.

My daughter and I established early on that we wanted ours to be a friendship and not a parent-child relationship. I think we're fairly successful. We now live far apart and I don't see her often. We call when we feel like calling. Sometimes I run into trouble in my own head—she could have called me . . . I'll get in this mood—I won't call her because she hasn't called me. But then I do—because I feel like it.

I am a significantly less apprehensive person since finding my daughter. After two and a half years, our relationship seems natural and normal. The first year stirred up emotions that were confusing and hard to identify for each of us. We agree that reunion has been a good thing on both sides and answers and settles more questions and issues than it raises.

I can't tell you how wonderful it is, how freeing, to no longer have to grieve for this child.

Some birthmothers discussed feelings of being a "bad" mother because they had relinquished their babies. This interfered at times with their confidence in mothering the children they later had. Adoption had a detrimental effect on their parenting skills.

An even sadder result is that many birthmothers never have another child. Marcia struggled after letting go of her baby daughter. For years afterward, she questioned whether she had made the right decision.

A big part of me died inside when I surrendered my daughter. I was so filled with grief that I had difficulty thinking about having another child. Somehow meeting my daughter almost two decades later allowed me to open my heart to the mother inside me, and to finally grieve the loss of my little girl.

There were moments during my search and reunion process when I thought the grief and pain would never end. Now I know it will never really end. It is much lighter now and I can manage it far better than I could before our reunion.

Today, I am a deeply fulfilled mother of a four-month-old boy. My daughter and I continue to write. She recently wrote to congratulate us on the birth of our son. She also said that she would like to come visit us this summer. I am so delighted. I pray that we can continue to develop a relationship.

Being a birthmother has been a continuous process in learning how to let go and to love unconditionally. For these life lessons, I can now see the hidden grace in the deep suffering I've experienced. I know it's partly why I am the loving, compassionate, nonjudgmental woman I am today. And I also know why I so treasure every moment with my little boy.

Perhaps one of the most useful comments about relationships between birthmothers and their birthchildren was made, not by a birthmother, but by an adoptive mother. Marie had these insights into why her daughter Alison and Alison's birthmother, Betsy, were able to be so comfortable with each other.

Alison and Betsy's relationship is solid. They are mother and daughter in some ways; in other ways, they are just friends. Their relationship just happened, quite easily and naturally. I think the reason for this is that *there were no "have to's."* Betsy never loaded Alison up with guilt trips. No questions of "why haven't you called?" or "why aren't you staying in touch?" Months might go by and Alison won't have called or written and Betsy will call and say, "Hey, let's have lunch."

Lots of birthmothers seem to dump on their kids. They feel a need for constant reassurance. They're scared that their birthchild is just going to drift away. So they hold on too tight, demanding a closeness that frequently isn't realistic or possible. Betsy has wisely always given Alison the freedom to make the relationship what she wants it to be. Hence, they are close.

There is great wisdom in this observation, not just for triad members, but for anyone in life. Relationships simply cannot be forced. When expectations and demands for closeness exist, resistance if not outright rejection is sure to follow. An axiom for a reunion might be to avoid "have to's" if you want to create something permanent.

I find the stories these women have told to be quite haunting. As young women, they were placed in the position of making decisions that would have frighteningly powerful consequences on the rest of their lives. People used to argue that *they* were responsible for getting pregnant in the first place. They broke a rule and therefore have no rights. Others have said, "They were deviant to begin with, and that's why they're still having problems. They're unstable."

To believe such inane qualifiers is to deny the social wrong that was done to these women. They were badly counseled and treated inhumanely. I'm not saying that adoption was always a poor option. But the secrecy, control, and enforced denial that were—and in many instances still are—an inherent part of the adoption system are among the most uncivilized of pursuits ever undertaken by our "modern" society.

One has only to listen to these stories to realize that the system of adoption failed birthmothers. Somewhere along the road, we forgot the most primal of human instincts: a mother's natural inclination to protect and nurture her child. Without that instinct our species would not exist. Should it really be such a surprise that birthmothers have had a difficult time surviving this unnatural termination?

~ 13 ~

BIRTHFATHERS

WHEN DISCUSSING BIRTHPARENTS' SEARCHES AND REUNIONS, people generally are referring to the birthmother, not the birthfather. In truth, the birthmother is the one almost always sought out initially by the adoptee, and the birthmother is also the one more prone to search. This should not come as any great surprise. The birthmother was the one, after all, who bore the child, who paid the price emotionally and physically, and who had a direct physical connection with the child.

Most people assume the majority of birthfathers don't want to be found. This may be true. I don't know. Statistics indicate that the number of birthmothers who would welcome contact from their birthchildren is quite high—upward of 80 percent if not higher. But I could find no data on birthfathers. Are they harder to find or just forgotten? How many doubted their paternity? And how many never knew about the child they fathered?

Many view the birthfather as a nonexistent entity, invisible and unimportant except for a sperm or two. Yet, for the adoptee, the birthfather is part of their heritage. No matter what the birthfather's actions and attitudes were during the pregnancy and relinquishment, most adoptees who search ultimately wish at least to meet their birthfathers or learn something about them. I was no different.

A birthmother can feel enormous fear at the desire of the adoptee to contact the birthfather. She may never have told him of the pregnancy. Even if the birthfather was aware of the situation, a birthmother can still feel tremendous anger and resentment at her birthchild's desire to connect with him. These feelings are natural. The birthfather rarely paid a price for bearing the child, and frequently just walked away. As my own birthmother said, "Why should he have the privilege of knowing you? He did nothing but turn his back on both of us." When I wrote him a letter, it sent her into a weekend-long crying jag. I never intended to hurt her. But finding out where I came from included knowing something about *him*. Rationally, I know she understood this need. But rationality is often difficult to maintain in a reunion.

Just because I was interested in meeting my birthfather, however, did not guarantee that he was interested in meeting me. I sent him a discreet letter. He did not write back. I tried to reach him by phone. I didn't badger him. I nudged. I was perplexed by his complete lack of interest. How could he not be curious?

Three years went by. Once or twice a year I'd try to reach him. My efforts were always covert and judicious. I never wrote him or phoned him at home, only at work. I never identified myself to anyone but him. Still, he seemed threatened by my contact. I felt sad that I made him uncomfortable, but I felt I needed to meet him once to put my mind at rest. Someone once told me, "If accidental paternity carries any responsibility, it's a half-hour over a cup of coffee to answer any questions that might exist." I needed that half-hour.

Once, while I was a guest on a radio talk show, the host told me the story of a young adoptee who had searched. The young man had emotional problems and was desperate to meet his birthparents. When he finally located his birthmother, she wanted nothing to do with him. "It was a very bad situation all the way around," the talk-show host remembered. "What about people who *don't* want to be found? Their attitude seems to be a strong argument against people searching at all."

I confidently rattled off some statistics as I answered him, but I found myself asking inwardly, What about them? How can one search and still accommodate birth relatives who angrily oppose any contact? I asked myself those same questions about my own birthfather all the time.

Almost three years after my first letter to my birthfather, I called to let him know I would be passing through his area and wondered if he would be willing to meet briefly. There was something different in his voice. Suddenly, I knew he was going to say yes. Why? What changed?

Certainly he'd had time to absorb the reality of "me" and to feel he had some control over the situation. Maybe he knew I'd finally "go away" if he satisfied my desire to meet him. Had I been fair to cajole this reluctant dragon into my half-hour over a cup of coffee?

"This must be the end of a long trail for you," he said.

"Yeah, it is."

We stood several feet apart in an empty parking lot. The

coffeeshop where he'd suggested we meet was closed. I followed his car a half mile down the road to another one. We parked, and walked up the steps to the restaurant, as if this were a business meeting. The waitress seated us. We were both reserved. He didn't let his guard down. I didn't want to overstep any boundaries. No one around us would have guessed by our demeanor the drama that was going on.

It was a very different reunion from the one I shared with Lee and her family. There were no joyful hugs, no comparing of physical features, no flurry of questions and answers. My birthmother had welcomed my "intrusion." My birthfather did not. Yet this reunion with him was equally poignant.

I liked him instantly. He had always been very cold on the phone. But in person, behind his reserve, I saw a human being whom I automatically liked. I could see he still didn't understand why I had searched. I could feel him thinking, "Why not leave well enough alone?"

In advance of this meeting, I had given a great deal of thought to what I would ask him. Lee had been so receptive to me that I never hesitated to ask whatever popped into my mind. This situation was different. I decided ahead of time to avoid questions about his personal life, his family. What did I really want to know? What did I have a *right* to know?

"If I had only one question to ask you it would be this," I told him. "I have always felt my parents are my parents, but I never had a sense that their ancestors are my ancestors. Can you share any of your family history?"

He paused for a moment, then told me a sketchy history of his parents, grandparents, and great grandparents: their nationalities, careers, and migrations. It wasn't earth-shattering or exciting information, but it was a treasure trove to me. When you don't have something, it can seem incredibly valuable. He was giving me knowledge of my ancestors —something priceless to me.

"You might be disappointed," he began. "It's been my experience that reality doesn't usually live up to fantasy."

"Reality is what this is all about," I replied. I fully believe that. I needed to see him, to hear him, to know a few pieces of my heritage to be able to feel complete. No one can fully understand this need unless they're adopted. As we talked for a brief forty minutes, pieces of information filled blank spaces that had existed for so long in my mind. In reality, the information was not all that important. Susan Darke of The Adoption Connection says, "It isn't what you find but that you find it." What mattered most to me was that I now had knowledge of my roots. It gave me perspective, clarity, and peace of mind.

Neither of us finished our coffee. We walked to the parking lot and stood awkwardly for a few moments. I asked if I could take his picture and was glad when he nodded yes. A picture lasts forever. I was surprised when he gave me a hug goodbye. I watched his car drive away until I couldn't see it anymore.

That was two years ago. I've not heard from him since, not that I expected to. Will I ever see him again, contact him again? I don't know. Right now, I feel that's up to him. Do I expect anything further from him, to meet his family, his children? His life is his life, and mine is mine. I received what I had sought and felt I had a right to: knowledge about my roots.

Some might view this differently, and say I have a right to know his children—my half-siblings. All individuals need to come to their own conclusions about their personal situations. I believe knowledge of my origins is my right. But to me, a relationship is something different. It's a wonderful thing if it happens, but it's not a given, nor do I believe it should be forced upon someone. I know if I imposed myself on my birthfather I might cause disastrous problems in his life. Some would say, "Good—it's time he paid for what he did." But it isn't only my birthfather whose life is involved. His wife and children know nothing about me. I am concerned about the effect of my introduction upon them.

Others, however, might say I never should have forced a single meeting on him. What about people who don't want to be found? What about promises made decades ago that their lives would never be disturbed? Was it fair for me to seek out my birthfather, simply to satisfy my own need for information? Just as important a question to ask, I believe, is whether it would have been fair for my birthfather to deny me that one meeting forever.

I don't know whether my birthfather is the exception to the rule. Maybe, like birthmothers, most birthfathers *do* want to know what happened to their birthchild. One thing is certain: searchers must approach possible birth relatives discreetly, with as much information as possible. Birthfathers (and alleged birthfathers) are perhaps more vulnerable to cases of mistaken identity than others within the triad. One person whose story illustrates that strongly to me is Hugh Hefner, the playboy of the century.

Just a few weeks after I began my search in late 1983, a friend sent me a magazine article about Hefner's reunion with his long-lost son. The young man's mother had revealed to him when he was eighteen years old that Hugh Hefner was his birthfather. Unsure how Hefner would react to the news, the young man, whose name was Mark, waited eight years before contacting him. Hefner was shocked and surprised, but he believed the story. He remembered Mark's mother.

Considering the number of Hefner's purported dalliances, it was, surprisingly, the first time Hefner had ever been approached by a stranger claiming to be his child. Rather than deny his paternity, Hefner was gracious and accepting. He recalled the first moment he met Mark. "I walked into the room, Mark extended his hand, I put my arms around him, and we both started to cry." The reporter observed, "When the two are together, they constantly laugh, touch and pat each other on the back in a sort of ongoing reality check."[1]

I remember looking at the full-page picture of them together. They looked happy, and so much alike. It validated, for me, my own search efforts. Birthparents could welcome contact. Reunions could have happy endings. Hefner was compassionate and caring, accepting Mark as his son.

Months later, a story in the *Los Angeles Herald Examiner* refuted this fairy-tale story. A blood test had revealed Hefner and Mark could not be related. I remember how badly this news made me feel. They looked so similar. I'd wanted it to be true. I can't imagine what this revelation was like for Hefner or for Mark. A publicist from *Playboy Magazine* was quoted as saying that it "was a surprise. He looked like Hefner . . . the boy believed he was [Hef's] son" based on the information his mother had supplied.[2]

While working on this book, I contacted Hefner. I'd always wondered about what happened next. Had he stayed in touch with Mark? They'd spent time together, begun forming a relationship, only to find out it was all an innocent mistake. How had this whole situation made them feel?

While he declined an interview, Hefner acknowledged that the subject was too deeply personal and painful to discuss. I would imagine the same holds true for Mark and his mother. Their story is a lesson that everybody is vulnerable in a reunion. Perhaps more information might have saved everyone a lot of grief.

Maybe because of my own birthfather's ambivalence and resistance to a reunion, I was surprised that most of the birthfathers I talked to seemed extremely glad to have been found. Many, like Jeremy, always wondered what happened to the child they fathered, but felt they had no right ever to search for.

We were just friends, Heidi's birthmother, Cindy, and I. I was twenty-three, struggling to start my career, financially unstable. When she got pregnant Cindy kept bringing up the suggestion that we could get married. I just didn't see any way that could happen.

Cindy's mother called me the day the baby was born. I still remember that phone call. Her mother said, "She had a baby girl. I thought you'd like to know." Click. I thought it was extremely nice she'd let me know. Cindy's father hated me. He hated her—hated the situation.

I went to the hospital the day the adoption agency was coming for the baby. Heidi was born in the same hospital where I was born. It felt strange walking in there that day. Cindy and I came into the room together. I held Heidi for a few moments, then passed her back to Cindy. When the agency worker came over, a tug-of-war ensued. Cindy couldn't let go. The agency worker finally had to be firm, and took the baby away. I remember how empty that room became. Here we were, a mother and a father, and the baby, her clothes, everything was gone.

I drove Cindy home. Her father met us at the door and started screaming at us. He'd never had his chance to say his piece. I never saw her again after that day. I can't imagine what life was like for her in that house.

I got on with my life. Married. Had three daughters. I thought of Heidi every so often. I knew she was out there, somewhere, but felt I had no right to intrude on her life. I didn't know what she knew. What if her parents had never told her she was adopted? I left the need to reconnect up to her, but I always hoped she'd come to my door.

I had bought a used 1966 Volvo when my kids were little. I love that car, and have it to this day. It's old, beat-up, black. My kids hate it. But it's from '66, the year that Heidi was born. It became my symbol of part of my past—the part that I was supposed to forget about.

Out of the blue, Cindy called me one day. Heidi had called her. She was now twenty-one years old. Was it all right if Heidi called me? I was thrilled. Ecstatic. I wanted to know everything about her, what she looked like, what she was like as a person. We talked on the phone and agreed to meet that same weekend.

She looked beautiful. I remember staring at her. She did all the talking, I did all the looking. We sat and talked on a park bench until it got dark. I asked her if she would forgive me for not ever being there for her when she was a kid. She said yes.

My marriage, at the time, was on shaky ground. My wife felt very shut out that I was going to meet Heidi alone. I was adamant that this was my time alone with my daughter. My wife felt diminished, because she wasn't the mother of *all* of my children. Her reaction when I left to meet Heidi was "if you go, don't come back." When I came home that night, I was locked out of the house. I couldn't get in.

A week later, my wife and three kids met Heidi at

a restaurant. Everybody liked everybody—my wife felt better then. She was more a part of it. But our problems were coming to a head.

Heidi was probably a catalyst for my divorce. She didn't cause it at all, but she forced me to take a good hard look at myself. Meeting Heidi, I had a snapshot of twenty-three years. I suddenly saw myself going through this passage of time still repeating the same mistakes. My marriage was a shambles but I wasn't willing to admit it. I had kids whom I was estranged from even though I saw them every day. I wasn't a good communicator. I couldn't show them love.

About a month after the initial reunion, I told Heidi that I needed to slow this down. I needed time. I didn't want her to call me. I would call her when I was ready. Heidi was hurt that I was pulling back. She told me she'd been rejected once, and she wasn't going to be rejected again. She'd give me some space, but she wasn't going to go away.

In a way, Heidi was the first person ever to accept me unconditionally. She gave me time to adjust. This was in July. She was to be married in September, and her wedding gave me a great opportunity to sort out who I was in her life—who she was in mine. The event forced clarity. It was obvious to me that I was her birthfather. But I was not her dad. I went to her wedding but I did not go to the reception. I felt my place was not there—that part of the day belonged to her adoptive family.

Heidi has enriched my life in many ways. She has helped me open up. I communicate more honestly in my relationships with all the people I love. Meeting her opened up all the things I needed to talk about: pain, grief, and loss. I have nothing to hide anymore. Heidi has validated me, and a difficult choice I was a part of. I can't imagine my life without her.

Jeremy was well prepared for Heidi's arrival, but he never would have searched for her, feeling the risk of causing her harm if she had not been told she was adopted was too great. He believed that only Heidi had the right to search.

But some birthfathers *do* choose to search. Like many birthmothers, they feel the need to locate their birthchildren and give them the option for contact.

Charlie wanted to locate his birthdaughter for years. He was beleaguered by feelings of guilt and concerned that he be there for her if she ever needed him. He felt the urge to connect. A group of adoptees finally "gave him permission."

When deciding to "surrender," I was focused on getting out of a bad situation. I had gotten someone pregnant. I was not in love with her. I focused on the problem. It didn't kick in until later that I'd given away my child. I remember vividly how I felt after I'd married and my next daughter was born. I started to realize what I'd done.

I felt all along that I was this bad guy. The penalty was that I would never get to see my child. I had a lot of guilt. At some point, I decided I owed my daughter access to me if she ever needed to find me. I realized it was my job to keep my file at the adoption agency up to date, in case my birthdaughter wanted or needed any medical information. The agency worker was surprised by my interest. I was the first birthfather who'd contacted her, although she heard from many birthmothers.

I joined a support group. Initially, all of the members were birthmothers, who focused on how they were victims (and they were). Then I met with a group of adopted males, who began to change my perspective. In talking with adoptees, I began to see how *they*, too, had been shortchanged. I realized a huge part of adoptees' lives didn't make sense. I began to feel that it wasn't fair to Rachel (my birthdaughter) that she wasn't automatically allowed access to either me, her birthmother, or the information we could provide her. By then she was twenty years old. I felt compelled to search. I felt it was for Rachel, not for me, and that it was the right thing to do.

After I found her, it took me a long time to write her a letter. I got her address in July. I didn't write until November. I knew she would ask me about what went on at the time of surrender. I wasn't proud of what I had done. Her birthmother was quite a nice person. We dated for months, then began seeing each other less and less. I cut it off. So cool. I found out a month later from a roommate that she was pregnant. I decided to go to Europe and never come back. But I did come back.

Now, here I was twenty-two years later trying to write this letter. "Hello, my name is Charlie and I am your birthfather. My purpose for writing to you is not to intrude in your life or make you uncomfortable, but rather to let you know who I am and where I am. I want to let you know that I am available to you on any level you may choose. . . ."

Rachel was staggered. Her husband and brother were both angry, thinking, how dare I write to her. How dare I impose myself in her life. But she wrote me back, telling me she needed time to think things through. I reassured her by letter that all the choices were hers.

That was our last contact for about a year. She wasn't ready. I was quiet about the wait. I knew that sometimes all an adoptee ever needs is one letter or a photo. I was prepared for that. Then she called me the following October. She said she'd be up in my area the following June. Would I like to meet her then?

We met in the lobby of a large hotel. I brought my family, my wife and kids. Rachel came with her husband. Even though the lobby was crowded and I was forty feet away from her when I first saw her, I knew it was her.

We closed the restaurant at one in the morning. I cried several times during our time together. As the night wore on, Rachel herself began crying. It was then that I knew this was as big a deal for her as it was for me.

I've enjoyed getting to know her parents. Her dad and I talk frequently on the phone, once a month or so. Their support has helped. This is not a competition.

Reuniting with Rachel has been an unbelievable experience for me. I can't really describe it. I had felt like this part of my life was dragging me under. Meeting my birthdaughter has given me a sense of peace. It hasn't all been perfect. One day Rachel yelled at me, "Why didn't you keep me?! I was a good kid!" It hurt but I knew she had to get feelings out. You don't go through this without a lot of anger.

Today we're pretty close. Before we met, I thought chances of that happening were pretty slim. I feel very lucky, especially when she tells me she loves me.

Birthfathers, like birthmothers, can have an expectation for a relationship with their birthchild. Robert, whose search is documented in Chapter 6, would have liked more of a relationship with his birthson, but he feels grateful and happy for whatever they can have together. His belief in his son's right to know his origins and his birthfamily was not shared by the birthmother, however.

Mark was in his mid-twenties when I located him. I remember how overwhelmed I suddenly felt when I got his phone number. Thinking about contacting your birthchild is one thing. But when it's suddenly in your power to do it—that's something else. I knew it was a phone call that I couldn't come back from.

He was a bachelor living with a couple of other guys. When I called, there was a lot of background noise; one of his roommates answered. My company makes telephone-recorded announcement systems. I know what my voice sounds like on the phone. When Mark came on the line, I heard my own voice.

I asked him a couple of questions and then said, "I'm your birthfather."

Mark said, "Huh? Hey, guys, keep it down. This guy's got some information about my birthfather."

The room quieted and I repeated, "I *am* your birthfather."

Mark said, "No kidding?! I've been looking for you!"

We talked for an hour—my wife, Elyse, sat beside me. Mark was very receptive. I knew right away that he was my kid—I couldn't get a word in edgewise (I'm known for being very talkative).

I told him to get a piece of paper, and then I gave him all the information that I could: his original name, my name, his birthmother's name, and told him he had two half-brothers. I thought it was his right to know all of this. I wasn't going to hide anything from him.

I express-mailed him pictures of our family. I expected to get some from him, but I never did. I felt rejected. I called him back. He just didn't realize how important this was to me. He's young, busy.

The second time I talked to him, I told him I wanted to write his parents a letter. I didn't want to hurt them or have them feel I was sneaking around. Mark was way ahead of me. He'd already told them. I wrote his parents a letter, and his father called me after they got it. He handled the whole situation magnificently. He could have tried to drive a wedge between Mark and me, but was very accepting. In reality, I'm nothing. I'm the genetic link only. He's Mark's father.

The following year, Mark and his girlfriend came to visit us two days after Christmas. It was very emotional, very exciting, when he walked off the plane. I took him to a huge reunion of my family. My family welcomed him with open hearts—they knew I was not going to deny this kid being a part of our family. My mom has an embroidery on the wall with the names of all her grandchildren on it. She added Mark's name to it before he came. I think he was very touched by this.

When Mark was here, we took lots of pictures. He and I talked about a strategy for contacting his birthmother [see Chapter 6 for the earlier part of this story]. Julie had been completely averse to finding Mark, but I knew she might be living with the same fears I had had about the well-being of our birthchild. I felt Mark deserved to know her, and felt that she deserved to know that he was well. So I wrote a letter to Julie, enclosing some of the pictures from Mark's visit.

I really wanted her to open up her life to this kid. I agonized over the letter, changed it, had other people read it to make sure it was perfect. I encouraged her to take a chance, give Mark a call.

Two weeks later, a yellow envelope without a return address arrived at my office. I opened it up. Inside were shredded pieces of the letter I had mailed Julie, as well as all the pictures of Mark I had sent, cut to shreds. She also included a letter to me, saying how dare I contact her. She was happy. I'd invaded her privacy. She demanded I stay out of her life, and the same went for Mark. I knew she was hurt, feeling cornered, and that she was striking out.

I let Mark read the letter. His response was that her writing that letter might have been the best therapy she'd had in twenty-five years. I hope he's right. I know he wants her to be happy.

I'm very proud of Mark. I have many fatherly feelings for him. There are times when I'd like Mark to come into my life and be another son, but that is obviously not going to happen. Where I'd like to see him a great deal more, he could probably take it one way or the other. He's distant at times, and culturally different from us. My one disappointment is that he's not reached out to me. I spent so much time worrying that I'd find this kid who was going to have trouble in his life, I guess I was surprised to find a kid who didn't need me. But meeting Mark has made me whole. It's been a totally positive experience for me and my family.

Sometimes, when birthparents and birthchildren meet, they can find themselves feeling a strong attraction to each other. Pat Sanders and Nancy Sitterly explain: "These situations should not be interpreted as that dread taboo of incest. . . . It all boils down to that incredible need to be close to someone who might have been ours from the beginning."[3]

Although this response is normal, it's important for the birthparent to remain in charge, and not let feelings get out of control. Jon spent a great deal of time educating himself about postadoption issues before his reunion with his birthdaughter. He feels this understanding helped him recognize what was happening when he met his daughter, and to react to his feelings appropriately.

My daughter was born in 1969. Her mother and I had been high school sweethearts and we were engaged when we found that she was pregnant. We got married right away. I was in the Army, stationed in the South, and our families were all in the North. My wife did not want her family to know that she had become pregnant before we were married, so she wanted to place our child for adoption.

Our daughter was born on a Saturday morning. The following Wednesday afternoon we went to the adoption agency to sign the papers. They told me that my daughter was in the next room and I could see her if I wanted. I said I couldn't bear to see her if I couldn't raise her. We signed the papers and left, and never talked about our daughter or having any other children for ten years.

We divorced in 1978, mainly because the pain of the adoption had surfaced for me and my wife refused to talk about it. A month later, I began to search for my daughter. It took me five years to find the name of the couple who adopted her.

In March of 1984, I wrote a letter to the adoptive parents explaining who I was and asking how they felt about communicating with me. I mailed the letter on a Monday afternoon. Three days later, on Thursday, the phone rang and it was my daughter Karen! We spoke for about forty-five electrifying minutes. The first question she asked was if she had any brothers or sisters. She told me that she always wanted to know who her parents were and my finding her was a dream come true. We both told each other, "I love you." After our call, I was so ecstatic at finding my daughter and knowing that she was alive and healthy that I didn't sleep for three days.

The next day we both wrote letters and put pictures in the mail. The following Tuesday, for the first time, we were able to see what each other looked like. There was absolutely no question she was my daughter.

Three months later, I decided to drive back east to see Karen. During my week-long drive across the country each day I would call her. When I finally arrived in her hometown, Karen stood me up! At the last minute, she became apprehensive about meeting face-to-face. She was only fifteen years old. Because I had been to many workshops on reunions at adoption conferences, I knew something like this might happen. Reunions don't always move directly from Point A to Point B, but can be circuitous and have any number of ups and downs. Both sides need to give the other plenty of room and understanding.

I told Karen that I respected what she was feeling, that I still loved her, and that we would set another time to meet when she was ready. I left without seeing her.

For the next six months, Karen and I continued to

phone and write letters regularly. Finally, Karen said that she was ready to try again. We arranged that I would pick her up from school when her classes were over in the early afternoon.

Karen's first words when we met were "Wow, nice car!" She later admitted that she was *very* nervous and it seemed to be the easiest thing to talk about. I was so happy to finally meet her, to hug her, to tell her in person that I loved her. Being with Karen that first time was very mixed emotionally for me. I was happy to finally be with her, but sad when I realized how much I had missed of my beautiful daughter. I felt like laughing and crying at the same time.

During our time together, I couldn't take my eyes off her. I had always loved my daughter from the day she was born—not a day went by that I didn't think of her. Now, finally having met her, I felt something else: it was as if I was with her mother all over again. When Karen first walked toward me, I was astounded by how much she looked, walked, and acted like her mother. At one point, when we were talking, I reached over, squeezed Karen's hand, and told her that I loved her. This was my daughter, but she was so very much her mother—even Karen's hands looked and felt like her mother's.

Because I had spent five years educating myself about adoption and reunion, I was very aware of the attraction that may occur between parents and children who have been separated by closed adoption. Sometimes, when parents are reunited years later with their grown sons and daughters, the birthparent may experience some of the romantic feelings they had felt years before for the other birthparent. It's almost like a time warp, in which one jumps from the past to the present. This is a natural reaction to the unnatural process of separation by closed adoption. However, it's important for those being reunited to know how powerful such feelings can be and keep them in their proper parent-child perspective. Because of my awareness about this issue, it never became a problem in our relationship.

Since our first meeting nine years ago, Karen and I have seen each other regularly. Although we were once separated by adoption, we are now—and will always be—a family.

It is difficult for Tom to look back on when his girl-friend became pregnant in high school. He was barely concerned about her feelings, nor did he think much about the baby. Thoughts of the son she surrendered for adoption wouldn't begin to haunt him until years later.

We were just teenagers in high school when Mary got pregnant. We'd both had pretty sheltered lives, and when we got a taste of freedom in high school, we went kind of crazy. . . .

We didn't know anything. Not like kids today. Mary didn't tell me for a while, then when she did tell me that she'd missed two of her periods I didn't even know what that meant.

I was a jerk. I never considered her feelings. I said, "How could you do this to *me*?!" She was so sweet— she said, "I'm sorry, I'm so sorry." We procrastinated another month. We had no idea what to do. Finally, Mary's grandmother noticed that Mary was looking pregnant, and she told Mary's parents.

Her parents were obviously upset, and came over

to talk with my parents that same night. I was real brave—I just took off from my house and didn't come back until they were gone. So our parents talked. Marriage was out of the question back then—you ruined your life if you got married in high school. Mary was to be shipped off to a nearby city to have the baby, and then it would be put up for adoption.

Her father came looking for me one night, and when he found me, he really laid into me. He didn't hit me, but it felt like he had. I had ruined their little girl. I had destroyed all their lives. Obviously, they weren't very fond of me.

So Mary went into seclusion. We talked before she left. I told her that maybe adoption was for the best. A month later, I got up the courage to go see her. The hospital where she was being kept would let the girls out for a short time once a week. We met for a soda. I'd never seen a girl who was really pregnant before. She was as big as a house. It shows what I was like then. That's what I can remember from that day—that I couldn't believe how huge she was. The rest of it I just blocked out.

In late September of 1970, she had the baby. She told me it was a boy, with red hair and blue eyes. By this time, I had graduated from high school and was playing with a band. Mary went home and began her senior year of high school. We simply got on with our lives. That's what everyone expected us to do. That baby boy was never mentioned for years.

I played in the band for a year, but the music scene at the time was getting pretty scary—drugs and stuff. I finally decided to get out. Vietnam was just about over. I decided to go into the army. I was changing. But one part of me that had never changed was how I felt about Mary. I was in love with her. I always had been. We kept in contact. When I entered the service, we wrote letters to each other. When I was on leave, we got together. My parents were supportive. Mary's parents, at first, knew nothing about our renewed relationship. But when they found out, they felt that I had grown up a lot, and they were accepting of me. When I got out of the service, Mary and I ultimately married and moved, starting a new life together.

During this whole time, the "incident" was never mentioned. Not once. It was like it hadn't happened, like this baby didn't exist. Then our son Thomas was born.

Thomas was born in late September, only two days before our first baby's fifth birthday. He had red hair and blue eyes. Mary and I looked at each other when she was first holding him. I knew what she was thinking. There was another one just like him out there. For the first time, we talked about our first child. We hoped he'd been adopted by a good family, that he was safe and well. We tried rationalizing it—we'd done the best thing. Right?

That's when it started. We began to realize what we'd lost. Every time Thomas's birthday came around, we'd feel like there was another birthday that we should be celebrating. When our son Josh was born, it was the same thing. He had red hair and blue eyes. Every Christmas, every birthday, I could see Mary was thinking about "him." Finally, one day Mary said, "I've got to find him."

I was not initially supportive of her desire to search. I had never seen the baby. I couldn't relate to him. I didn't have any visual memory of him. For me, there was nothing tangible to look for. That's how I felt: he was mine . . . but he was not mine. But if Mary wanted to search, then I would support her. I agreed it was time to look.

We didn't know what to do. We went to the library and found every book we could on adoption. We hired a private investigator and spent upward of $15,000 on the search. This was about all the savings we had, but it got us nowhere. The investigator was just ripping us off. Then my wife read an article about this amazing woman Sandy Musser. She contacted Sandy, and I was impressed by the materials Sandy sent us. Finally, we hired her to help us find our son. She called us only three days later and told us what his name was and where he lived.

I was a basket case. I cried for a week. I hadn't expected this to make me so emotional, but it did.

Peter was his name. He was now over eighteen. Mary and I talked a lot about what we should do. We tried to put ourselves in the position of his parents. We decided to talk to Peter's mother first.

Peter's mother was initially very receptive on the phone when Mary called. She said she always knew this day would come. But then the conversation began to sour. She told Mary that this kid meant everything in the world to her. "How do I know you're who you say you are?" It went downhill from there. Since Peter's mother wasn't receptive to his meeting us, we ultimately decided to contact him directly. Mary wrote him a nice letter, which explained everything. She told him we'd gotten married, and that we had three other sons (by now, our son Kyle had been born). We had not yet told Thomas, Josh, or Kyle about their older brother.

One day, not long after Mary had sent her letter,

it was raining. I do construction work, so I had to call it quits for the day. I got home and took the mail out of the mailbox and there was this letter in it from Peter. I opened it, scanned it. There was a picture of him inside, this big, stocky, red-haired, blue-eyed man. I fell to my knees and began to sob.

When Mary arrived home with the kids she found me kneeling in the driveway, crying. We took the letter inside and read it, and reread it a dozen times. "Thank you for not forgetting me. . . . I've thought of searching for you but didn't for fear you'd reject me." Some of what he shared with us seemed so ironic. His life had paralleled Thomas's in so many ways. Same sports, same interests. When Peter was in his early teens, his father had been killed in a car accident—on my birthday.

Peter was excited in the letter, and in our subsequent phone calls. He'd been raised as an only child. He was so excited to have brothers. For the first time we told Thomas, Josh, and Kyle about the brother they never knew they had, and they were as excited as Peter was.

We flew out to meet Peter for the first time. We got ourselves a room at a Ramada Inn and waited for him to arrive. Snow occupied us as we waited. It was the middle of winter. My kids had never seen snow before, and I hadn't seen it in twenty years.

When Peter arrived, it was just incredible. I had imagined him as this tough city kid: jeans, a T-shirt, and a pack of Marlboros rolled up in his sleeve. Our sons were raised in this little town. I thought there would be a big difference between our kids and Peter, but I was wrong. They were amazingly alike. I looked at him in shock—he has the same build as me, the same red hair and blue eyes as Thomas and Josh. There was no disputing they were brothers.

We couldn't keep our hands off each other, hugging and laughing as we talked through the night. We stayed a few more days, and managed to find as much time as possible for each other. We hated to leave . . . hated to leave.

It was a great reunion, and in the years since, we've kept up constant communication and have had numerous visits. The tough part has been that Peter's mother feels very threatened by us. She's never agreed to meet us. This isn't what we wanted to have happen. We never wanted to make this into a competition. Peter's in a difficult spot sometimes. He enjoys spending time with us, but is made to feel disloyal. It hasn't interfered with our ability to have a relationship with him, but I know it's awkward for him, and that frustrates me. It doesn't have to be this way.

Most marriages don't survive for twenty years anymore. For the relationship that Mary and I have to have made it through everything we've had happen, we feel lucky. Peter is a part of our lives. He's part of the cement which holds us together. He's part of our history, and we are part of his. I feel that Mary and I, in meeting Peter, have come full circle.

He's a great kid. A fine young man. I love him with all my heart.

It's interesting that for many of the birthfathers I interviewed, their awareness of their child is dormant until after their next children are born and they assume parenting responsibilities. Before this, all they seemed cognizant of was that they got a girl pregnant. They seemed detached from the fact that a human being was created.

The strong need by the majority of these birthfathers to connect with their birthchildren is compelling. They have not suffered the same levels of anguish as most birthmothers, but the relinquishment of their child has left an inescapable void. The compassion and responsibility they demonstrate indicates that the casual "boys will be boys" attitude isn't necessarily a lifelong affliction.

~ 14 ~

ADOPTIVE PARENTS

When my mom passed away in 1987, I stayed in the San Francisco Bay area an extra two weeks to pack her things. I was three months pregnant with my first child, and reeling from the fact that life could be so unfair that she would be denied the chance to ever hold her grandson.

As I packed up cartons to send home to Massachusetts, I came across one of Erma Bombeck's books, *Motherhood: The Second Oldest Profession.* My mom, born and raised near Bombeck's hometown of Dayton, Ohio, adored her books. Whenever a new hardback came out, it was a surefire winner for me to give as a Christmas present.

Picking up the book, I noticed a page had been purposefully bent back. It was the only page in my mom's entire library that was marked. I sat down amid half-packed boxes and read three pages of a chapter entitled simply "Pat." Words and sentences jumped off the page at me.

So you're Joanie's "real mother." . . . I look at you and I don't know why all these years I've felt threatened by the ghost of a "real mother." . . .

. . . I do know why. All these years you have been the object of my love and gratitude, frustration and pain, blame and compassion. But mostly you have been the object of my envy. You had that wonderful experience that I would have given anything to have. The movement inside me of a girl child who would one day look at me and see me as "real."

No one can give it to me. No one can take it away from you. It is there.[1]

Erma Bombeck, so well known for her humorous jabs at life, had, with words uncharacteristically serious, forced me into my mother's skin. I sat on the floor of Mom's living room and cried as I read this, for at that moment I knew she must have grappled with these same feelings, yet we had never talked about it. Reading this passage, I had to wonder if she really had known how I felt about her. Had she marked those pages because she had doubts after over three decades that she was "real"? It was a question that could never be answered. I wished I could have five minutes more to put my arms around my mom and reassure her of the feelings in my heart.

How would my mom and dad have responded to my reunion? What kind of pain and loss would they have experienced? How would they have coped with their feelings? Would my reunion have made them feel more "real" or less "real"? And most important, how would the reunion have affected our relationship?

In interviewing people for this book, I found myself listening acutely to the adoptive parents who told their stories. Could I find answers to my own questions from the experiences of others? Although every reunion is unique, there are common experiences and emotions that adoptees share. Do adoptive parents also have universal feelings?

As I sat in a local coffeehouse one morning interviewing Marie, I didn't want her to stop talking. In temperament and personality she reminded me a great deal of my adoptive mother. Was what Marie shared with me a mirror of what my own mother would have felt had she lived?

I am an adoptive mother of a grown son and daughter, both of whom have searched and been reunited with their birthfamilies. I have strong beliefs about adoptees' connecting with their biological families. It seems fundamental to me that every person has a right to know their origins. In fact, I can't imagine anyone bringing a child into this world expecting protection (like sealed records) at the expense of that child.

Still, many people seem uncomfortable with the notion of an adoptee wanting to search. I remember once, when my son, Richard, was a teenager, I was concerned when I discovered that he had started smoking. One of my neighbors told me not to worry about it. Later, when Richard wanted to search, that same neighbor was horrified and appalled. She couldn't believe I wasn't upset. I have trouble understanding how someone could be so casual about a sixteen-year-old possibly ruining his lungs and future health, and then reacting so strongly about his healthy desire to know his origins.

Richard was two when we adopted him. As agencies advised you to do back then, I set about making him fit into our family. We knew nothing. I wasn't mature enough to understand his needs. Actually, the way society viewed it, he had no needs. Now that he had a family, everything was supposed to be perfect. I was a little rough on him sometimes, trying to make him act like everyone else in the family. While he was acting out his anger at his early severed relationships, I was frustrated that he didn't behave nicely like my nieces and nephews, who had had a stable environment their whole lives.

As he got older, Richard began to feel angry. He began to ask a lot of questions that I had no ability to answer. I didn't even know his nationality. I remember having asked the agency worker what it was when we adopted him and she had snapped, "Why is *that* important to you?" I withdrew, feeling like I shouldn't have asked.

One of the saddest moments I remember was when Richard was a teenager and played on a basketball team. All the kids had shirts made up with these nicknames on the back, and all the nicknames had to do with each kid's nationality—Irish, Italian, German. Whatever. Richard had his made to say simply RICHARD. It was a moment that put me in my son's shoes. I began to realize how much information was denied to him.

At eighteen, Richard decided to search. I was happy for him and glad to do what I could. During the search, Richard had a timetable, which I didn't understand at the time. It was very slow. I have some regrets over my help in his search because I think he needed to dictate the speed with which this all happened. We helped facilitate the reunion too quickly. Once Richard had his birthmother's name, he was satisfied. I couldn't believe he wasn't dying to call her. We went six months or so and then we stepped in to help. That was eleven years ago. It took me five to six years to realize that we pushed too hard. We should have just let Richard take the next step. I know now that adoptive parents should only be there when *asked*. I'm not saying that adoptive parents shouldn't be involved in the search, or a part of the process. I might have felt betrayed if I hadn't been a part of it. But the adoptee has to be the one in *control*.

My daughter Alison's reunion was quite different. She was in complete control of everything, and her reunion was a lot healthier. Alison's very direct. When she was eighteen, she went straight to the agency and said, "I want to know." The agency said they would go to the birthmother and ask, and Betsy, Alison's birthmother, was willing.

The same social worker who had carried Alison in to me when we adopted her now brought Betsy in to meet Alison. That was beautiful to me. It felt like a circle closing.

Betsy has been wonderful. She called me that first night so just she and I could talk. She wanted to give Alison a high school graduation gift and wanted to make sure that was all right with me. I appreciated it so much that she included me. I'd advise any birthparent during a reunion to try to do that—give the adoptive family some sense of control. It makes everything better, more comfortable. Betsy has always been respectful of my relationship with Alison, just as I am respectful of the birth bond that they share.

I'm very clear about my relationship as my kids' mother. I've never felt threatened by their need to connect with their birthfamilies. I'm not saying I've never felt painful emotions about any of this.

For example, I've got very large feet. I have. I've

always hated them. Alison has these wonderful, small feet. I have lived vicariously through those feet. I love shopping for shoes for her.

One day, Betsy invited us to her house. Alison was wearing brand-new cowboy boots. Betsy was admiring them. Well, they have the same-size feet, so Alison slid off a boot to let Betsy try it on.

Suddenly, I was angry. Jealous. Threatened. I wanted to shout, "Get your foot out of that boot!" An irrational reaction, but the reality is Betsy's ability to wear that boot had beaten home to me that those were not *my* feet. Alison is my daughter, but physically she is not a reflection of me. I have had to accept that.

I must acknowledge that I have worked through my childlessness but not my infertility. Recently, I was at the funeral for Alison's birth grandfather. I stood in the cemetery and looked at all these gravestones, generations of them, with this family's name. And I was aware that Alison was a part of this, where I was not. I thought, "My daughter's children and grandchildren may be drawn to this cemetery someday in search of ancestors. I won't have anyone looking for my stone." I had an overwhelming sense of something being lost in my life because I have no offspring. Kind of a loss of immortality.

I believe this is at the root of adoptive parents' fears if they've adopted because they were unable to conceive. The search and reunion aren't what causes such pain for adoptive parents. It's confronting that infertility, that lack of genetic connection to the next generation, that they're really dealing with, whether they're aware of it or not.

I never fully faced my own infertility until my kids

searched. I found I needed to look back on my infertility and grieve it. I became so much more aware of my feelings once my children found their birthparents. Yet, contrary to what most people assume, I don't regret having to confront these long-buried feelings. I have seen the most amazing period of growth in myself. I needed to resolve this, and be aware of it. It has strengthened me.

Marie has had eleven years to work through a lot of feelings, and she will admit that her perspectives are constantly evolving. But she never did feel threatened by the search. Her constant focus seemed to be on her children's needs and not her own. Gail, another adoptive mother, has had a similar focus.

> We made our family through adoption. That is the central miracle of my life. We adopted each other. They are our right children. A bigger hand than our own put our family together. If one learns lessons in life, that is mine.
>
> I didn't know anything about birthparents until a few years ago. We never thought to invite the four women who had given birth to our children into our consciousness. I wish I could say I thought about them on their children's birthdays or Mother's Day but I didn't. I was oblivious.
>
> Our education began after we moved to a new state, when the need to connect with new people drew us to an adoption-support-group meeting. A new chapter began in our lives that night. My husband and I, fired up by the stories of search and reunion we heard

at the meeting, went home and encouraged our children to consider their own searches.

"No way!" one of our sons responded. "You're my mom and dad. I don't need to know anything else."

"You do!" I argued, high-pitched with the fervor of a convert, inspired by the idea that he did need to know, that no adopted person could feel emotionally complete unless he or she touched roots. I pressured my children toward search for three reasons: their own emotional health, their birthparents' relief, and to assuage my guilt for all my years of ignorance.

At the time, two of my children decided to search, two did not (all in early adulthood). The hardest thing for me was to butt out. Each of them had to be in charge of his or her own decisions and processes. I could offer support, nothing more. They had to live their own lives.

Then one day, my son Seth phoned to say he had his birthmother's name and address. We all waited anxiously for her response to his letter. What if she didn't answer him? What if he found her curled up in a fetal position in a crack house? What if she broke his heart?

My first glimpse of her face in a snapshot Seth showed us knocked me out. She had his face. All of a sudden she was real. Now what had we done? Yes, she was thrilled Seth had found her. Yes, she wanted to meet him. Though happily married, she had not had other children. I found her letter to us both comforting and scary. I was at once intimidated, convinced that Seth was doing the right thing, and aware of how grateful I was to this woman. Her loss had been our gain.

Our family is connected in such a way that anything affecting any one of us impacts everyone else. Our oldest daughter, married and a mother herself, gave voice to some of my own darkest fears, worrying that the appearance of other parents would somehow dilute our family, that her brother wouldn't be her brother in the same way anymore.

Seth came home from his reunion six inches taller than when he left. I was surprised, I told him, that such a *mensch* could become so much more of a *mensch*. He smiled, saying that questions he hadn't thought to ask himself had been answered. He felt great, he said, and it showed.

I would have believed that the love, pride, and satisfaction I have always felt as Seth's mom could not increase . . . but they have. Seth has become more fully himself; there is more of him to love. I think that solving this central puzzle in his own life on his own has increased his confidence and opened him to the world in a way most people never get to experience. His growth through reunion directly benefits our relationship with him. What could be better for any parent than to see their child flourishing?

Two of my children still have no desire to search. I no longer think every adopted person has to do a search to feel whole. We are all different. Not everyone is Alex Haley. The search for roots takes different forms.

Any underground fears I had of losing my child because of his other parents have been laid to rest. I feel connected to them through my son in the same way I am connected to my husband's relatives through marriage. We all know who we are. We are all connected. I expect we will grow closer and closer over time.[2]

Another adoptive mother went against the wishes of her husband and other relatives to help her son search. She felt that connecting him to his birthfamily was critical to his personal growth. Her willingness to risk approval in her family is a testament to the length a parent is willing to go to help her child thrive.

We tried very hard to be good parents by helping our son along, providing him with opportunities, giving him a good education, teaching him values, and making him feel secure in a good family. He seemed oblivious of it all. Nothing seemed to stick. Sometimes I felt he wanted no part of us. He seemed to resent the fact that we adopted him. Maybe it was all too much for him. As a result, he gradually set himself outside the circle, always on the outside looking in—in school, socially, and even within the family.

During his teen years, we discussed searching for his birthparents. He seemed very excited at the prospect. As time went on, however, he seemed to lose interest. Every time I brought up the subject he said he wanted to search "someday." I offered to pay for the search, but he never picked up on it.

As an adult, my son did not seem to be moving forward. I continued to wonder if the blank spaces in his life might have something to do with it. Ultimately, I not only encouraged my son to search, I initiated the search for him.

I did not have the support of the rest of our family. They felt I shouldn't be the one to promote the search, even though I had my son's approval. But I had a gut feeling that it was important to do this. To this day my family will not discuss it with me. I get a silent response. But I have to trust that I did the right thing, and move on. My only fear was the uncertainty of not knowing if he would be welcomed by his birthmother.

When we located her and my son sent her a letter, she responded immediately, almost as though she were waiting for this contact, or had expected it, and her response was positive. She would meet with him and "explain things."

I drove my son to meet his birthmother. He seemed very nervous, almost acting silly before the meeting. I did not participate in the actual reunion. I felt it was their time to be alone together. I wasn't afraid I was going to lose my son to his birthmother.

The similarities that he discovered are fascinating. His handwriting is similar to his birthmom's, and his eyes are exactly like hers. His build and appearance are similar to his half-brother's, and his career is similar to his birthfather's. For me, it was the most amazing realization how much his genes have governed his life.

I don't know yet how the reunion will play out, and what will ultimately come of it for us all. But I feel I better understand my son from this experience. If only I had known about his background when he was growing up. I wouldn't have tried so hard to make him into the person *I* wanted him to be.

It would appear from both this woman's story and Marie's story, that adoptive parents feel their lack of knowledge about the birthparents and their backgrounds ultimately hurt their child. The encouragement of agencies to parents to "make him fit" or "make her like your own" is a denial of significant aspect of the child's persona.

Adoptive parents can feel threatened by search and reunion. In fact, some feel the search and subsequent reuniting are a violation of their legal rights as parents. This was true for Lenore, the mother of two children: an adopted daughter and a biological son.

My husband and I adopted our daughter in 1970 through Catholic Charities. She was a typical child, with typical problems. Then, when she became a teenager, we began having problems. She became secretive, and kept very much to herself.

At age eighteen, she became pregnant. Her baby was born with severe birth defects and died at two weeks of age. Her anger and turmoil increased. We argued constantly. She ended up moving out of our home for a few months. She returned to live with us for a short time, and then we had the worst argument we've ever had. She moved out, and we had very little contact with her. This was the worst time in my life as a mother, not knowing where my child was or how to reach her.

The search and reunion occurred during this period of estrangement. It was not an easy event for us.

In October of 1990, my husband and I received a letter from a woman saying she was a confidential mediator acting on behalf of our daughter's birthmother, who was interested in locating our daughter. I was devastated.

I verified and confirmed that this mediator was who she said she was. Then, when she called me on the telephone, I spilled my guts to her about some of what had happened. Her call came at a time in my life when I was grasping for any help I could get for our relationship with our daughter. I asked to have some time to locate our daughter, and to let her know what was happening. We felt it was our responsibility to do so. The mediator called the birthmother, then called us back, saying that we had some time. This was in the fall.

I was very threatened by all of this, but continued to try to locate our daughter. Three months later, I learned where she was staying, but was waiting for the right time to contact her. Then my hand was forced with the final letter from the so-called confidential mediator, informing me that our daughter and the birthmother had already been reunited.

The meeting was, and is, not a problem for my husband and me. Our daughter was always raised knowing she was adopted, and that if she ever found it necessary to search, just to let us know, she would have our support. We just asked that it not be done behind our backs.

We feel our constitutional rights, and our right to privacy, were taken away from us by this court-appointed confidential mediator, and that she overstepped her boundaries.

I called our daughter. She was very defensive, owing to the length of time since we had last communicated, and to the fact that the mediator had told the birthmother some of the confidential information I gave her, and the birthmother had asked our daughter about it.

We were not allowed to know much about the birthmother. I felt betrayed, hurt, and most of all threatened by a woman who had relinquished her rights so many years ago, and a daughter who had always said she wanted nothing to do with the people who gave her away. I was upset by our daughter's secretiveness, so I started asking questions about the birthmother and her family so I could feel included. Finally I asked to meet the birthmother.

Fourteen months after our daughter's reunion with her birthmother, my husband and I drove to the city where the birthmother lives. Our daughter was not with us for the meeting. We took her birthmother a single red rose, the symbol of love. What else could we feel for a courageous woman who made it possible for us to have our beautiful daughter?

The meeting went well. We shared fears, joys, and hopes for the future. We shed tears together, and came to the agreement that what we all wanted for the future was that our positions as our daughter's parents would not be taken from us. We wanted the birthmother to share a place in our daughter's life, too. We felt good about the meeting, and hope we made friends.

As adoptive parents, we hope and dream for our daughter that her life can become a complete circle and filled with love and happiness, and that we can all be a happy family.

Aaron and Louise have eight children, all adopted, ranging in age from fifteen to twenty-seven. They began their family in the late sixties, firmly holding to the belief that every child is entitled to be raised in a loving family. They weren't trying to make any social statements nor were they seeking notoriety. They just kept adding to their family until they felt they were too tired, too old, and too much in debt.

After Louise and I decided to adopt, we proceeded with two traditional adoptions of Caucasian babies. The first child was Jacqueline, a three-week-old baby, born in 1966. Sam came two years later when he was two weeks of age. Louise and I regard their birthmothers as generous and courageous in giving their children up for adoption. We believe they acted, with great pain, in the best interest of their children.

In 1968 we decided to adopt an African-American child after learning that many of these children were going unadopted. Sarah, a three-month-old brown-skinned African-American child, came into our home.

In 1970, ready for another child, we received Thomas, an eleven-month-old, physically healthy, dark-skinned black boy, born to a thirteen-year-old child. Ours was his third home—his first permanent home. He sobbed bitterly for the first week. He was shy and anxious for two years. After that, he became a good-natured, trusting, outgoing child and adult.

We were managing quite well with our four children and felt ready for a fifth. The children that seemed most in need were Vietnamese-American children over two years of age—children fathered by American soldiers. We were referred for assistance to Naomi Bronstein, a Canadian mother of fourteen children, mostly adopted. In March of 1973 we received a letter and an undeveloped roll of film, which introduced us to Hien, a four-and-a-half-year-old child born to a Vietnamese woman and an African-American soldier. She looked like a sad, sad little girl.

Our four children took Hien in hand. She stayed close to them. They taught her to use the jungle gym. They taught her to speak English. After four weeks of silence, she walked into the kitchen and began speaking fluent English. We offered her the name Anne. "No, I am Hien." She has remained Hien.

In 1974, we agreed to take two Vietnamese-American half-brothers, David and Robert, aged eight and nine. They had the same mother and two different Caucasian American-soldier fathers. We corresponded and sent pictures.

The Vietnam war was winding down, and we feared they would not get out of the country. It was now days before the fall of Saigon. At 6 A.M. on April 14, 1975, we learned that a C-5 transport carrying 317 Vietnamese orphans had crashed. Sabotage was suspected. Our boys were two of three thousand children waiting to be evacuated. It was unlikely, we believed, that they were on the plane. But at 1 P.M. that day, we learned that all of the children from Allambie, the orphanage where our boys had been, died in the crash. Our one-year relationship with these children ended. Our hopes and dreams were shattered. Friends and relatives came to our house to console us. It was a house of mourning.

At 10:30 P.M. we received a phone call from a man in Jamaica Plain telling me that his son, who was working in Saigon, had been swimming in the Exxon executive swimming pool with our two boys. Was this phone call a cruel hoax? How could they be alive? We later learned that Naomi Bronstein, who was flying thirty-four Cambodian orphans to Montreal, stopped in Saigon. She told her friends in the orphanage that she knew us and would take the children to Montreal on her flight. David and Robert were the only two survivors from Allambie. All of their friends died in the crash.

In 1977, Louise wanted one more baby. I told Louise that we were too tired, too old, and too much in debt. She looked me right in the eye and said, "Not yet." In the midst of our discussions, we received a phone call from Catholic Charities. They had a healthy African-American six-month-old whom they were having a difficult time placing and asked us to adopt. So a beautiful little girl came into our lives. We named her Naomi after Naomi Bronstein.

I always felt that Jackie, our first child, experienced the particular stress of being the wonderful and perfect only child who was then displaced seven times. When Robert arrived, she even lost her place as the oldest. In addition, she had to carry the brunt of racial prejudice in order to defend her siblings.

With this background, it was particularly sweet for Louise and me that Jackie and her birthmother, Hope, found each other just one year ago. As a single twenty-year-old woman amidst family stress, Hope put her daughter up for adoption believing it was in the best interest of the child. She subsequently married and had four miscarriages. But she is not childless.

Now Hope has found her child (even though she's all grown up), and Jackie is an only child again. We all have spent good times together. Jackie has been glowing since finding Hope. She said that the day she met Hope was the happiest in her life because she was surrounded by all the people in her life who love her.

Jackie told us when she was reunited with Hope that her biggest worry was us. She didn't want us to feel hurt or left out. It was her worry, not ours. She kept asking, "Are you sure it's all right with you that I meet her?"

Louise and I feel very fulfilled that Jackie has had such a wonderful experience meeting her birthmother. Hope is long-lost and rediscovered family. Her very presence, as well as the tact and sensitivity with which she reunited with Jackie, was an act of generosity and further expands our family.

Personally, I would feel very happy having all my children find their birthfamilies. But whether they ever decide to is up to them individually.[3]

Some adoptees grow up and become adoptive parents. How does the issue of their own child's growing curiosity about their roots affect an adoptee who becomes an adoptive parent? Patty has these perspectives on her dual role.

My adoption story is twofold. First, I am an adoptee. Second, four years ago my husband and I became adoptive parents.

At various times growing up I remember asking my parents about my adoption—the way other kids asked their parents about their births. My recollection is that I was told my birthmother was a young woman in college when she became pregnant with me. I was also told that I was in a foster home for six months because my birthmother had a difficult time deciding what to do.

I have no medical history whatsoever. That's one thing my parents wished they had more information about, and now as an adoptive parent myself, I understand their concerns.

I don't know my birthmother. She is a stranger to me. The person I've become, the values and beliefs I possess are all because of my adoptive parents and the experiences they gave me. I recognize that I have a birthmother and birthfather, but I've never had any longing to find either one. I have always held on to the belief that my birthparents continued on with their lives and that I have no bearing on their lives now.

I'm secure with the family I have. I'm secure with the knowledge I possess regarding my adoption. There were times when I was growing up that I wondered if I looked like my birthmother, but that small amount of curiosity was never reason enough for me to try to open a past that isn't there.

One of the things my husband and I felt strongly about was that we wanted a closed or traditional adoption. We didn't feel that in trying to make our family we would be ready to incorporate other people that come with an open adoption.

When we were being interviewed by the adoption agency we were asked how we'd feel if our child decided to search for his or her birthparents. Our daughter, Maryjane, knows she is adopted. At three years old, she doesn't understand all the related issues, but in time the pieces will be filled in for her. She also knows that Mommy was adopted, that her two uncles were adopted and that two of her best friends were also adopted. So she has a pretty broad base of experienced people around her. If, however, she expresses an interest to search, we can only hope that it will be when she is an adult. If her interest occurs during adolescence, at which time I'm sure every parent feels a tug-of-war, we three will have to sit down and discuss the reasons she feels she needs to search at the particular time. We will have already given her all the nonidentifying information and birth statistics we have available, just as my parents gave me when I asked. I'm not sure that an adolescent is prepared to handle all the emotions and ramifications, both positive and negative, that can occur in a search.

If she is an adult and wants to search, we will still want to discuss her reasons. We will also be sure that current literature is available regarding searches and the outcomes they can produce. We want her to be fully aware of everything before committing to search. We are her parents and will be there for her always in whatever way we can. I can only hope that we will make her feel as secure and loved in our home as I was in mine, and that she'll accept herself fully as an adoptee.

Patty is secure in her views and choices. There are many triad members that will not be comfortable with Patty's position, arguing that it is a throwback to the fifties. Patty is aware there are those who take exception to her views. But, as she points out, adoption is always very emotional, and opinions are varied on the issues at hand. I cannot argue with that.

Sheridan understands adoption from every angle. As an adoptee, a birthmother, and an adoptive mother, she literally represents the triad. Unlike Patty, she feels that the connection between adoptees and their birthfamilies is of great consequence. She feels that the continuity between the birthchild and his or her family is about life, that we can't separate from each other for very long and survive.

I am an adoptee. I'm also a birthmother and an adoptive mother. My daughter Judy was adopted in a closed adoption as a three-week-old infant. She was adopted through the same agency where I had placed my infant son for adoption thirteen years before. As a result of my connection to all aspects of the adoption triad, Judy has grown up in a home that talks openly and freely about adoption, and honors her birthfamily in our lives.

From the time Judy became verbal, she expressed a desire to meet her birthmother. When she was twelve years old, together we initiated a search for her birthmother, Robyn. We traveled to our state archives, researched names and dates around the time and place she was born, and were fortunate to locate Robyn in just one day.

This was a very special effort for Judy and me to share. The "process" is much longer than a day and is, in fact, still going on. Assisting Judy with the search for her birthfamily—her search for herself—she got the message that I truly accept her, all of who she is and where she comes from.

Judy, Robyn, I, and my husband, had a wonderful first coming-together in our home four years ago. Judy and Robyn spent time alone at first. Then we joined them to share photo albums, stories, questions, information, and thanks. Robyn stayed late into the night, talking, laughing, and crying, as she joined our family. This reunion was special for all of us. A short conversation the following day had an even more profound impact on Judy.

Robyn had driven home late that night. Early the next morning she called Judy to let her know she had arrived home safely. She went on to say, "By the way, Judy, I forgot to tell you the most important pieces of all—after you were born, I got to hold you."

Judy responded, "You did?! Oh, that's neat."

Robyn continued, "And guess what else, Judy—I gave you your first bath."

Judy was transformed by this. "You did? You gave me my first bath?!"

Robyn replied, "Yes, I cried a million tears, and you were soaking wet."

No one but Judy's birthmom could have given

Judy that message. Judy now knows deep in her psyche and soul that from the moment she was born she was loved.

Isn't that what every mother wishes for her child?

More and more adoptive parents are sensing that a connection to and acknowledgment of those roots is vitally important. In fact, many are coming to see this as a basic right of their adopted children. Russ was able to comprehend this early on.

From the beginning thirty-three years ago, I felt that our opportunity to parent was a direct result of another person's decision to give her child a better chance to survive, grow, and become a well-adjusted adult.

I couldn't and wouldn't ignore the fact that our adopted children were born into an existing family with certain genetic connections, which would always be present. It was, and is, their human right to have access to all of the facts of their birth and heritage.

Too many persons, through ignorance and probably through false basic information, try to keep the adopted person in a childhood state. Even as an adult they are commonly referred to as an adopted child! The fact is, they do grow up to be contributing adults. We must acknowledge this fact by allowing them the right to control their own lives.

Some adoptive parents feel they may lose their children when search issues come up. I have learned in raising my children that the bonds of our years and experiences together can never be lost to me or to them. The birthparents or original family has never been a threat to me. Just the opposite. I looked forward to meeting and knowing them. Like finding a long-lost member of the extended family. Birthfamily members could fill in the blanks of the birth and give to our children in ways we were unable to. Why deny this opportunity?!

When our son became ill at age sixteen, it was a parenting choice to aggressively search for his roots and medical background. As a youngster, he had expressed an extreme interest in knowing his origins. He wanted answers to questions we were unable to give because of limited information supplied by the adoption agency, even after seeking more information because of health matters. With his successful search and the benefits derived, we, as a family, embarked on the searches for the original families of our three other children as well.

Others would ask us why we were opening up a can of worms! We did not establish the connection with this attitude. We felt we were doing something positive for our sons and daughters, and still feel good about the decisions today, many years down the road.

Russ's wife Carol echoes him strongly.

I personally felt connected to the original families as I watched our sons and daughters grow and develop into the unique individuals they are today. I cared deeply about the unknown families who had allowed us the joy of becoming parents through adoption. I knew our happiness had come through their difficult decisions, pain, and loss.

As adoptive parents, we had fantasized about the reconnections with the original families. We wondered if they, as extended parts of our family, would gather together with us through the years. It has not turned out that way. Relationships between adoptees and original families are most often individually geared to their needs—not ours.

Our family remains secure in our love for each other. I believe the truth, found through search and reunions, has given our whole family the freedom to move on with our lives in more complete ways.

Adoptive parents face their own issues of loss, and searches and reunions by their children can force them into facing that pain. Yet many, like Russ and Carol, feel so secure in their role as adoptive parents that they are able to encourage their childrens' needs to reconnect with their birth families.

Certainly, having supportive adoptive parents helps an adoptee begin to reconcile the many issues that arise during these life-changing events. The fear of being disloyal or of hurting one's adoptive parents can be an immense barrier to the adoptee, and parents need to realize how vital they are to the healing process. As Marie told me,

> You can't hold on too tight. You have to keep that in mind when you're an adoptive parent. You have to hold your kids with open arms. They need you to do that.

~ 15 ~

THE FOURTH SIDE
OF THE TRIANGLE

THE LITERATURE AVAILABLE ON POSTADOPTION ISSUES has begun to increase in recent years. Yet, in spite of all the works now in print about searching and reunions, there is a large group of people about whom little has been written. They are the "fourth side" of the triad: the spouses, brothers and sisters, aunts and uncles, sons and daughters, and grandparents of adoptees, birthparents, and adoptive parents.

While they may not be the direct focus of the search or reunion, the lives of these individuals are nonetheless greatly impacted. Spouses, in particular, seem at risk. The upheaval of a reunion tests the bonds of even a strong marriage. I believe it is no coincidence that divorce followed many of the reunions included in this book.

Dirck Brown and Lucille Buergers write: "The reunion can create feelings on the part of the spouse that he or she is being displaced. . . . Searchers need to understand that spouses may be fearful that the search and reunion will bring about unwanted changes in the marital relationship. Fears of being displaced, rejected, not being included, feelings of rivalry and jealousy are just some of the emotions commonly experienced by the spouse."[1]

Perhaps one reason that reunions can be so devastating to a marriage is that individuals can't and don't anticipate the difficult emotional transition that invariably occurs. Most families don't have any foundation of experience from which to understand a reunion in advance. Again, that is why support groups are so invaluable during the search. Long before a reunion begins, one can become familiar with the emotional ride that will happen.

Still, while reunions can cause tremendous strains on some marriages, they can also be beneficial and enhance relationships. Mark found his wife's search for her birthdaughter to be a bonding experience.

My wife Marsha's reunion with her birthdaughter was difficult at times. The adoptive parents were very threatened when Marsha first wrote to them. They had a sheriff bring a summons to our house saying that Marsha could not go within one hundred yards of their daughter. There was to be absolutely no contact. All Marsha's letter had said was that she had been thinking about Amy for a long time, and would love to meet with her if her parents thought it was appropriate.

They hired an attorney to draw up an agreement that there would be no contact until Amy was eighteen. Then the lawyer called to say that the adoptive mother had talked with Amy, and that they would be willing to let Marsha meet with Amy if we would pay the attorney's fees. We agreed and Marsha and Amy finally were able to meet.

The search and reunion has been good for our relationship. Two things brought us a lot closer. First, Marsha felt I supported her. This reunion was a long time in coming for her. She had been thinking about searching for Amy, but didn't feel she could do it alone. It helped that I could be there for her, and that she needed me to be there for her.

Second, the reunion provided us a way of understanding each other. This is my second marriage. I have a daughter who is thirteen from my first marriage. There are some similarities between being a birthparent and being a noncustodial parent. We both have children with whom we have a blood tie but no real parental relationship. Just being related isn't the same as being there day to day for your kid.

When my daughter would come to visit us, even though Marsha and she knew each other, there would be this jolt when she would come. I'd lavish time and attention on my daughter, and Marsha would be confronted by the reality of my other marriage.

A birthmother's reunion with her child is also a consuming event, one that demands all the birthmother's attention. In that sense, this whole experience has brought us closer together. It's given us more empathy for each other.

Siblings experience some difficult issues when a brother or sister lost through adoption returns for a reunion. Many feel displaced, sensing that the birth order has changed. The oldest may no longer feel like the oldest. If there are a number of siblings in a family, jealousies can develop over who is closest to the new relation. And certainly reunions can cause other children in the family to feel threatened as their parent(s) deal with the return of the lost child. Just as with members of the immediate triad, empathy and understanding are needed by all members of the extended family throughout the difficult postreunion period.

Hannah met her half-brother a decade ago when she was twenty-five years old. It was an event she was unprepared for, and an intrusion she did not welcome.

As I entered the kitchen one day, I couldn't help noticing the look on my mother's face. She was greatly upset. I asked what was wrong. What happened changed things in my head and heart in ways I probably wasn't ready to handle.

The day before, my mother had received a letter from a man stating his birthdate and the conditions under which he had been put up for adoption. Evidently it all clicked, and my mother realized this person was her son. Conceived by rape, "Sam," was put up for adoption and given to his adoptive parents immediately after birth. Since that day, there had been no communication with him—only heartbreak for my mother. Now—thirty-seven years later—here he was.

My first reaction was to hug my mother and console her as much as I could. I felt her pain. My mother had suppressed many emotions and now the wound was reopened. I asked her what he wanted. Naturally, it was to meet her.

It's important to mention that my father knew nothing about this. My mother dealt with the entire reunion with Sam without his ever knowing. To this day he still doesn't know.

In some ways, I've always been a parent to my parents. Now, I acted as an intermediary on my mother's behalf. I contacted Sam to set up a meeting. When they first met, my mother cried and embraced him. The whole thing seemed to help her heal in some ways.

I kept three steps back emotionally. He was very nice and so excited that he had half-sisters. I wasn't quite so excited. After the meeting, Sam began calling my office at least three times a week. He was very emotional about this and couldn't understand how I could handle it as well as I did. He is twelve years older than me! During his frequent calling I also had my mother's feelings to deal with. She began resenting the fact that I knew for fear I might tell my father. I told her I would never do such a thing, and I was hurt by her thoughts.

Sam became a pest. I told him he had to stop pressuring me into accepting him as my long-lost brother. As far as I was concerned, he wasn't my brother. My mother gave birth to him and that was it.

My sister came to town to meet him. Miss Emotional cried and embraced Sam. She couldn't understand why I felt the way I did about him. I explained I had been the "adult" for everyone. From day one I listened to my mother and Sam about all their emotions. What I wanted to say was "Doesn't anyone care about my feelings in this whole thing?"

After a while, my mother decided she didn't want to hear from Sam anymore. I think she was afraid my father would find out. My sister kept in touch with him for a while. Then he stopped communicating with her.

Now, ten years later, I've had a chance to look back. Sam's arrival in my life had a definite impact on me. Because of my family dynamics it caused a lot of confusion. It was not a joyous reunion, although it did seem to heal my mother in some ways. It certainly made me understand a lot more about her, her relationships with men, and, most of all, why she'd been so self-destructive through her life.

If it could have all just slowed down a bit. It was too much, too fast. There was not enough time to process what was happening and gain a perspective on it.

It's interesting to note that in the past year I've thought about Sam and wondered where he is. I actually feel like I'd like to get to know him. Maybe *I'm* finally ready for a reunion.

The secrecy that continued during this reunion certainly interfered with Hannah's ability to feel comfortable with the knowledge of Sam. Placed in the perilous position of sharing a secret within her own home, Hannah could only resent the intrusive needs of this stranger. If her mother and father had had a more open and secure relationship, perhaps Hannah would have been less resistant to Sam. What's equally important in Hannah's story is that she needed time to get ready to know him. He pressed hard for something Hannah was not interested in or ready for. It can't be stated enough times that when a reunion carries expectations and "have to's," resentment and resistance will exist.

Prior knowledge of Sam might have helped Hannah come to terms sooner. Yet some siblings, without ever knowing about their mother's "lost child," are immediately ready for a reunion. Mary never knew about the son, Paul, her mother had had to give up. When he called fifty years later, Mary had to deal not with his existence so much as with the fact that he had been kept secret.

I first learned about Paul when my mom called me and told me about him the day after she'd received his letter. I had mixed emotions concerning the secrecy of it all. It was hard for me to believe my mother had not shared something so important with the seven children in our family. After talking with her, I soon realized that God must have intended she have a child for this other family. And I realized how very difficult it must have been for her to live with her secret. So I elected to build on the relationship with Paul, instead of harboring feelings of anger at being kept in the dark. I knew all the wishing in the world wasn't going to change things.

I couldn't afford to fly in for the reunion with Paul, so I surprised my mother by making the seventeen-hour drive with my sons. It was quite emotional when we met. We stood embracing each other. Paul began to sob. He was indeed surprised and pleased that my sons and I had come. Later that day I grabbed some chocolate-chip cookies and two glasses of milk and Paul and I went to the top of the stairs in my sister's house and just talked, relating fifty years of stories.

We've tried to get to know each other better. Each time I leave him, it becomes more difficult. I can honestly say that I've grown to love him like a brother.

Age may have something to do with one's ability to process the relationship with a sibling lost through adoption. Yuri was only twelve when he learned about his full sister over a decade ago. His white mother and black father were not married when their first child was born, and were encouraged to put her up for adoption. Yuri still vividly remembers the moment when he first learned of her existence.

I was deeply engrossed in an evening game of Monopoly with my oldest friend when my parents called me into the other room. I looked at my father and found him sullen and pensive, as if a certain uncomely destiny was finally upon him. My mother appeared quite apprehensive. Inside me there came a welling of dread. I expected the worst. My mother told my father that she did not wish to say anything. The timing was wrong. My dread increased. My dad tried to reassure my mother, and then asked me what I would think if they were to tell me that I had a sister. They had asked me this question on previous occasions, but I had never really taken the proposition seriously. However, my parents' demeanors told me immediately that the question was no longer a matter of idle speculation.

With no further introduction and much to my mother's dismay, my father explained to me that I did indeed have an older sister whom my mother had placed for adoption at birth. He produced a small schoolbook photo of a brown-skinned girl, about seven years old, who wore a blue velour shirt. She had green eyes, ponytails in braid, and a nervous smile. I had actually seen the photo before, but was told it was someone my mother knew through her job as a social worker.

I remember a brief sensation that something was missing, that suddenly there seemed a gap that should be filled. That sensation passed quickly and I could not readily process the information further. I knew nothing of this sister and had no real desire to. I returned to my game of Monopoly and greedily vanquished my friend with only faint twinges of emotion. I was scarcely moved.

Ultimately, I spoke over the phone from time to

time with my sister. When we finally met, our visit was strained and anticlimactic. I am a reserved person and she is even more so. It seemed that our every moment together was influenced by the question "So where does this lead?"

Now, more than a decade has passed and my relationship with my sister has remained at a standstill. I still know relatively little about her. She remains quite reluctant to bridge that gap. It would be wrong to say that I have no feelings for her. It would be likewise incorrect to suggest that my feelings are in any real way deep or developed.

Birth grandparents face a variety of emotions. Some, still embarrassed and concerned about "what everyone will think," even decades after a relinquishment, refuse to acknowledge that their son or daughter had a child out of wedlock. They don't understand the need for a reunion, and are upset when it occurs. Old values and principles sometimes die hard. Yet other grandparents yearn for an opportunity to meet that birth grandchild and to have a relationship.

Ray and Elaine both wish they could get to know their granddaughter. Even though Elaine met her and Ray has corresponded with her, they have never achieved the closeness they would like to have. Ray feels as he grows older that time is running out.

We were penpals briefly. She sent me a blown-up photo, and I sent one of me. She wanted to know about her ancestors, and I related all I knew. Her letters, though, were few and far between. I felt her drifting away from me. Having had a catastrophic illness, I felt it was urgent to keep up a dialogue with her in hope of one day getting to meet her. I get the feeling that she is having trouble coping, so a reunion with me and my wife seems remote.

My feeling is she should never have been adopted out. My daughter never gave us a chance to voice an opinion. But it's history. We must live knowing our flesh and blood will never be a part of this family. It's very hard for me to accept.

Ray's wife, Elaine, shares his sadness. To her, life seems less complete without this granddaughter as an ongoing part of it.

I got a chance to meet her in person once when I was visiting her hometown. She came in the evening with a sweet girlfriend and our visit was wonderful! She was very like her mother, my daughter, and I was so happy to be with her even for such a short time.

It comforted me greatly knowing that my granddaughter was with such kind and good people. But their gain and happiness will always be my sorrow and loss. I will never recover from the loss of this wonderful girl. And I know my daughter thinks about this girl every day as I do. I feel sorrow for my daughter. I feel our family is missing a great deal and that we will never be whole.

Adoption creates such a paradox, at times. This couple is grieving the loss of their granddaughter. Yet she is alive. The relationship they desire with her is elusive. Who are they to each other? The past is impossible to recapture. How do people resolve their grief over what is lost when what was lost exists, but by a different definition?

Sometimes the first person the searcher contacts is not an immediate family member. This can be an advantage. A cousin or an uncle or a grandparent can work as an intermediary. It obviously depends upon the person and his or her sensitivity to the situation. At other times initial contact with an extended family member can work against the searcher. There has been more than one reunion stalled by the decision of an intermediary to take control of the reunion process.

Being the first family member contacted by Lisa, I first felt joy in knowing she was alive and well. Second, I felt the burden of whether or not to proceed with the reunion attempt. The birthmother, who is my cousin, was undergoing radiation treatment for cancer at the time. I did not expect her to live long. She was also suffering from severe emotional problems. Her husband of forty years had just left her and she was in financial straits. I did not know what other members of the family knew of Lisa's existence. I seriously doubted that her aunt or her half-brother knew that she had been born. Her grandmother was in her eighties. I did not know if she would realize any benefit by knowing Lisa. All indications were that Lisa was a lesbian, and I did not know how that would be accepted by other family members. With these conditions, it was difficult for me to decide to proceed with the reunion. I felt I had fulfilled my obligation to Lisa by sharing her family heritage, giving her the genealogical records, etc. I felt a blood loyalty to my cousin, Lisa's birthmother, to abide by her extreme desire to leave the doors of the past closed.

The contradiction here is that this cousin was choosing to keep the door to the past closed without ever consulting other members of the family. Over two years would pass before Lisa was "allowed" to meet her birthfamily. Her maternal aunt was delighted to finally meet her niece.

My first feeling was a rush of excitement and delight, with immediate curiosity. Who did she look like? What kind of person was she? How did she feel about the family who gave her up?

I was so excited I wanted to call everyone and share the news. I went around for several hours in a happy haze. But the news that my sister, Lisa's birthmother, didn't want to be reunited worried me. My relationship with my sister had been shaky for several years. I didn't know how to approach this subject with her. And since I didn't have any of the facts about Lisa's birth, I was as much in the dark as Lisa was. I didn't sleep that first night, wondering if I truly wanted this person, this stranger, in my life.

Yet, even with my personal doubts, I had strong empathy for Lisa. I could imagine what it must be like not knowing what her birthfamily was like. Were we honest? Healthy? Normal? I felt a need to reassure her that it wasn't her but the situation that created the decision for adoption. I wrote Lisa to arrange a meeting with her as soon as possible.

Several years have now passed since Lisa and I first met. My feelings for her have been good from the start. My husband and children (Lisa's cousins) have been equally happy to have her in our lives as a member of the family. She has had a very positive effect on us all. My sister, Lisa's birthmother, has yet to agree to meet her. She is mentally ill, so I work on being understanding of my sister's viewpoint. But it is hard at times. I try to accept the situation as it is, but there is small hope for the impossible—that my sister ultimately accept and welcome her birthchild into her life as the rest of her family has.

Meeting Lisa has taught me many things. I now know that adoption leaves deep emotional scars on everyone involved. Also, people need to be themselves in a reunion. You can't force feelings. You need to allow time for affection to grow. Despite my sister's actions, I feel finding answers is worth the risk of rejection. Most importantly, I've learned it is possible to develop a caring relationship with someone, even after being separated for a lifetime.

When reunions are covered by the media, they tend to be one-dimensional. Because of the time constraints of most programs, it isn't possible to capture the subtleties going on with each individual. Nor is everyone comfortable airing his or her innermost thoughts and feelings in front of a studio audience.

Thus, the portrayals of reunions are almost always black or white. The event is either a good one or a bad one. The participants must be either happy or sad. The issues that arise must, by virtue of time constraints, be oversimplified and homogenized. But a real reunion obviously is not an event that can be described or understood in a thirty-second sound bite or even an hour-long talk show. To truly understand the dynamic nature of the reunion process, one must take into account everyone involved.

Within a single family, the reunion will affect people in many different ways. Each individual will bring his or her own set of hopes and fears to the table. Nothing illustrated this better to me than the diverse reactions within my own birthfamily during our reunion. Lee's children and their families, as well as her fiancée, Don, each had a different response to my appearance, and the ups and downs that followed. For some, the journey was easier than for others.

My brother Jim, for example, took the entire episode in stride. He was excited, but he kept his feet on the ground.

"She found us! She's alive! Cecelia found us!"

Those few words were to change my life. At that time, I was unsure how to react to this new person about to enter my life. That same night she called me, and after speaking to her for a while, I couldn't wait to meet her.

The three weeks between that first phone call and our face-to-face meeting allowed me and my wife, Cheryl, time to assess the situation and what this new relationship might bring our family. Cheryl and I decided that when Jean came to town we would just let things happen as they may—take it all in and then see what developed. We had already had the benefit of several phone conversations with Jean, which allowed us to get to know her a little better. It seemed very easy to communicate with her, and we found we had a lot in common. When the day came to finally meet her, it was like meeting a long-time friend. I was euphoric!

I found myself engulfed with wanting to know everything about her and wanting to spend more time with her. Fortunately, over the following five years Cheryl and I were able to visit with, and be visited by, Jean and her family. These visits enabled us to have long discussions about ourselves and our new relationship. I enjoy talking with her about our dreams and goals for the future. I have found that I have a tremendous amount of pride and respect for her. Jean is my *sister*, not my half-sister. She has brought a new dimension into my own family and she holds a special place in all our hearts.

Jim's wife, Cheryl, helped to make my acceptance by Jim uncomplicated. Level-headed and practical, Cheryl acted as a mediator, encouraging open communication within the family, as the initial reunion melted into reality.

After that warm July-evening telephone conversation between my husband, Jim, and his newly announced sister, Jean, my mind rushed with many thoughts. Initially, I too was caught up in the fascination and anticipation of this new person. Who did she look the most like? Whose mannerisms did she share?

The first meeting between Jean and the Iacarella family was exciting yet overwhelmingly stressful. Many people with very high expectations, and the *People* magazine coverage. As an onlooker, I saw eight different relationships to be established, yet only one Jean. The family was amazingly accepting and welcoming of Jean, but everyone had individual expectations and needs. I decided I would disappear into the background during this initial contact. I would be a support for my husband during this loving, emotional, exciting, and difficult time. Yet I couldn't help wondering what would come to be after the unfair and unrealistic first interaction.

Jean and Jim meshed well since they shared common interests in sports, music, and education. I observed Jim wanting to know more about Jean's past. This is one thing that put Jim's interaction with Jean apart from that of most of the other siblings. He realized that Jean's past made up a big part of who she was. She was his sister, but she hadn't grown up an Iacarella. He took the time to learn about her and accept her as her own person. Together they established a relationship of respect from which to build on, mature, and cherish.

Five years after the reunion of Jean with Jim and the Iacarella family, I can't help but reflect on the event and realize how this has changed the lives of everyone involved. Much anxiety, difficulties, and turmoil for some. Much growth, healing, and joy for others. Jean and her family have truly enriched Jim's life, my life, and that of our three sons, Taylor, Collin, and Reed. I really look forward to the times ahead that we can share.

My brother Mike had a much different reaction when he first heard that I had called his mother. Although everyone else in the family had prior knowledge that I existed, Mike had no recollection of ever being told about a long-lost sister. Perhaps he just blocked any memory of a mention of me from his mind, for to Mike my mere existence was initially cause for embarrassment.

I remember my sister Sue (we lived next door to each other) came running out of her house. "Mike! Call Mom," she said. "You've got a sister you didn't know about and she just talked to her!"

"I have a what?" I snapped back, as a sinking feeling started to grow in my stomach.

"You have a sister that Mom gave up for adoption thirty-three years ago, and now she's finally called Mom! Isn't that great!"

"Big deal," I said, which got a very nasty response from Sue. As I went into the house, I sat down to ponder what had just transpired. A host of feelings rushed through my brain. Who was this person to upset my well-ordered family and life? Why was everyone getting so excited? So what if my mom got knocked up before she met my dad. What were people going to think? I became more embarrassed the more I thought about it. I wanted to get my thoughts on something else, but by then I was obsessed with the situation.

What was I going to say to her? I had no history with this person. She was probably some flake from California whom I'd have nothing in common with. I bet she was fat. She most likely ate better than we had since she hadn't had to fight so many people at the dinner table for her food. She probably had gotten to travel more than we had too, and experienced things I could only dream about. Maybe she was the lucky one. . . .

"I don't care," I told myself over and over again. Yet, even though I was mad and embarrassed over the situation, I still had this growing curiosity to find out about this entity that was related to me. I started thinking more about her place in the family and how she would fit into the pecking order. I wondered if she was overwhelmed by the sheer numbers of the siblings she had found. I speculated that my mom and this new sibling looked alike. I look too much like my father, so I knew we wouldn't have any resemblance to each other. I didn't know if resemblance was important or not, but was I supposed to like this new person just because we shared some genetic patterns?

The next few days, everyone in the family had spoken to the new sibling except me. I was so difficult to get a hold of anyway, but maybe subconsciously I was avoiding the whole ordeal.

The phone rang on Sunday evening. "Hello, Mike?"

It's amazing what the sound of a voice can communicate. A lot of fear and anxiety left me with those first few words. For some reason, I could detect intelligence and a sense of stability in this person's voice that was very comforting to me. I knew nothing about her, yet we had no problem conversing. Her interests and passions were very similar to mine. Everyone in my family is so different from each other; however, this stranger and I had some common threads.

Jean and I spoke for several minutes, and after the conversation ended, I realized that this was a special person. She was now a part of my life forever, no matter what I did. The way she looked was now totally insignificant to the scheme of things. I needed to concern myself as to how I would fit her into my life.

On the day of the reunion, emotions in the family were running high. I felt sorry for my mom because this was twice the emotional burden for her. When we met at the baggage checkout, Jean was mobbed by all the siblings, in-laws, nephews, and nieces. Everyone hugging and kissing except Mom and me. We kind of got left behind. My family let their Italian emotions take over, which was understandable since it was a very dramatic event.

After a brief moment, I parted the sea of relatives and allowed Mom to meet Jean for the first time. It was my first sight of her also, since I was unable to see her through the herd. I could not believe how much she looked like my mom. There was no doubt about this one being related.

Once Jean and Mom exchanged pleasantries, I thought it was my turn. I put my hand out and said, "Hi, Jean, I'm Mike." I knew a handshake seemed a little cool, but I felt a hug or a kiss at this time would be empty and untrue. I barely knew her.

A lot has happened to me since Jean came into my life. She has had a tremendous impact on me and has changed me forever. We've shared enough experiences now that I'm offended if I don't get a hug and a kiss when we meet.

Of all my brothers and sisters, the one most eagerly awaiting my plane that first day was Sue. She had had a desire to find me since the birth of her first child, and had actively encouraged her mother to search. Sue and I talked for hours over the phone before the reunion. Her expectations of a special closeness to me were understandably high.

My mother took me aside when I was sixteen and carefully told me that I had an older sister who was given up for adoption. I was taken aback but not shocked. Maybe there was something inside me that always knew something was missing. I felt anger for not knowing her. I also felt sad for my mother, who loved her and was suffering from this separation. I wondered if this missing sister was dead or alive—if she was safe, happy, or sad. And mostly I wondered if she knew about us.

I always thought of her on her birthday and on Christmases and other holidays. When I had my own first child at twenty-three, I really wanted this missing piece of the puzzle found. My mother was so happy to hear that we kids shared her desire to find her missing daughter.

When my mother called five years later, telling me that Jean had found her and wanted to speak to her, at first I wasn't sure what she was talking about. Then it hit me. The sister I had never known had found us. The hairs on my arms actually stood up. When Jean called me later that night I was in shock. I couldn't stop saying, "I can't believe this is you!" I told Jean she had to call the rest of the family and to prepare herself for a long list of phone numbers.

When we finally met, I couldn't believe she was in my sight. She was real. This was no joke. She looked like my brother Bob's twin. Trying to hold back tears and failing, we all embraced.

We had a wonderful day, everyone was riding on cloud nine. Nobody could burst this bubble, I thought. But I was wrong. Reality burst the bubble the very next day. Suddenly, there was this tension that I couldn't understand. Jean went to a movie with my brothers, and I found myself wondering, What on earth is going on? You can go to a movie any day, why go now? Where is our rap session? Why aren't we getting to know each other?!

I couldn't believe all these emotions surfacing. Why was I having trouble with this wonderful event? I just wanted all these bad feelings to go away.

My dream didn't come close to what reality brought me. I'm not sure what my expectations were, but I didn't anticipate having any problems with this. I thought there would be this easy, relaxed attitude. Pull up a chair, make yourself at home, you're with family now. I guess you could say that was part of my dream. But my dream was just that—a dream.

There is no way to prepare yourself for this kind of

reunion. After we said our goodbyes and Jean went home, I really missed not being able to get to know her. I would call her and try to get a conversation going, but it felt like we were strangers. I could feel her pulling away—wanting distance. It was strange. I felt as if I was being rejected.

There was this feeling of insecurity that hovered over me. I felt that at any moment she could just drop out of our lives. I never knew if I was talking too much or too loud. I worried about things I never thought twice about before. I felt, one wrong move and who knows, I could be yesterday's news. It was so awkward for me to handle. I didn't want to push it or blow the chance of really getting to know her. I felt I had to constantly play by her rules, waiting until she was ready to talk or make the next move.

I felt angry. Why had she looked for us if she was going to pull this "I need my space" routine? This was my sister. I was so impatient. I wanted everything to happen yesterday. My persistence in getting to know her was actually pushing her away. She was brought up differently and handles things differently. The hard reality of finding a new family member is you have to start from square one and get to know her as a totally separate individual.

The reality of my arrival was no talk-show fairy tale although that's how it would have appeared had we been on one. The varying reactions to the reunion caused tension within the Iacarella family at times. I remained wonderfully oblivious of this, living my busy life half a continent away. I was in hiding.

Everyone coped with his or her own adjustment to the

situation, which was certainly exacerbated by my overt discomfort with Lee. Some of her kids felt understandably protective of their mother and angry at me. Others tried to empathize with both sides. Divisiveness was rife.

While each of the kids was concerned about their mom after the reunion, no one knew or understood what Lee was living through day to day better than her fiancée (now husband), Don. He was with her when she got my first phone call and he was with her through her bitterest moments. Most certainly, my arrival in Lee's life affected their courtship and the first year of their marriage in profound ways. Don says:

Lee and I met at a Parents Without Partners function. After a long night of talking about everything, we went out on a formal date. Lee listened to me talk about my family breakup, and the pain of having my children angry with me. She related stories about her own life, including her lost daughter, Cecelia. Both of us had had a lot of hurt, and by sharing it we developed a common bond.

Even though I had joint custody of my children, and visitation rights, for the most part I had been unable to see or even talk to them. So I knew what it was like to lose a child, not to death, but to not knowing, to not see them grow or be there when they needed help. It was a real void—a black hole in my life.

I was at Lee's house when she received the phone call from the priest asking if she wanted to talk to her daughter. When she realized it was her lost daughter, she almost fainted, then said, "Yes!" When Jean called a few minutes later, Lee had a nice conversation with her, answering lots of questions about her past. She tried to be unemotional, but she was shaking the entire time.

She was at first very happy. But, rather quickly, I noticed a change. She started to relive everything, from bad memories about the birthfather to her time in "seclusion" in California to when she gave the baby away. To protect herself, these events had been buried in her subconscious. As they came back, she fell apart. She was very angry.

I remember when Jean called to tell Lee she had found her father. Lee turned into a basket case. She could not sleep without dreaming about what had happened. She expressed absolute anger toward him. He had basically gotten away with everything. There was no penalty for him, no public shame, no ostracism by society. He had had the economic means to help support the child he fathered, but he did nothing. Lee never received anything either. I'm not talking about money —just an apology, or empathy. A little human kindness would have helped her back then.

About the same time all this was going on, Lee was having to answer a lot of questions her kids had and talk to a reporter from *People* magazine. On one hand, Lee felt it was important to tell her story. But on the other, she was the one who had had a child out of wedlock. Given her generation, her status as a birthmother, and the fact that she was also adopted, these were sources of enormous guilt and pain.

When Lee went to Minnesota for the reunion, she was scared to death. I was not part of the big mess, even though I spent a good deal of time helping Lee with her emotions. At the time, her family was dealing with a new person—Jean. They didn't need another new person—me.

During the reunion, Lee never had the chance to deal with her emotions one on one with Jean. All of her emotions went underground. *People* magazine came out. Other people outside the family got to read a great story and several of the kids had fun with the publicity. Good!

Sometime after the article came out, we visited the town in Oregon where Lee grew up. We stopped to buy gas at a small grocery store, and a customer who had vaguely known Lee as a child stopped her and asked, "Aren't you Lee? I saw the *People* article. . . . Everyone has read it. It took a lot of courage." I'm not sure anyone other than Lee knew just how much courage! She commented when she returned to the car, "Well, I guess everyone knows about me now!" Her voice was both negative and positive at the same time.

After Lee and I were married, we moved to Minneapolis. I thought a lot about Jean. She was a lot like me. I came into Lee's family, too, a family of adults whom I did not know and who did not know me. But Jean had one advantage: she could withdraw from people when things got tight. She lived a thousand miles away with her own family and children. To her credit, after withdrawing, she made a real effort to improve understanding. And to the family's credit, Lee's children also worked to make things better. Time and effort can solve most problems.

I was on the outside of this much of the time. I felt they all had lives which I could never truly be a part of. Over the years, I have gotten to know and become friends with, and yes, love, Lee's children and grandchildren. But they are not mine. So when Jean said to Lee, "You're not my mom," I understood.

After all is said and done, everything that Lee and her family have gone through I feel has been more than worth it. I feel better for having been a part of Lee's family and the reunion. Her own search for her birthparents goes on with all the support, love, and help I can give her.

Lee was fortunate to have had Don beside her as a friend and supporter throughout the early days of reunion. It says a great deal about the foundations of their relationship that they survived the turmoil.

These few stories barely touch on the mountain of experiences and feelings that are felt by extended family members during a reunion. Certainly, anyone doing a search or entering a reunion needs to be aware of the far-reaching effects that that first phone call will have, not just on birthparents or adoptees and adoptive parents, but on the myriad family members who surround them.

~ 16 ~

THAT HANG-UP
WITH WORDS

SUSAN DARKE ONCE TOLD ME ABOUT a phone call with her birthson shortly after they were reunited. "I can remember him struggling with what to call me. First I was Mrs. Darke, then I was Mom and then I was Susan. Eventually he wasn't calling me anything at all. I realized he was feeling uncomfortable, so I asked him to call me Susan. I literally heard him relax. That's what he's used ever since."

An adoptee interviewed for Jill Krementz's book *How It Feels to Be Adopted* remembered having similar discomfort in her first reunion with her birthfamily. "They had a big family gathering, which included [several members of my birthfamily]. . . . I was too overwhelmed by it and felt uncomfortable. Everyone treated me like a relative, which bothered me because I didn't feel that way. At one point, someone who was talking to me referred to [my birthmother] as "your mom" and I didn't like that at all and said so. If I hadn't said anything I would have felt guilty and that wouldn't have helped in the long run."[1]

Lee, my own birthmother, wrote of the time following our reunion: "Jean is so hung up on labels and names. I'm definitely not her mother, but I struggle with 'What am I?' Her two little boys are related to me, but how?"

Language, or at least my preoccupation with it, also drove my sister Sue crazy. She wrote, "When people call my sister Jean my half-sister I just cringe and say, 'Which half is my sister?' I know adoptees have their mothers and sisters and brothers and nobody wants to confuse anyone, but do we have to label everything? What is my mother supposed to refer to Jean as? A daughter? A birthdaughter? A fetus?!"

Language can present an enormous problem after a reunion. "Mother," "father," "daughter," "son" are powerful words, words that automatically conjure up specific images and expectations. They reflect love and sacrifice, role models and teachers, home and family. But within the adoption triangle, these words can cause confusion, fear, and misunderstanding.

When adoptees meet birthparents, what words define their unique relationship? The words we use to define how we relate to each other can be extremely important because they not only help the "outside world" understand these unique ties, but they help members "inside" the adoption triangle, family members and those directly involved, to better understand themselves.

Lee is accurate in what she wrote about the months following our reunion. I *was* hung up on labels and names. I struggled to define who she was in relation to me in my adult life. She had carried me for nine months, given birth to me, then courageously let me go. Many would say, and did say, that she was my mother. But I disagreed. She was special in my life, and I cared about her well-being, but I was not willing to have anyone call her my mother. For me it just didn't seem realistic.

To me, Mom is the woman I had known my whole life, who changed my diapers, made dinner every night, read stories, sang me to sleep, comforted me when I was sick or frightened, and proudly taped my homework to our refrigerator. She let me have two horses, two dogs, a cat, homing pigeons, lop-eared bunnies, a hamster, a parakeet, a duck, a baby buzzard, and sixty-four rats—even though she wasn't fond of animals. She got out of bed with a 104-degree fever and the flu to take me to school when I missed the bus. She was always there. She trusted me when I was a teenager, and never questioned my nomadic lifestyle when I was an early adult. We stood beside each other at funerals and weddings, were there for each other in the tough times, and shared the laughter in the good times. We had a lifetime of experiences together that defined us as mother and daughter. What should I call this other woman in my life? What should she call me? And, just as important, by what words should others understand our relationship?

I believe there are no words that currently exist in our vocabulary that accurately describe the relationship between adoptees and their roots. I know I don't represent all adoptees when I say this. Some feel comfortable calling their adoptive mother and their birthmother both "Mom."

Paul remembers the way his very first conversation with his birthmother began. "I told her that I had this urge to call her Mom. She reminded me that I had a mother that brought me up, and that she was my mother. I said, 'But she's been gone for twenty years.' So my birthmother said to call her whatever felt most comfortable for me. So I said, 'Okay . . . Mom.' "

Diana had a similar experience. "My birthmom doesn't replace my adoptive mom in any way—nor does she want to. She has respect for my parents and feels thankful to them because she knows I'm happy and successful. Because of the way my birthmom has handled all of this, I've never felt threatened by having a very close relationship with her. I have no problem calling her 'Mom.' I like calling her 'Mom.' I feel I have two mothers."

For many people, language presents no issue, no barrier. Some people might feel that a discussion of the language we use to define relationships is splitting hairs. Who cares about mere words? Does it really matter how we define our bonds with people?

I believe it matters a great deal. Language is the primary tool we use to communicate with each other. The exactness of word meanings helps us to be clear and succinct in what we say and imply. Through language we achieve understanding. And when language fails, the results can be threatening.

A young man recalled his first meeting with his birthmother. "I had really enjoyed talking with her. She filled in so many blanks for me. Then she introduced me to a friend of hers as *her* son. I found myself all of a sudden feeling, hey, I'm not *yours*. It made me mad. I couldn't wait to get away from her, to go home. That was five months ago. She keeps calling, writing, but all I want to do is ignore her."[2] Would this young man have been less threatened by his birthmother if she had had other words at her disposal to define their relationship? What if she had introduced him as her "*birth*son"? Would that have made any difference?

Some adoptees, who never felt a part of their adopted homes, perhaps *are* looking for a mother or a father when they choose to search. But I wasn't. I searched, not to find parents, but to find pieces of myself that were missing. I don't intend to make it sound like all I wanted was to locate a data bank. I wanted to meet a special person. She had given me life. Finding Lee and her family was a joyous occasion, yet almost immediately a level of discomfort developed. The idea of calling Lee "Mom," and of having others refer to her as my mother set off all sorts of alarms inside of me. Giving her that title felt wrong and disloyal. My adopted mom had just died eighteen months earlier and she was irreplacable in my heart. To say that Lee was also my mother seemed to threaten the memory of the only real mother I had ever known. So for me, much of the difficulty in our reunion grew out of the language our society used to define who we were to each other.

I am not alone in my concern over how to define my ties to my birthfamily. Other adoptees have described similar feelings. Amy Dean, in her poignant *Letters to My Birthmother* writes:

> I wish you [her birthmother] would stop identifying members of your family as *my* sisters, *my* aunts, etc. That makes me feel like I'm being pulled into your family before I'm ready.
>
> I just don't think of *your* family as *my* family.
>
> I don't know if I ever will. . . . It's *you* that I wanted to find, not a family.[3]

Another young adoptee interviewed by Jill Krementz recalled:

> It upset me when [my birthmother's] friends would say stuff like, "So you're Alison's daughter." I didn't know what to say. I sort of went along with it because I didn't know what else they would call me, but by not saying anything, I felt like I was taking away

something from my mom. It's confusing because I don't know how to categorize my relationship with Alison. I don't want to think of it as purely biological, but I don't know how else to define it. I feel ridiculous introducing her as "my friend," and yet I certainly don't think of her as my mother.[4]

Bill, an adoptee, has tried to illustrate this confusion with an unusual analogy. "As humans, we tend to describe the unknown by comparing it to things that we already know. What do frogs legs taste like? Kind of like chicken. Are they chicken? No. And neither is your birthmother 100 percent your mother nor your adoptive mother 100 percent your mother. Each has a quality all her own and each holds a different meaning for the adoptee. Judging their quality by their likeness to a traditional family relation of the same name only leads to frustration. You wouldn't judge the quality of frog legs by their likeness to chicken, would you? Nor can you judge your birthmother by her likeness to your adoptive mother."

When Bill met his own birthmother he had a hard time deciding what to call her. "I even felt uncomfortable using her first name. For two years or more I often avoided conversation that would involve having to call her anything. I just decided to let time take its course and a name would eventually develop. Now, five years later, I feel comfortable calling her by her first name, but refer to her differently to different people: By her first name to some, 'birthmother' to others, and even 'mom' in the third person when talking to my two new sisters. But I don't call her Mom when speaking to her. That is a very powerful word and—it is someone else's name."[5]

Certainly at issue here is that our language can set up

adoptees for feelings of divided loyalty. If they acknowledge birthparents as "Mom" and "Dad," adoptees can instantly feel at risk of either hurting or alienating the parents who raised them.

During the past two decades, various people and organizations have tried to solve this linguistic dilemma by creating new phrases. Once one becomes involved in a search, this new terminology becomes a part of one's vernacular. Words like "birthmother," "natural father," "genetic or biological parent" join "adoptive parent" as words we toss about to explain our ties to the people in our lives. Yet I question whether these pasted-together terms adequately help outsiders or insiders understand and feel comfortable with these unique bonds.

For example, the title "natural parent" which is often used is a nice phrase, less harsh and clinical than "biological mother" or "genetic father." Yet, if the person who has conceived a child is the natural parent, then what is the person who has raised the child to be called? The *un*natural parent? My mother was many things, but never unnatural. Of the commonly used terms I have chosen *birth*parent as the most comfortable. The birthmother and adoptee do share conception and birth.

Yet, for many in the triad, even this term seems inadequate. Adoptee Karen Tashjian, in a short essay she wrote called "You Name It," stated that "Birthmother is starting to sound like cold lingo to me. First mother is sounding better. First is not best . . . or worst . . . just first. Birthfather seems to be a term in conflict with itself, since biological fathers had little to do with the actual birth. First father."[6]

Adoptive mother Gail Steinberg feels the language for who we are, to put it bluntly, "stinks." She feels that the term *birth*mother is misleading because it implies that the relationship ends with the process of giving birth. Nor does she like the title *adoptive* parent. "The legal process of adoption (which allowed us to make our family) is no longer a component of our parenting."[7]

It's interesting that adoptees are rarely referred to as the "natural son" or "birthdaughter" of a birthparent. They are always referred to as just "sons" and "daughters." Yet frequently the terms "adopted son" or "adopted daughter" is used to describe the relationship between the adopted parent and child. I find this odd. It seems to demote the adopted parent, linguistically at least. At what point does society recognize an adopted child as just the son or daughter of the parents who raise them?

No wonder people fear reuniting adoptees and their birthparents. They do not trust the bonds that time and experience can make.

When I met Lee, it was a wonderful event, but it was also a painful and awkward time. Well-meaning comments made establishing a relationship with my birthmother threatening. "It must be wonderful to have found your *real* mother." "What does your adopted mother think of your mother?" (This from people who didn't know my mom had died.) "Isn't it great you now have a *new* mother?" I found myself feeling defensive, and I would explain *ad infinitum* that my adopted mother was my *real* mother.

Was I overly sensitive? Yes. But my point here is not how I felt but what those words did. *They drove me away.* They interfered with the beginnings of my relationship with my birthmother as much as did her instinctive need to mother me.

Mother. Daughter. The images and expectations I attach to those words are deep and strong. These words did not adequately define this new relationship. The language failed us, and instead of creating understanding, it created a barrier.

Why was my search immediately interpreted by many as a search for parents? In part, I believe, because of the words we use. If I was looking for my birth*mother*, then I must be looking for a mother.

The underlying reality of this whole problem is, of course, not the language itself but the *relationships* that the language supposedly represents. Is a birthparent really a *parent*? Is a birthmother really a *mother*? Are these appropriate words to assign to these relationships? Would triad members benefit from the creation of a new terminology?

There are a lot of people who would oppose my notion of creating different words to define these nontraditional relationships. They would say my idea is hogwash, and that my discomfort with calling Lee "Mom" is a sign that I'm in denial. I would have no argument with that accusation.

Denial was a strong emotion I experienced in the early stages of my reunion: denial of the profound relationship that in reality *does* exist. I spent over three decades ignoring my birthmother's role in my life. To acknowledge it was as threatening as anything I've ever faced. The concept of having two mothers seemed as sacrilegious to me as there being two Gods. To alter my belief system felt like denouncing everything I hold dear. Yet adoptees face a unique and perplexing circumstance. The reality is, two mothers do exist. One gave birth. The other nurtured and raised.

We react most strongly when there is something to react to. At the root of my problem with what to call Lee was a truth I was afraid to face: I have two mothers. I gasp even now as I write this. It's a round statement that doesn't fit into my square definition of family.

I'm not the only one who has had difficulty accepting

this fact. Our entire society has yet to recognize this reality. In a misguided effort to "protect" everyone involved, reality has been avoided. America launched into a game of "let's pretend" with its twentieth-century system of adoption. A major part of the game was the rule that knowledge of the birthfamily was of little importance to the adoptee *or* the adoptive parents.

Nothing illustrates the "let's pretend" aspect of adoption better than the amended birth certificate. It's a legal document that's an outright lie. It says that the adoptive parents *gave birth* to the adoptee. Creating a legal document that doesn't reflect the truth is unhealthy for everyone involved. It encourages people to live in a fantasy rather than reality. It forces the denial of a human being's origins. Other countries show greater respect for an individual's heritage. In France, for example, in a simple adoption, the birthparents' names are not removed from the amended certificate. The adoptive parents' names are *added*.

In his book *Surrogate Motherhood*, Thomas A. Shannon points out: "To dismiss [the biological relatedness of the child] as insignificant or morally irrelevant is to eliminate a significant aspect of our being."[8]

Later, he cites British sociologist R. Snowden, arguing that "the nurturing of the child is insufficient of itself to endow full parent status. The nurturing role may be seen *socially* as the most important but the genetic role is also an essential component."[9]

I swallowed hard when I first read that. It took me a long time to embrace the concept that I do have two mothers. Yet acknowledging that reality does not change my frustration with our language.

What words would better describe these relationships? If used over time, could new titles help people better understand these unusual ties? Could they help alleviate the threat that our current language often seems to create?

It's a subjective issue, one that each individual will have personal opinions about. For me, the creation of new and better words to define these special relationships would have helped enrich my understanding of, and comfort with, the reunion process.

With all this said, what will I call my own birthmother? I will still call her by her nickname: Lee. Maybe Bill said it best: "Mom" is someone else's name. But to me Lee also deserves her own title, one that reflects and honors her unique role in my life.

~ 17 ~

COMING TO TERMS

I BELIEVE THAT HEALING IS THE goal of the search and the reunion. Yet I am no expert on healing. I'm not a psychologist or a counselor, nor have I completed my own "work" on the impact adoption has had on my life. Although my reunion was five years ago, that's really not a long period of time to have dealt with the numerous issues that arise. Sharon Kaplan Roszia, of Parenting Resources in California, once surmised that for every year a birthparent and birthchild are separated (and the deeply rooted issues of adoption are avoided), it takes that many years, plus one, to heal.[1] I was thirty-three when I had my reunion with Lee. According to the above timetable, I'll be an advanced soul by the time I'm sixty-seven. I ought to have a lot more to say on all of this by then.

In writing this chapter, I feel like a woman in the early

stages of labor, trying to describe giving birth. I know what's coming, but I haven't experienced the gamut of sensations yet. I don't have all the answers. Maybe no one really does. Maybe each of us, individually, must find his or her own way. We must come to our own terms with the events and people that have shaped our lives, create our own definition of what it means to heal.

For me, reconciling my adoption losses has, to this point, involved certain steps: acknowledging the losses, giving myself permission to come to terms with them, learning to look inside myself for the solutions, and setting achievable and empowering goals.

The search itself seems to me a big step toward healing. It is an acknowledgment, whether conscious or subconscious, that a deep and profound loss exists, which requires attention. When someone decides to search, the reasons may be articulated as "I'm curious," or "I want to know my medical background." These are external reasons—rationalizations that society (and triad members) can both approve of and understand. But there are deeper, less visible, motivations, which will only become clear as the search and reunion unfold. It's important to listen to yourself throughout the process. What is your search *really* all about? What's going on under the surface? Self-knowledge is the key to healing.

The idea that there is a wound that needs healing isn't necessarily easy to accept. Triad members can bristle and feel instantly defensive when introduced to the concept that adoptees will face hurdles that people raised by biological parents won't ever have to confront.

No one wants to acknowledge feelings of abandonment or rejection. No one wants to be labeled as "different." No one wants to have a finger pointed at him or her, with the

statement attached "There's something wrong with you."
But that's not what this is all about. There's nothing
"wrong" with adoptees. There is, however, something
wrong with the secrecy and pretending that are a part of
traditional closed adoption. As Robert Andersen writes,
"Adoptees are often encouraged to ignore adoption as a fac-
tor in their lives. This relative indifference to the issues of
adoption, often taken by adoptive parents and society in general, might be as big a trauma as the adoption itself."[2]

By denying the significant trauma of having these primal
bonds severed, adoptees become numb, and wall off a por-
tion of their psyche. This does not, however, diminish the
significance of the event. As Clarissa Pinkola Estes points out
in *Warming the Stone Child*, "The original abandonment has
meaning to it. It is not some senseless event like a dog being
run down on the highway."[3]

Recognizing that triad members have issues that need
addressing does not mean there is something pathologically
wrong with them. They have suffered a loss that they have
never been given permission to feel and resolve. Pushing this
loss to the side without acknowledging it and paying attention to it can cause problems.

Personally, while I began to be aware that there were
problems inherent in adoption that may well have had an
impact on my life, I did not find it easy to accept the idea
that these couldn't be healed overnight. As I began to resolve some of my feelings following my reunion, I sought a
quick fix. I wanted a weekend retreat, a book, a videotape
—something fast somewhere, so I could finish all this adop-
tion/loss business and be done with it. But resolution of
these issues is not a simple task accomplished over a weekend, or even a year.

In fact, when I interviewed one psychologist for this

chapter, and I mentioned that I thought healing was a goal of the search and reunion, the psychologist responded with the assertion that adoptees could never fully heal. The separation from one's birthmother created an injury that was impossible to repair fully.

After the interview, I found myself upset, even angry, at this comment. How could something that had happened to me when I was three days old affect me for the rest of my life? I didn't want to embrace such a thought. Its implications for my own self seemed too harsh to consider. After all, I'd had a happy childhood and felt strong love for (and had been loved by) my adoptive family. Why should I have any problems to deal with at all? I just couldn't buy it. The idea seemed Calvinistic, dooming all adoptees to a life of pain and despair. Suddenly, even though I accepted that adoption carried inherent problems, I no longer wanted to acknowledge that being adopted had affected me in any way. I didn't want to consider myself damaged goods for the rest of my life. But there was a small voice deep inside me that asked, "What if it's true?"

Is healing impossible for an adoptee? What about other members of the triad? Isn't it possible ultimately to incorporate all this knowledge into oneself, and get on with one's life? In fact, couldn't one be *empowered* by the process?

I believe that coming to terms with these issues *is* possible. If I didn't believe that, I wouldn't encourage people to search. What would be the point if all one would gain would be pain and confusion? To me, none of this effort would be justified if there were no chance to benefit and grow from it.

The notion of having wounds that were impossible to heal was what bothered me most. Forever is a long time to hurt. But was that what this psychologist was really saying?

My response to what had been said needed closer examination. I decided that my main difficulty with this statement was the way it was framed. "You have a wound that cannot heal." The very words made me feel damaged. Crippled. Disfigured. What if what I needed to do was reconcile a *loss*, rather than heal a wound? Looking at the issue in that context, I began to feel more comfortable. Losses of special people in our lives are never fully resolved. That's both accepted and acceptable.

For example, my dad died almost thirty years ago, when I was nine years old. I grieved for him when he died, then ultimately got on with my childhood and the business of growing up. But there have been certain times when I must again work through this loss. When I graduated from high school, when I attended his alma mater, when I married, when I had children: all these events were times when I was keenly aware he was missing from my life, and I needed to resolve new feelings of loss. Even minor events have caused me to experience sadness, acknowledge his loss, and come to new resolutions.

A recent event brought this home to me. Fishing had been an important part of my dad's life. It was his favorite pastime and passion. Fishing had been his way of connecting with friends and family. I had shared many special moments with him on the shores of the Feather River.

When my son Kristoffer was four years old, he went fishing for the very first time. He caught a fish on his very first cast into the pond. I couldn't believe it. I watched as he patiently reeled it in, and proudly stood to have his picture taken. Immediately I wished my dad could have shared this moment. I knew how much he would have enjoyed being there, and how much he would have enjoyed teaching his grandson the art of being a fisherman. I felt my loss of him all over again, suddenly sad that my sons would never be able to sit side by side with their grandfather, fishing poles, tackle boxes, and sandwiches wrapped in wax paper between them, watching the sun rise. It'll never happen.

There are ways for me to deal with this renewed sense of loss. I can share with my children pictures and stories of my dad. I can make my memories of him survive for them. I will never stop missing him, but I believe I have reconciled his loss. I just need readjustments now and again. No one begrudges me moments like this when I miss my mom or dad. Why should coping with the loss of my birthfamily be any different?

Looking at the issue from this slightly different perspective made it easier for me to accept that coming to terms with adoption losses can be a lifelong process. Brodzinsky, Schechter, and Henig write: "The path to psychological maturity may look, at first glance, as though it's straight and narrow. But it usually turns out to be littered with rocky spots and obstacles. . . . That's what happens too in dealing with adoption: it's an issue that emerges, seems to be settled, and then reemerges at some later point along life's path."[4]

Thus, different things need to be dealt with at different times. As one moves from one phase of life to another, adoption issues will be dealt with anew. I began to view my processing of adoption issues as similar to dealing with any other major loss in my life.

But losses through adoption, for an adoptee, birthparent, or adoptive parent *are* different, because we've been conditioned to believe we aren't supposed to feel *anything*. Most people will see a triad-member's pain as grieving for "air," grieving for something intangible, something that we've never even seen. Few people will understand that for everyone connected by adoption there is profound loss. They will question how someone could miss or feel the loss of people they have never known. Further, few will understand why finding one's birthfamily doesn't automatically fix these losses.

Recently, a good friend of mine, who's known me since I was an infant, said, "I have to be honest with you. I don't get all this angst adoptees exhibit on these reunion shows. Why can't all these searchers just get on with their lives? I mean, all of us have tough things to deal with. No one has a perfect family. Here you've got these couples giving these kids a good home. Why isn't it enough?"

I heard her questions and wondered how to answer—not because I didn't have something to say but because there was so *much* to say. I didn't know where to start. I was reminded that it is very difficult for someone who has not been adopted to understand what it's like to be an adoptee. It's difficult for someone who has never surrendered a child for adoption or suffered through infertility to understand what it's like to be a birthparent or an adoptive parent.

Her questions lead to what I see as the second step in healing: *giving yourself permission to deal with adoption losses.* Her questions also inspire further questions.

Why is this need for birthfamilies to reconnect so hard for some people to understand? How could someone *not* need to know their birthfamily? If adoption is a social conveyance created in the "best interest of the child," why is society not listening to those children now that they are grown? How could the vast majority of American citizens not be able to see that closed records are a violation of an adoptee's civil rights? Most importantly, it made me wonder how people can begin to deal with their losses if they are not supported and encouraged to do so.

Is it because America is a melting pot that we so easily

push aside the importance of one's roots, one's clan? Is it because of our desire to blend together as a nation that society tacitly accepts the idea that ties to our "tribes" are of no consequence or meaning? Shannon writes: "The motive, or the end, of parenthood is surely the creation of a whole person, and this takes within its grasp both the *begetting* and the raising of the child."[5] Resolving adoption losses would be so much easier if society, as a whole, would embrace this statement. Connecting with one's birthparents is a natural need. The birthfamily is a part of the adoptee; knowing who they are should be an adoptee's birthright, not a closely guarded secret.

But I believe many adoptees are afraid even to acknowledge this natural (and healthy) desire because they are made to feel that this yearning is disloyal and inappropriate. For adoptees to survive and be accepted, any desires to discover their birthfamilies must be buried deep in the subconscious. There it will remain dormant until it surfaces, triggered by some climactic event: the death of a parent, the birth of a child. Such events open the portals to the subconscious, at which time the adoptee may realize the need to resolve this primal loss—a lifelong amputation. Yet the awakening of the desire to search does not mean that an adoptee will feel permission to do anything about it. Searching is still, to many, a taboo.

One of the better-known opponents of search and reunion has been columnist Ann Landers. I contacted her in the early stages of writing this book and she generously consented to an interview. Any discussion of the validity and necessity of search and reunion is incomplete without an understanding of why many people remain against it.

Landers wasn't totally opposed to reunions. She felt that such endeavors were acceptable if:

The adoptee and the birthparents and the adoptive parents all agree that this is what they want to do. . . . [But] I would only support taking this on if all three parties are not only comfortable but enormously enthusiastic. Comfortable isn't enough. They must desperately want it *and* be prepared for the worst. Sometimes, even though they are eager and willing, it turns out to be a disaster, and then they're sorry.

She said her major objection to reunions is that people have their lives disrupted. "I've heard from so many people who have had horrible experiences." She is most concerned for the adoptive parents because:

They're the ones who have the most legitimate complaint and they're the ones who have the biggest heartache. Here they have adopted a child with the understanding that the child would be theirs and they would never hear from the birthmother again. Then suddenly, fourteen years later, here she comes. They [birthmothers] often hire detectives. They get the records and the adoptive parents are absolutely defenseless. . . . When parents adopt a child, many of them live in mortal fear that the birthmother is going to look them up and take the child away.

A lot of people will find Landers's focus appalling. They will point out that she is willing to listen to (and publish) an adoptive parent's pain, while ignoring the pain of the adoptee or the birthparent. They will argue that no one can own a child. The child isn't *theirs*. But I think Landers's words are important to hear: ". . . [they] live in mortal fear. . . ." People are resistant to understanding the root of the issues at hand because they are afraid. Certainly anyone undertaking a search must try to be sensitive to that fear. They shouldn't, however, allow their sensitivity to stop them from searching at all. As Clarissa Pinkola Estes writes, "It is never a mistake to search for what one requires. Never."[6]

Perhaps the most important thing that Ann Landers imparted to me was this:

> I've heard from very few people actually who say, "Gee, I found her and we all get along fine, and my natural mother loves my adopted mother." What I'm getting is, "I should have listened to you. I've had nothing but trouble. . . . I can't get rid of my birthmother. She is camping on my doorstep."
>
> My conclusions are based on what I hear from my readers.[7]

As she spoke, I thought about the fact that I'd never written to her about my own reunion. I'd never written to my adoption agency or that hospital or a judge or anyone. How were they ever to know the value that my reunion has had in my life?

I also wondered, if I had written to Ann Landers during the first year of my reunion what would I have said? It was a confusing time. Following the initial reunion I experienced a wide range of emotions I never anticipated. I vacillated between feeling joy and frustration, happiness and anger. Mostly I felt threatened. It took a long time for me to understand and move beyond those emotions. Fortunately, my birthfamily was patient, and wanted to see our relationship through to fruition. We stuck with it, and the result is that what I feel today is light years from what I felt five years ago.

I'm thankful I searched. I believe the ultimate outcome

is healthier for everyone, including the generation that follows me. My own children will not only know their genetic heritage but now have a whole new group of people to enjoy in their lives.

But a mere five years ago I would have expressed all of this differently. I never regretted the search, or finding my birthfamily, but I certainly had moments when I wished my birthmother would just go away. Dealing with her meant confronting deep, painful, long-avoided issues. How many people does Ann Landers hear from who are in the unresolved stages of their reunions?

While I don't agree with her perspective on all of this, I was grateful to her for this insight: I learned we are not going to educate anyone about the importance of adoptees' reconnecting with birthfamilies if those of us who have had positive experiences remain silent. People who are unhappy and frustrated are much more likely to ask for advice. Ann Landers, and anyone else for that matter, cannot come to any other conclusions unless they receive communication from people who have had favorable experiences.

Of what relevance are Ann Landers's views on the subject of healing? Her stance is certainly relevant in the context of permission. If the search and reunion are important first steps in resolving adoption losses, these can be scary, seemingly disloyal acts to take without support. As psychotherapist Nancy Verrier writes, "One of the ways in which society might help the healing process for adoption triad members would be to withhold judgment about those adoptees and birthmothers who are searching for one another."[8]

But as long as the needs of the adoptive parents are seen as paramount, society will not endorse the need to search. Verrier continues, "There is often a failure to realize that the adoptive parents' feelings pale in comparison to the painful feelings experienced by their child due to that early separation."[9] Only when the best interests of the adoptee become the primary focus will search and reunion begin to be seen as necessary and healthy steps.

There are such paradoxes here. We have made something so basic and natural as one's ties to one's biological family into a threatening ogre. The ones who have the hardest time with this are the ones who hold on too tight. Their message is the wrong one: "I'm afraid you'll find out you're not really *mine*." The message should be: "You are a human being. Go and do what you must to be strong and thrive in this world. I'll still be here." We must learn to trust the bonds that time and experience can make. Strong bonds will not be broken.

There are bright spots on the horizon. I was surprised and pleased that many agencies are beginning to respond to the needs of both adoptees and birthparents. Many are rethinking how they view the issues that adult adoptees face. In my own town in Massachusetts, in a region of the country that is often seen as conservative and resistant to change, some social-service agencies are quite progressive, and willing to accommodate needs they never foresaw decades ago. I asked Mary Ann Ulevich, a social worker, how her views have changed over the many years she has been involved in social work.

When I first began to do searches for birthparents at the request of adoptees, I, like my colleagues, naïvely asked, "Why do you want to do this?" We believed that something must be awry with the bonding in the adoptive family. Part of our assessment was to decide if the request was "valid." Through scores of searches and interviews with all members of the adoption triad, I now consider all requests for a search to be valid, and my question generally is "Why now?" Frequently, an adopted person, ready to assert her or his "right to know," is taken aback by my willingness to help. The search is then a shared one, an adoptee for a background, a social worker for enhanced understanding.

Through years of counseling birthparents, preparing adoptive families, and talking to adoptees, I have come to understand the powerful need to know about one's heritage. Information is essential and helpful, not destructive. When I shared her birthmother's history revealing a musical talent, an adoptee tearfully told me of her own love for the symphony. Another young woman was so excited that she and her mother were the same height. If this minor information is so eagerly embraced, I can only imagine what meeting birthparents must mean to adopted persons.

My agency recently changed its policy to include searches initiated by birthparents. These requests have been much fewer than those initiated by adopted persons. I am not sure why, but birthparents that I have located at the request of their birthchildren have told me that, even though they have frequently considered a search, a range of reasons have kept them from doing so. These reasons include guilt, fear, insecurity, and a wish not to intrude. I look forward to continue learning from birthparents, as well as from adoptees and adoptive parents, about lifelong connections.

Mary Ann is an empathetic human being and she has worked hard to educate herself. In an ideal world, all social workers, as well as society, would make similar efforts to support the needs of triad members.

For me, the third step in reconciling adoption losses has been *learning to look inside myself to find answers*. During the process of healing, one's focus must ultimately turn inward.

Meeting a birthparent won't fix that initial loss and all the subsequent issues which may have evolved for the adoptee. Finding that birthchild won't erase decades of pain, or dissolve years of suppressed anger experienced by the birthparent. Yet, all too often, people search and reunite with these kinds of expectations. A letter to Ann Landers's column displays what such expectations cause during a reunion. In it, a twenty-seven-year-old adoptee was frustrated at having been found by his birthmother. The adoptee wrote:

> My birthmother seems to be a pleasant person, and the medical knowledge she has given me has been helpful. However, I did not want to be found, and it has caused a great deal of stress to me and my family.
>
> My birthmother continues to call me, and she wants very much to be a part of my life, but this is *not* what I want. This may sound harsh, but I already have a loving family, and I want my life to remain the same as it's been for the last twenty-seven years, without my birthmother in it.[10]

If this letter is similar to the majority of letters that Ann Landers receives from adoptees, her conclusion that reunions are invasive and disruptive is understandable. The adoptee in this letter had every right to be upset.

Searches and reunions are complicated events. People get into trouble when they search with an expectation of a relationship. In my opinion it is acceptable for a birthmother to contact her birthson to put her mind at peace. However, she should not expect more.

All those who undertake searches need to be willing to put themselves in the shoes of the persons they seek. They need to respect the private lives and needs of those individuals. They need to *listen*. To do less may indicate the searcher isn't ready to handle a reunion.

There are three axioms that can be helpful to remember during a reunion.

1. Only you can heal yourself. No one else can resolve your losses for you. You are the only one who has the power to do that.

2. Accept that there are some things you can control and some things you cannot. The past cannot be changed. The future is somewhere around that bend where we cannot see. You can only control the present. You can only control yourself.

3. Wait the bad feelings out. Expect that it will take time for everything to work out. People will need time to work on their own personal issues.

Just becoming aware of the impact adoption has had on one's life doesn't immediately reconcile those lifelong losses. Awareness just makes the issues more visible and hopefully more manageable. It's hard to work on something when you're in the dark. It's a lot easier with the light on. That's what searches and reunions do. They illuminate one's deepest feelings and needs.

How does one "heal" from within? By asking oneself empowering questions, by initiating an inner dialogue. Estes concurs. "Asking the proper question is the central action of transformation—in fairy tales, in analysis, and in individuation. The key question causes germination of consciousness. . . . Questions are the keys that cause the secret doors of the psyche to swing open."[11]

Find private moments to contemplate the following questions at different times. You may find that the way you answer them three months after your initial reunion may differ enormously from how you answer them three years later.

QUESTIONS FOR POSTREUNION[12]

What about the reunion makes you feel thankful?

What has been difficult?

What's the least you are willing to accept?

If your initial contact resulted in a rejection or a denial, how long are you willing to wait before you make contact again?

Have you been able to take a breather?

Are you making sure you get a lot of rest?

If you're an adoptee, are you feeling somehow disloyal?

If you're a birthparent, are you surprised at the levels of anger you're experiencing?

If you're an adoptive parent, do you feel your relationship with your child is threatened?

If you're an adoptive parent and you're angry, who are you really angry at?

Are there people who understand your situation that you can talk with?

Have you had the opportunity to talk about your reunion experience with others?

What kind of relationship do you want to have with your birthchild or birthparents?

What kind of boundaries would make you feel comfortable?

How patient are you?

How do you think your birthchild or birthparents feel?

How do you think the adoptive parents feel?

Can you try to put yourself in each person's position—to empathize with them?

These questions can help you deal with your own issues, and help you focus on yourself. Solitude can help you hear your inner voice. What's on the surface, in the tidepools of your mind, may be quite different from what exists in the depths of your soul.

The last step I have taken in healing (so far) is *establishing goals*. This process begins with questions like "What do I want to have happen?" My goals have probably been similar to what many others hope for during postreunion. I wanted to have a comfortable relationship with each individual in my birthfamily. I wanted to deal with the lifelong impact adoption had had on my life—an impact I only began to become aware of after my reunion. Mostly, I wanted to find ways to have all these issues empower me, not disable me. I wanted to work on this, and at the same time get on with my life.

To achieve any of these goals would involve effort and even some pain. Any task we undertake that's difficult brings us to the question "why?" Some will say, "Isn't it easier to just avoid all this stuff the rest of your life?"

I must admit there have been moments when I've wondered what's the point. It's such hard work at times. Why do it? The only reason is that the present and future could be better. Much better. But it can take time to decide to deal with these issues. I think many people put off deciding to come to terms with adoption's impact on them until it's too painful *not* to.

I never really had a problem with being adopted, never really felt conscious pain or loss, until I began writing the first draft of this book. Suddenly, adoption was in my face night and day. By necessity, in my working hours it was all I talked or thought about.

As I listened to others, I analyzed and reanalyzed my own feelings and experiences. On certain days I'd feel very down. On other days, I'd sail on an even keel. But I never felt up. Writing made me deal with a lot of issues that were not fun to face on a daily basis. To me, there was a powerful lesson in how this narrow focus affected me emotionally.

What you focus on affects your emotions. It's simple. If you choose to focus only on what is upsetting to you, then you must realize that you have made a choice. We may not have the power to control the past, or our emotional reactions to certain events, but we do have the power to control *what* we focus on.

I cannot see living my life as if I were in the spin cycle of a dryer. Part of coming to terms, for me, is accepting the losses. I can't change them. But, as Robert Andersen writes, "One does not need to alter history to change the experience of it."[13]

Adoption creates losses—but it also creates gains. We all have the ability to choose which aspects we want to focus on: what we do have, rather than what we will never have, what we can do, rather than what we can't change.

Thus a goal for me has been to focus on the benefits of being an adoptee—not just the love and experiences I share with all my families, but also the gifts that come from working through the losses. Facing and surviving any trauma is empowering, not disabling. Author Sue Miller once said, "If we don't have the experience of sorrow and pain, we are not as wise and compassionate."[14] There are unique strengths and insights to be gained through being an adoptee, a birthparent, and an adoptive parent. There are gifts to be derived from search and reunion experiences, no matter what the outcome.

I was at the American Adoption Congress convention a year ago when a woman with a subtle southern accent gave a speech. Every time she said the word "adoptee," it came out sounding like she'd said "adaptee."

Adaptee. I like it. It fits. That's what adoptees truly are: human beings who've adapted to a unique situation. The dictionary defines the word "adaptor" as meaning "a device that connects pieces of equipment that were not originally designed to be connected." Interesting.

What have my own search and reunion taught me? I know where I came from. I have a more complete sense of myself and a better understanding of all the relationships in my life. In an odd way, I feel I have more personal power. I own my past. Now I can go forward with more confidence.

How will all of this affect me in the future? What insights will I have when I'm sixty-seven years old? It's impossible to say. All I know for certain is that it *will* continue to affect me. Adoption is a part of who I am. It is one of the defining experiences of my life.

I have more distance to cover. There are walls that need

tearing down. Although I was the one who searched for my birthmother, it felt sacrilegious to invite her into my life, as well as to accept her invitation into hers. It felt inappropriate to acknowledge two sets of parents. But as time goes on, I wonder why having more people to love and enjoy should pose such a threat. Why should it feel disloyal to have two families? Can't they all be embraced and incorporated into my life, as in-laws and special friends are? Does joining my birthfamily have to be interpreted as somehow diminishing to my adoptive family and the memory of my parents? The answers to these questions lie within me. They are threatening, disloyal, and diminishing only if *I* choose to see them that way.

I may never be close to all my birth relatives. We live thousands of miles apart, and lead quite separate and busy lives. We *are* related. Like distant cousins at a family reunion, there is a recognition, a bond. It will always be there.

I have learned a lot about families and life and myself from meeting Lee and my brothers and sisters. Our reuniting was much more complex than I ever anticipated. I would have to say that the experience has been one of both pain and joy. Just like giving birth.

The mark of your ignorance is the
depth of your belief in injustice and tragedy. . . .
What the caterpillar calls the end of the world,
the master calls a butterfly.

—RICHARD BACH, *Illusions*

ACKNOWLEDGMENTS

I ALWAYS THOUGHT THAT WRITING A book was a solitary task, pursued alone and accomplished solo. Little did I know.

There are well over a hundred people who have contributed to this effort in one way or another. I feel odd that only my name is going on the title page. Suffice it to say, I wish we all could fit there.

Foremost to acknowledge are the seventy people who contributed their personal stories to *Birthright*. It is only through their many voices that the lifelong effects of adoption can truly be seen. Without question their collective narrative will aid others in understanding the search and reunion process. It would be interesting to see where they all are in five years, and what new perspectives they will have to share, for their stories here reflect only how they feel *now*. They may have evolved to a different way of feeling even by the time this book is in print. Each and every one of them has my deep appreciation and admiration.

Above all I thank my birthmother, Lee Porter Iacarella Beno. She not only had to cope with the trauma of our reunion, she also had to deal with a book being written about it. Her personal contribution to this text is greatly appreciated. Mike, Sue, Jim, Cathy, Robert, and Charles—my brothers and sisters by birth—have each taught me different things about being part of a family. My special thanks go to Mike and Sue, and Jim and his wife, Cheryl, for making the time and effort to contribute to the book. And a very special thanks to Lee's husband, Don.

Several people were responsible for getting *Birthright* into print. My undying gratitude goes to Jill Kneerim, my agent, who believed this book was a worthy project and never threw in the towel. Her tenacity, encouragement and professional acumen helped make *Birthright* a reality. I am grateful as well to Lori Lipsky for bringing the book to Penguin and for her early guidance as my editor, and to Frances Jones who contributed to the final draft. Lastly, I am obliged to my editor Nicole Guisto and Beena Kamlani, who steered *Birthright* through the final stages of production and helped enhance the text in significant ways.

Five special people took the time to read through the original manuscript. Their insights were a godsend, arriving at a point when I was deep amid the proverbial trees, no longer able to see the forest. I'm most grateful to Edith Wagner, Mary Jo Rillera, Marilyn Popko, Sheridan Robbins, and Susan Darke for their reviews. Susan also helped in a hundred other ways, from helping me locate numerous people to interview, to providing advice on searching and the reunion process. She has been both a guide and an inspiration. Also Sandy Musser, whose mission in life has been reuniting families, provided invaluable assistance and was always willing to help in any way she could.

A number of professionals generously gave a great deal of their personal time to help me in the course of writing this book. I am particularly indebted to Dirck Brown for his counsel over the years, and to Annette Baran whose generosity is exceeded only by her wisdom.

I'd also like to thank Robert Andersen, Erma Bombeck,

Josh Butler, Louis Chang, Mimi Cotter, Steve Dacri, Amy Dean, Clarissa Pinkola Estes, Bill Gage, Jim Gritter, Ann Henry, Richard Johnson, Sharon Kaplan-Roszia, Sheila Klopper, Virgil Klunder, Jill Krementz, Sondra Neuberger, Mike Ryan, Tom Shannon, Joe Soll, Reuben Tannor, Nancy Verrier, Tony Vilardi, Edith Wagner, and Kenneth Watson for their contributions.

Many friends sustained me during both my search and reunion, and my days at the typewriter. I especially acknowledge:

John Riley, who taught me how to search; Liz Miles, who once asked questions I didn't want to hear, but needed to think about; Pat Spratlen Etem, for being honest about my early writings; Kim Sandmann, who has never been afraid to tell me the truth; Carol Hebert, who reminded me that every day is precious; Linda Warden, who has always, always been there; my cousin, Larry Black, for being my touchstone; Kathy Hill, Beth Borchelt, Robin Reardon, Val McClain, Joy Hagin, Kathy Long, Duane Hickling, and my cousin Dave Garber for always knowing the right thing to say; and to my "other mothers," Jackie Warden, Lue Jones, Susie Reardon, and my aunts Marty Garber and Rena Sacconaghi Black for their love and unending support.

My sons Kristoffer and Jonathon gave up a lot of time with Mom so that I could write this book. I wish to thank Kristoffer for never erasing my chapter files off the hard disc, even though he tried several times, and to thank Jonathon for telling me that he put a gummy bear inside the laser printer. (It still works!)

The person who sustained me most of all was my husband, Jon, who willingly read every draft of the manuscript and never said a discouraging word. He also never gasped, clutching his chest apoplectically as he opened the phone bill during the months I conducted interviews, nor did he ever complain about the numerous weekends he was required to spend as a "single parent" while I sat hunched over the computer keyboard. I could never have written this book without his love and support.

It's impossible for me to know how my parents, Betty and Lou Sacconaghi, would have felt about my search and reunion, or about my many public writings about the subject. All I do know is that they loved me, and taught me to have the courage of my convictions. A great part of who I am is a result of my relationship with them, and hence, I feel they are in large measure responsible for this book.

NOTES

INTRODUCTION

1. Barbara Gonyo and Kenneth Watson, "Searching in Adoption." *Public Welfare*, Winter 1988, p. 14.
2. Ibid., p. 16.
3. Lisa DePaulo, "The Baby Chase." *Special Report* magazine, Jan./Feb. 1993, p. 15.

CHAPTER 1

1. Robert Lasnik, *A Parent's Guide to Adoption*. New York, NY: Drake Publishing, 1978, p. 92.

CHAPTER 2

1. Annette Baran, personal interview, February 11, 1993.
2. Co-created by the author and Annette Baran.

CHAPTER 3

1. Virgil Klunder, *Lifeline*. Cape Coral, FL: Caradium Publishing, 1991, p. 29.

2. Jean Paton, "The Intermediary." Cedaredge, CO, *Orphan Voyage* Newsletter, 1978.

CHAPTER 5

1. Dirck Brown, "Search and Reunion." *AdoptNet Magazine*, March/April 1992.
2. Ibid.
3. Gail Steinberg, "A View of Reunion." *AdoptNet Magazine*, Sept./Oct. 1991.

CHAPTER 7

1. Thomas A. Shannon, *Surrogate Motherhood*. New York, NY: Crossroad Publishing Co., 1988, p. 1.
2. Jean A. S. Strauss, "Origins" Column, *Reunions Magazine*, Summer 1991, Vol. 1, No. 4.
3. James Gritter, *Adoption Without Fear*. San Antonio, TX: Corona Publishing Co., 1989, p. 4.
4. Florence Rondell and Ruth Michaels, *The Adopted Family*. New York, NY: Crown Publishers, 1951.
5. Ibid.
6. Gritter, *Adoption Without Fear*, p. 3.
7. Robert Andersen, *Second Choice: Growing Up Adopted*. Chesterfield, MO: Badger Hill Press, 1993, p. 140.

CHAPTER 8

1. Susan Schindehette, Sue Carswell, and Maria Eftimiades, "A Victory of Faith." *People*, March 8, 1993.
2. Jean A. S. Strauss, "Origins" Column, *Reunions Magazine*, Spring 1991, p. 7.

3. David Brodzinsky, Marshall Schechter, and Robin Marantz Henig, *Being Adopted: The Lifelong Search for Self.* New York, NY: Doubleday, 1992.
4. Inventory co-created by Annette Baran and the author.
5. Robert Andersen, *Second Choice: Growing Up Adopted.* Chesterfield, MO: Badger Hill Press, 1993, p. 105.
6. Ibid.

CHAPTER 11

1. Disneyland used to use ticket books for rides, with tickets lettered "A" through "E," the "E" ticket being for the "best," most exciting rides.

CHAPTER 12

1. Nancy Newton Verrier, *The Primal Wound.* Published by the author (919 Village Center #9, Lafayette, CA 94549), 1993, p. 176.

CHAPTER 13

1. Gail Buchalter, "Up Front—Hugh Hefner." *People*, December 5, 1983.
2. Frank Swertlow, "Play Boy." *Los Angeles Herald Examiner*, June 15, 1984, p. A2.
3. Patricia Sanders and Nancy Sitterly, *Search Aftermath.* Published by the authors, 1981, p. 37.

CHAPTER 14

1. Erma Bombeck, *Motherhood: The Second Oldest Profession*. New York, NY: McGraw-Hill Book Company, 1985.
2. Gail Steinberg, "View of Reunion." *AdoptNet Magazine*, Sept./Oct. 1991.
3. Aaron Lazare, Keynote Speech, National Conference of Christians and Jews, Worcester, Mass., November 18, 1992.

CHAPTER 15

1. Dirck Brown and Lucille Buergers, "The Role of the Spouse in the Search and Reunion Process." *AdoptNet Magazine*, Sept./Oct. 1991.

CHAPTER 16

1. Jill Krementz, *How It Feels To Be Adopted*. New York, NY: Alfred A. Knopf, 1982, 1991, p. 83.
2. *The Adoption Connection Newsletter*, Peabody, Mass., 1982.
3. Amy E. Dean, *Letters to My Birthmother*. New York, NY: Pharos Books, 1991, p. 88.
4. Krementz, *How It Feels To Be Adopted*, p. 52.
5. Bill Wattendorf, *The Adoption Connection Newsletter*, 1992.
6. Karen Tashjian, unpublished essay, 1992.
7. Gail Steinberg, "View on Adoption." *AdoptNet Magazine*, Sept./Oct. 1991.
8. Thomas A. Shannon, *Surrogate Motherhood*. New York, NY: Crossroad Publishing, 1988, p. 75.
9. Ibid.

CHAPTER 17

1. Sharon Kaplan Roszia, 4th Annual National Conference on Open Adoption, Traverse City, Michigan, April 30, 1993.

2. Robert Andersen, "The Nature of Adoption Search: Adventure, Cure, or Growth?" *Child Welfare*, Jan./Feb. 1988, pp. 623–632.

3. Clarissa Pinkola Estés, audio tape *Warming the Stone Child*. Boulder, CO: Sounds True, 1992.

4. Brodzinsky, Schechter, and Henig, *Being Adopted: The Life-long Search For Self*, p. 4.

5. Thomas A. Shannon, *Surrogate Motherhood*, p. 44.

6. Clarissa Pinkola Estés, *Women Who Run with the Wolves*, New York, Ballantine Books, 1992, p. 186.

7. Ann Landers, interview, January 18, 1993.

8. Nancy Newton Verrier, *The Primal Wound*. Published by the author (see note 1, Chapter 12), p. 154.

9. Ibid.

10. Ann Landers column, February 24, 1993.

11. Estes, *Women Who Run with the Wolves*, p. 52.

12. Inventory co-created by Annette Baran and the author.

13. Andersen, "The Nature of Adoption Search: Adventure, Cure, or Growth."

14. Carol Flake, "The Good Novelist," interview of author Sue Miller, *Boston Globe Sunday Magazine*, April 11, 1993, p. 27.

APPENDIX A

THE SEARCH CHECKLIST FOR ADOPTEES

— 1. Create a search journal.
— 2. Discuss the search with your parents.
— 3. Locate your amended birth certificate.
— 4. Retrieve a copy of your final decree.
— 5. Retrieve your petition to adopt.
— 6. Contact the adoption agency.
— 7. Contact the law firm or attorney who assisted in your adoption.
— 8. Contact your delivery physician.
— 9. File waivers of confidentiality with the adoption agency, law firm, and courts.
— 10. Attempt to retrieve your original birth certificate.
— 11. Apply for medical records from the hospital where you were born.
— 12. Contact a judge about opening your records.
— 13. Formally petition the court to open your adoption records.

— 14. Register with the International Soundex Reunion Registry. (See address, Appendix B.)

— 15. Check both county and state records for marriage and/or divorce records for either birthparent.

— 16. Learn about the adoption laws for your state.

— 17. Check county or state death records for birthparents and birth grandparents.

— 18. Write to the Adoption Regulation Unit in your state to access your adoption records.

— 19. Send for a copy of *Where to Write for Birth, Marriage, Divorce, and Death Records*: Superintendent of Documents, U.S. Government Printing Office, Washington, DC 20402.

— 20. Order a copy of the *Guide to Genealogical Records in the National Archives*: The National Archives, Washington, DC 20408.

— 21. Find maps for the areas where you're searching.

— 22. Create a profile of the hometowns or regions where each of your birthparents was said to have been from.

— 23. Create a list of all the libraries in your area and in the localities where you are focusing your search.

— 24. Check local newspapers from the area where you were born for birth announcements.

— 25. Check local newspapers from the area where your birthparents were born for *their* birth announcements.

— 26. Check local newspapers for wedding and engagement announcements for your birthparents.

— 27. Check obituaries in local papers where you believe birth relatives may have died.

— 28. Check in old city directories to try to locate your birthparents or other relatives.

— 29. Check in city directories to match an occupation to a name.

— 30. Check in city directories to locate former or current employers of your birthparents.

— 31. Cross-reference city-directory information year by year.

— 32. Check in city directories to locate old addresses of birthparents and possible neighbors.

— 33. Check phone books and national telephone-directory discs for birth relatives.

— 34. List yourself in the phone directory of the area where you were born, or in the area where you relinquished your birthchild.

— 35. Locate all churches of the faith of your birthparents in the area where they were living at the time of your birth—and now.

— 36. Check any possible surnames against a book of name derivations.

— 37. Check local churches in the area near where you were born for any baptismal records.

— 38. Check local churches in areas where you believe your birthparents may have resided for their own baptismal, marriage, or death records.

— 39. Join a local or national search and support organization, and sign up in their registry if they maintain one.

— 40. Create your own library of search and reunion books (see the bibliography).

— 41. Advertise in adoption-search magazines.

— 42. Advertise in newspapers where you believe a birthparent might now reside.

— 43. Order a copy of *How to Locate Anyone Who Is or Has Been in the Military.* 1–800–937–2133.

— 44. Contact old landlords for forwarding addresses.

— 45. Contact old neighbors for forwarding addresses and other information.

— 46. Visit old neighborhoods in person to locate past acquaintances of birthparents.

— 47. Check with former employers about possible forwarding addresses of birthparents.

— 48. Check old high school and college yearbooks.

— 49. Check with a high school or college reunion chairman about the current address of a birthparent or request a list of the entire class.

— 50. Contact a private investigator or consultant.

APPENDIX B

IMPORTANT ADDRESSES

REGISTRIES

International Soundex Reunion Registry—ISRR
(Soundex)
P.O. Box 2312
Carson City, NV 89701–2312
(Include a self-addressed stamped-envelope.)

SEARCH AND SUPPORT REFERRAL

American Adoption Congress (AAC)
1000 Connecticut Avenue, NW
Suite 9
Washington, DC 20036
800–274–OPEN

Independent Search Consultants (ISC)
P.O. Box 10192
Costa Mesa, CA 92627

Council on Equal Rights in Adoption (CERA)
401 East 74th Street, Suite 17D
New York, NY 10021
212-988-0110

SEARCH AND SUPPORT ORGANIZATIONS

Adoptees' Liberty Movement Association (ALMA)
P.O. Box 727
Radio City Station
New York, NY 10101-0727
212-581-1568

Concerned United Birthparents (CUB)
2000 Walker Street
Des Moines, IA 50317
515-263-9558

The Adoption Connection (TAC)
11 Peabody Square, #6
Peabody, MA 01960
508-532-1261

MAGAZINES

AdoptNet
P.O. Box 50514
Palo Alto, CA 94303-0514
415-949-4370

Reunions—the Magazine
P.O. Box 11727
Milwaukee, WI 53211
414-263-4567

People Searching News
P.O. Box 22611
Fort Lauderdale, FL 33335–2611

U.S. GOVERNMENT AGENCIES

The National Archives
Washington, DC 20408
202–501–5402

Social Security Administration
6401 Security Boulevard
Baltimore, MD 21235
410–965–8882

Passport Records
Department of State, Passport Agency
1425 K Street NW
Washington, DC 20524
202–647–0518

Immigration and Naturalization Service (INS)
U.S. Department of Justice
425 I Street NW
Washington, DC 30536
202–514–2000

BIBLIOGRAPHY

BOOKSTORES AND CATALOGS

The following organizations have a wide variety of adoption-related books and materials. Many carry hard-to-find books on how to search, and some carry large quantities of books no longer available from publishers.

The American Adoption Congress
1000 Connecticut Ave. NW, Ste. 9
Washington, D.C. 20036

Triadoption (R) Publications and Services
P.O. Box 638
Westminster, CA 92684

The Musser Foundation
P.O. Box 1860
Cape Coral, FL 33910

Orphan Voyage
2141 Road 2300
Cedaredge, CO 81413

Today Reunites Yesterday
P.O. Box 989
Northampton, MA 01061–0989

BOOKS AND THEIR PUBLISHERS

I would suggest any of the following books as resources for people coping with search and postreunion issues. If you are unable to locate any of these books through the publisher or a local bookstore, contact one of the organizations above to see if they have copies available.

SEARCH BOOKS

Askin, Jayne, *Search—A Handbook for Adoptees and Birthparents.* Oryx Press (4041 North Central at Indian School, Phoenix, AZ 85012–3397), 1982, 1992.

Culligan, Joseph J., *You, Too, Can Find Anybody.* Hallmark Press (9737 NW 41st St., Ste. 120, Miami, FL 33178), 1993.

Johnson, Richard S., *How to Locate Anyone Who Is or Has Been in the Military.* Military Information Enterprises (P.O. Box 340081, Fort Sam Houston, TX 78234), 1990.

Rillera, Mary Jo, *The Adoption Searchbook.* PURE, Inc. (P.O. Box 638, Westminster, CA 92684), 1981, 1993.

BOOKS ON ADOPTION

Arms, Suzanne, *Adoption: A Handful of Hope.* Celestial Arts (P.O. Box 7327, Berkeley, CA 94707), 1990.

DuPrau, Jeanne, *Adoption.* New York, Julian Messner, 1981, 1990.

Gritter, James, *Adoption Without Fear.* Corona Publishing (1037 South Alamo, San Antonio, TX 78210), 1989.

BIOGRAPHIES

Andersen, Robert, *Second Choice: Growing Up Adopted*. Badger Hill Press (P.O. Box 4066, Chesterfield, MO 63006–4066), 1993.

Dean, Amy E., *Letters to My Birthmother*. New York, Pharos Books, 1991.

Dusky, Lorraine, *Birthmark*. New York, M. Evans and Company, 1979.

Fisher, Florence, *The Search for Anna Fisher*. New York, Fawcett, 1974.

Gediman, Judith, and Brown, Linda P., *Birth Bond*. Far Hills, N.J., New Horizons Press, 1989.

Krementz, Jill, *How It Feels to Be Adopted*. New York, Alfred A. Knopf, 1982.

Lifton, Betty Jean, *Twice Born: Memoirs of an Adoptee*. New York, McGraw Hill, 1975.

Musser, Sandra Kay, *I Would Have Searched Forever*. Adoption Awareness Press (P.O. Box 1860, Cape Coral, FL 33910), 1979, 1992.

Reagan, Michael, with Hyams, Joe, *On the Outside Looking In*. New York, Zebra Books, Kensington Publishing, 1988.

Rillera, Mary Jo, *The Reunion Book*. PURE, Inc., Triadoption (R) Services (P.O. Box 638, Westminster, CA 92684).

——*Adoption Encounter: Hurt, Transition, Healing*. PURE, Inc.

Schaefer, Carol, *The Other Mother*. Soho Press (853 Broadway, New York, NY 10003), 1991.

PSYCHOLOGY

Baran, Annette, and Pannor, Reuben, *Lethal Secrets*. Calif., Warner Books, 1988, 1989.

——, ——, and Sorosky, Arthur, *The Adoption Triangle*. Corona Publishing (1037 South Alamo, San Antonio, TX 78210), 1978, 1984.

Brodzinsky, David, and Schecter, Marshall, *The Psychology of Adoption*. New York, Oxford University Press, 1990.

——, ——, and Henig, Robin Marantz, *Being Adopted: The Life-long Search for Self*, New York, Doubleday, 1992.

Kirk, David, *Shared Fate*. New York, Free Press, 1984.

Lifton, Betty Jean, *Lost and Found*. New York, Harper & Row, 1979, 1988.

Lifton, Betty Jean, "Journey of the Adopted Self—A Quest for Wholeness." New York, Basic Books, 1994.

Rosenberg, Elinor B., *The Adoption Life Cycle*. New York, Macmillan, 1992.

Silber, Kathleen, and Speedlin, Phyllis, *Dear Birthmother*. 1832.

Sorosky, Arthur D., Baran, Annette, and Pannor, Reuben, *The Adoption Triangle*, San Antonio, TX, Corona Publishing Co., 1978, 1984.

Verrier, Nancy Newton, *The Primal Wound*. Published by the author (919 Village Center #9, Lafayette, CA 94549), 1993.